5 Days to Power

The Journey to Coalition Britain

Rob Wilson

First published in Great Britain in 2010 by

Biteback Publishing Ltd
Westminster Tower
3 Albert Embankment
London
SE1 7SP

ISBN 978-1-84954-081-0

10 9 8 7 6 5 4 3 2

A CIP catalogue record for this book is available from the British Library.

Set in Adobe Garamond by Soapbox

Printed and bound in Great Britain by
CPI Cox & Wyman, Reading, RG1 8EX

For all my Wilsons – Jane, Joseph, Elizabeth, Fern and Megan

Contents

Acknowledgements

It has been an enormous pleasure and privilege to write this book, which would not have been completed on time without the kindness and help of others. I am indebted to my wife and children, who tolerated me writing much of this book on my summer holidays and continued to be excited about its publication every step of the way. I also owe thanks to my mother-in-law, Patricia Pozzi, for letting me use her office and beautiful new Apple Mac to tap away on.

I am also deeply indebted to all those who agreed to be interviewed for the book and there were many of them, nearly sixty in total. There are some interviewees, including MPs and senior aides from across the political spectrum, who would doubtless rather remain anonymous but nonetheless have my sincere thanks.

I would especially like to thank the following for giving their time so generously, as many agreed to see me twice and also to check and recheck factual information: David Cameron, Nick Clegg, William Hague, George Osborne, Andrew Adonis, Ed Balls, David Laws, Chris Huhne, Andrew Stunell and Danny Alexander. All were in the thick of the action as it unfolded and were able to give impressive recollections of incidents that took place.

Thanks should also be given to the many transcribers of interviews for their painstaking and accurate work and to friends and colleagues who have read draft passages and sections of the book.

Biteback Publishing and Iain Dale heard by chance that I was writing this book and rang me out of the blue to ask if they could publish it. I would have been waiting until May 2011 to publish were it not for their entrepreneurial creativity. They have been a pleasure to work with.

Preface

What took place over the five days after the 2010 United Kingdom general election, from Friday 7 May to Tuesday 11 May, was a simple and raw fight for the ultimate prize in political power that the country can bestow: the office of Prime Minister.

David Cameron and Gordon Brown were to be locked by the electorate into a fight for power that would ultimately depend on the calculations and personal affections of Liberal Democrat leader Nick Clegg. Unlike perhaps more Machiavellian contests for power elsewhere in Europe over the centuries, this was to be a very British power struggle. It was played out, in public at least, according to bureaucratic rules set out by the Civil Service, but also with respect for the ancient British traditions of decency and fair play.

Few, however, would have been in any doubt: Gordon Brown and David Cameron were both determined to do whatever was necessary to secure the position of Prime Minister for the next five years and return their party to power, and the process became a quite brutal examination of their individual political skill, emotional intelligence, physical stamina and resourcefulness.

For all the party leaders the 'five days to power' would prove a stiff test of their character and of their parties' core beliefs. Regardless of the long-term success of the government which ensued, the outcome has set the scene for the politics of a generation.

Introduction

The forging of a coalition government in May 2010 was a momentous event in British political life. Few of the electorate actively sought a coalition government. Many indeed believed that such a government would be weak, unstable and incapable of dealing with the country's massive economic problems. The Conservative campaign had played on the fear that a hung parliament (that is, a parliament in which no single party holds an overall majority of seats) would be destabilising and damaging for the country, partly as a way of targeting the Liberal Democrat vote.

But once a hung parliament had materialised, and produced a coalition government made up of the Conservative and Liberal Democrat parties, the new Prime Minister, David Cameron, was naturally keen for it to be seen as a significant moment in modern history. The Conservative–Liberal Democrat government represented nothing less, he proclaimed, than 'an historic and seismic shift' in British politics.

The sort of behind-the-scenes horse-trading and compromise which is routine in so many countries in Europe and beyond had simply not been a feature of post-war British politics. Single-party majority government – Conservative or Labour – had become the assumed 'British way'. Even during an election campaign in which all the polls united in shouting 'hung parliament', the Conservative Party leader gave little attention to the idea of a coalition, as opposed to a minority government of one hue or the other.

There had of course been a torrent of rhetoric during the general election campaign about 'new politics.' The country appeared to be yearning for a different style of politics and promises were made to the cameras by all party leaders to end the murky cronyism and bed-feathering that the public felt had been luridly exposed during the parliamentary expenses scandal. This episode, more than any other in recent history, saw the standing of MPs and the whole Westminster system sink to new depths in the public estimation.

As leader of a third party, Nick Clegg in particular was anxious to press his claim to represent a politics that was fresh and different, detached from the creaking established system. And as his star ascended after the first of the televised leader debates, both Gordon Brown and David Cameron enhanced their own rhetoric calling for a new kind of politics. They assured the electorate that they too, after all the scandals of New Labour and MPs' expenses, yearned for a new way of doing things.

Many were cynical. The electorate had heard plenty of talk of 'new politics' before – not least when Tony Blair swept to power in 1997 – and all too often the reality had failed to match the expectation. But as it turned out, the election of 2010 truly did produce something surprising and new. Few could have imagined quite how quickly a 'new politics' – in terms of the nature of the government, if not necessarily of its moral purity – would arrive.

Commentators frantically dug out their history books. Many – particularly those who chose to be sceptical about the coalition's prospects – reached straight for the famous remark by Benjamin Disraeli: 'England does not love coalitions.' Some quoted him further: 'Coalitions, although successful, have always found this, that their triumph has been brief.'

Sober historians were equally quick to point out that what Disraeli was talking about was short-term tactical alliances, not coalitions in the modern sense of a binding together of parties in government. More importantly, they noted, for much of English parliamentary history in the age of democracy, whether England loved coalitions or not, it certainly got them. Between 1885 and 1945 governments by more than one party were the norm and single-party government was the exception. In this fifty-year period, majority single-party government ruled for only ten years.

Some of these coalitions were 'national governments' in times of war, or great national crisis, but by no means all were. And the new government of 2010, of course, was quick to emphasise the critical budgetary situation which it faced and which had made the forging of a strong combination government so critical.

At one level, of course, coalition is simply a basic political fact. Just as evolution is written, if one knows where to look, in the bones and body structures of species now alive, so modern parties contain in their basic anatomy the vestigial shapes of once independent political groups. In the case of the 'Lib Dems', the conjunction of words says it all: the party was born as a coalition, between the Liberals and the Social Democrats. And the Conservatives have thrived in the past by absorbing once distinct groupings, such as the Liberal Unionists of Joseph Chamberlain. This fact has been the source of much anxiety for modern Liberal Democrats such as Charles Kennedy and Menzies Campbell, alarmed by the lessons of the 'history book' in terms of the grave dangers of partnership with the Tories.

At another level, of course, all parties are coalitions. Few could doubt that David Cameron and Nick Clegg have more in common with each other, politically speaking, than either does with the more extreme wings of his own party (to the right in Cameron's case, to the left in Clegg's). While in recent years the leadership of all three parties has scrapped over the middle ground, their MPs and party memberships fan over a broader spectrum.

But for all that coalition and compromise is a basic fact of political life, it remains the case that the events of May 2010 were truly remarkable in recent British history. Since the end of the Second World War, Britain has been a country of almost unbroken single-party government. Before 2010, every general election bar one has returned either Labour or the Conservatives to office with an overall majority (even if on three occasions that majority was measured precariously in single figures, and on two of those occasions it evaporated during the term after defections or by-election defeats). For over sixty years now the political culture of this country has been that elections are a 'winner-takes-all' tussle between the fighter in the red corner and the fighter in the blue corner – and preferably decided by a knock-out.

Nor was David Cameron wrong to assume that even without a majority, the outcome would be a single-party minority government. In the only post-war election to fail to return a majority – that of February 1974 – this is how it was done (albeit briefly). Such a surprise was this particular result that the Queen's presence in the country had not been assured: she was on her way back from a trip to Australia. The widespread confusion as to basic procedure which followed served to intensify the general fear in Britain of any election result which was 'inconclusive'. Hence the general anxiety – which must have puzzled many watching on the Continent – to have matters resolved within a few days, for fear first that the markets would take fright, and second that the population at large would react angrily to a perceived failure of the political class.

There is no doubt that those involved in negotiating the coalition behind the scenes felt the pressure of this unfamiliar national event. (Some seemed to regard it even as a 'national crisis'.) The way in which our politicians responded, and the way the deal was done – as well as the alternative arrangements which were explored – is a story that deserves to be told.

Access to key figures involved from all three political parties enables me to tell it in a manner and a depth in which it has not been told before. It enables me to shed further light and answer questions to which even the negotiators themselves would have dearly loved to know the answers. Which concessions were genuinely necessary to persuade the other party to agree to a full coalition? What was Labour offering in its desperate bid to stay in power? Could it have delivered it? What was said in the one-to-one meetings between the party leaders? What contact and preparation between the parties occurred before and during the general election? Were the different parties as straight-talking and honest with each other as they affected to be? Why did the Conservatives decide to offer a referendum on the Alternative Vote? When was the Liberal Democrat decision to do the deal with the Conservatives actually taken?

Naturally this book does have opinions, but it is not an attempt to write a Conservative account of what happened, nor to apportion criticism or blame to the various participants, their parties or their leaders. Wherever it was practical in explaining events, I have left readers to draw their own conclusions. Its main intention is to document faithfully and historically what happened, so as to provide a contemporary map of history in the making: the order things happened, the meetings, conversations, the documents and first-hand memories of the key participants.

The account in the following pages is based on almost sixty interviews with key players in the hung parliament negotiations, including Cabinet ministers past and present, MPs, peers and aides. Where the source of a quotation is not otherwise explained in the text, the quotation is taken from these interviews. The memory undoubtedly can play tricks, and participants' recollections of events are sometimes hazy. I have tried, as far as possible, to cross-reference participants' accounts of events.

If this book is accessible, interesting and readable to a wide audience and adds to the knowledge of what happened in those critical five days in British political history, it will have achieved its purpose.

PREPARATIONS

There have been a number of theories about whether 'backroom deals' were done between the parties before the general election of May 2010 took place. Perhaps no leader-to-leader contact, because that would have been too obvious and difficult to deny, say the conspiracy theorists, but many believe that there was detailed backstairs contact, discussion and preparation between the parties.

To some extent, of course, the lesson of history might have been taken to be: Don't bother! Hung parliaments have been very rare things in post-war British politics and coalitions entirely absent. Even on those occasions when just such a situation looked highly likely, ultimately the outcome was different.

For example, in 1992, when a hung parliament seemed assured and extensive preparation was undertaken, the parties' efforts turned out to be wasted as the electorate's fears about Neil Kinnock entering Downing Street crystallised, allowing the pollsters to be confounded and Conservatives to be returned with a surprise majority of 21 seats.

In 1997, work had gone into a possible new alliance between Labour and the Liberal Democrats. But the public handed New Labour a crushing majority, beyond what Tony Blair had dared contemplate, and one which made any thought of a formal coalition with the Liberal Democrats unnecessary. Thereafter the prospect of a coalition receded in the Blair era as it became clear that Labour would continue to win comfortable majorities, which is what happened in the 2001 and 2005 general elections. As these recent elections demonstrate, second-guessing the electorate can be presumptuous, and therefore fraught with difficulty.

Nevertheless, since November 2009 the opinion polls had begun to suggest the likelihood of a hung parliament, a likelihood which by 2010 had become unambiguous. The major parties began subtly to shift their election preparations. This meant that at the same time as members of each party pored over their rivals' policy documents and manifestos for areas of disagreement which they could target during the election campaign, they simultaneously studied them for areas of agreement which might help cement an allegiance if circumstances dictated.

Simply to say 'Let's prepare for a hung parliament' is of course to take no account of the almost endless range of slightly but critically different situations which might arise, given even minor variations in the electoral figures. And sure enough, as even those who had planned most assiduously would discover, elections find a way to spin things, to impart a subtle but significant twist, that none had anticipated.

Yet with the polls suggesting a hung parliament, it would have been a surprise if the political parties had failed to draw up detailed strategies to act as reference points.

Labour preparations – or lack of ...

Gordon Brown, it would appear, had made very little effort to prepare any groundwork. Before 1997 Tony Blair had taken great pains to woo the leader of the Liberal Democrats, Paddy Ashdown, listening to his concerns, making promises and dedicating the time required to make him believe a real process of change was under way. Having seen John Major with a small majority (then minority) government become almost a prisoner of the Conservative Party right wing, Blair wanted the option of a coalition as insurance against being reliant on his party's left wing. Brown had no such approach.

Yet Lord Andrew Adonis, the former Liberal Democrat who became a key adviser to Tony Blair and served as Secretary of State for Transport in the Brown government, believes that Brown had set out to woo the Liberal Democrats at the very beginning of his premiership. He cites the advisory positions given to Liberal Democrats in June 2007, directly after Brown became Prime Minister, and the offer of the job of Secretary of State for Northern Ireland to Paddy Ashdown.

Likewise Adonis draws attention to a speech Brown made about constitutional reform which was 'a big opening to the Lib Dems. So the opening to the Lib Dems goes right back to the beginning of the Brown premiership.' He also points to the fact that the Labour Party had a firm policy of holding a referendum on the Alternative Vote system, which would deliver at least a version of the electoral reform which the Liberal Democrats had long craved. Labour had tried to introduce such a referendum before the election and had put it in their manifesto.

There were existing close contacts between some junior members of the Labour Cabinet and Liberal Democrats, who were committed to voting reform. John Denham, Ben Bradshaw and Peter Hain were pro-electoral reform and known to have close links with senior Liberal Democrats – both inside and outside their 'shadow Cabinet'.

Jack Straw, who as Justice Secretary was responsible for the Constitutional Reform Bill that was debated in early 2010, also argues that a combination of the likelihood of a hung parliament and Labour's previous commitments made them reach out to the Liberal Democrats. But he is willing to recognise that there was a question mark over the extent to which the Labour Party genuinely wanted electoral reform or could deliver it, having talked about it for so long without action: 'There was a feeling we needed to show greater delivery on the issue of voting reform because we were being mocked for the fact that there had been a pledge for a referendum on the voting system in the '97 election manifesto.'

Like Adonis, Straw believes that Brown was genuinely committed to constitutional change and attributes the lack of progress to his focus on the 2008–9 financial crisis, which had consumed all of Brown's energy and attention. And as the Liberal Democrats were well aware, this was coupled with the internal problem that the Labour Party was utterly divided on the issue of electoral reform. The party could not be relied upon to vote in support of it, which meant that to deliver a solution it needed the Prime Minister's direct attention, and he was either not willing or not able to give it.

By late 2009 the polls consistently showed Labour in trouble, and a feeling developed that the party and government needed to be more imaginative and construct a better offer at the election. Crucially in the minds of those around Brown, it was believed that the party needed to reach out in a distinctive way to liberally-minded voters. It was part of a strategy to firm up the soft left vote, those who had drifted from Labour due to the Iraq War and as a result of concerns about civil liberties.

It would be true to say that there was extreme nervousness about voting reform within the government, and discussions about it at Cabinet Committees and in Cabinet were not without serious reservations and argument. But by late 2009 the proposal had gone through, despite some heated debate at a Parliamentary Labour Party meeting. The compromise settled upon was that backbenchers would agree to vote a bill for a referendum through the House of Commons but would not then be under any party obligation to support a public 'Yes' vote in a referendum campaign itself.

The Labour leadership managed to get a proposal for a referendum on the Alternative Vote through the House of Commons before the election, although it was ultimately blocked by the Conservative Party in the House of Lords in the 'wash up' at the end of the parliament. The Conservative Party opposed a referendum on AV (at the time) partly as a matter of principle, but also because it would cost £100 million – an expense which Dominic Grieve, then shadow Justice Secretary, argued could not be justified when there was little evidence that the public generally cared about it as an issue.

So it did not make it to law, but Labour did then include the policy in its election manifesto. Brown sought to emphasise the common ground in an interview with the *Independent* during the election campaign. 'A new politics demands a new House of Commons and new House of Lords. The Conservatives are against a new politics,' Brown told the paper on 21 April 2010. 'There is some common ground on the constitutional issues. It is up to the Liberals [sic] to respond.'

Despite the efforts of the Brown government, none of the key Liberal Democrats saw these activities as representing a deep commitment to political reform. During the campaign, Liberal Democrat leader Nick Clegg dismissed AV as 'a baby step in the right direction – only because nothing can be worse than the status quo. If we want to change British politics once and for all, we have got to have a quite simple system in which everyone's votes count. We think AV-plus is a feasible way to proceed. At least it is proportional – and it retains a constituency link.'

Clegg felt Labour's offer was insufficient to attract his party's support: 'The Labour Party assumes that changes to the electoral system are like crumbs for the Liberal Democrats from the Labour table,' he told the *Independent* on 22 April. 'I am not going to settle for a miserable little compromise thrashed out by the Labour Party.' Brown personally, Clegg had declared to the *Daily Telegraph* the previous day, was 'a desperate politician' who had 'systematically blocked, and personally blocked, political reform'.

As David Laws has since recalled: 'Gordon Brown came in and missed the opportunity to develop the agenda; he didn't really reach out to the Liberal Democrats because we saw essentially ten years that were a missed opportunity. Brown did become convinced of the need for a centre-left realignment based on electoral reform, but it was literally at one minute past midnight, when the election was lost – it was simply too late.'

The Liberal Democrats could not have been clearer that they wanted much more from Labour on electoral reform. In the Constitutional Reform and Governance Bill on 19 January 2010, the Liberal Democrats put down an amendment which would have changed the voting system for elections to the House of Commons to the Single Transferable Vote. This was surely a clue to Brown and the Labour Party about what any negotiations in a hung parliament should be about.

Brown's relations with the Liberal Democrats

Previous experience of coalitions or partnership between parties in mainland British politics has demonstrated the crucial importance of the personal chemistry between the party leaders.

In December 1916, following the resignation of Prime Minister and Liberal Party leader Herbert Asquith, Conservative leader Andrew Bonar Law was invited by King George V to form a government and become Prime Minister. However, he deferred to Lloyd George, whom he liked and trusted in a way that perhaps would not be possible in politics today. He had served in Lloyd George's War Cabinet, as Chancellor and Leader of the House of Commons. The huge mutual trust between the two leaders and the way their personalities complemented one another made for an extraordinary political partnership. Their partnership at the top of government saw their coalition re-elected by a landslide following the Armistice.

The respective personalities and easy relationship between James Callaghan and David Steel greatly facilitated the formation of the Lib-Lab pact in the late 1970s, and the continued existence of the pact owed much to the determination of the two leaders to keep it going.

The creation of the Joint Cabinet Committee, in which Liberal Democrats formed part of the Blair government's Cabinet Committee on constitutional issues, was the product of the close personal relationship between Tony Blair, Paddy Ashdown and Roy Jenkins. In Scotland, the level of trust between Donald Dewar and Jim Wallace has been described as the 'rock' on which the Labour–Liberal Democrat coalition was built in 1999.

Despite his repeated claims that 'I agree with Nick' in the party leaders' televised debates during the campaign, Brown had no relationship to speak of with Nick Clegg; quite the reverse. Those around the Prime Minister suggest Brown didn't care for the Liberal Democrat leader much, seeing him as 'a privileged public school boy whose politics were largely Tory'. He was dismissive of his intellect and disliked what he saw as his constant opportunism. The times when they did meet in private as party leaders, Brown found it difficult to control his legendary temper and indeed, on occasions, did not.

In one instance, in the run-up to the general election, Brown was keen to come to an agreement with other party leaders over MPs' expenses. He could see it was damaging both politics generally and – to the extent that a sitting government was likely to come off worst from this sort of scandal – his own re-election prospects.

At the height of the scandal, in an effort to put a lid on an affair that was damaging all parties and the reputation of all politicians, in April 2009 the three party leaders took part in a meeting at the House of Commons, attended also by each party's Chief Whip. Brown had proposals to replace MPs' second home allowance with an allowance based on daily attendance, and it was an occasion where there was both an obvious need and a genuine opportunity for effective cross-party collaboration.

But the meeting was anything but constructive and the leaders failed to reach agreement. On this issue (as also on others) Brown found Clegg 'unhelpful, obstructive, holier-than-thou' and resented his, as he saw it, public grandstanding over a scandal in which none of them had any business casting the first stone.

In general, as one very senior Liberal Democrat who went on to serve in the Cabinet recalled, 'Gordon didn't like Nick, didn't relate to him. There was a bit of old-fashioned class stuff involved and Gordon was someone whom you needed to show respect to, not just the office he held, him personally. There was a way of dealing with him but I don't think Nick ever got to that level.'

Unable to contain his annoyance, Brown let rip at his younger rival in a quite extraordinary way. A bad-tempered row erupted, with a number of intemperate contributions. Clegg described Brown's proposals at one stage as 'barking mad' and demanded to know what the point of having a meeting was when Brown wanted only to lecture them about his proposals rather than discussing the reservations or ideas of anyone else present. One of those in the meeting was sufficiently enraged to describe Brown as 'an obnoxious bastard'. In general, Clegg felt, Brown's attitude to his party was one of maddening condescension: he had 'a demeanour towards the Liberal Democrats that if only we just grew up and wised up we would fall under Labour's wing.'

These reports are perhaps unfair to Brown, as Clegg and Cameron no doubt played their part in this meeting breaking down with such acrimony and recrimination. But whatever the rights and wrongs of the matter, the key thing was that the Liberal Democrat and Conservative leaders came away with a clear and shared sense that Brown was difficult to work with, to say the least. In Cameron's opinion they formed then, as well as on other occasions when they worked together (over the Gurkha controversy, for example), a mutual sense of the other as reasonable and straight-dealing.

This early awareness that each could collaborate with and trust the other – at the same time as they both found the Prime Minister infuriating – would be more important than either could then have guessed.

Rather in the manner of Edward Heath before him, Brown had failed to establish a meaningful long-term relationship with the Liberal leader before political circumstances forced them into coalition discussions. Although Brown would have been well advised to have been courting Clegg, he never really tried – until it was too late. Instead there was an atmosphere where the two leaders clearly didn't care for each other and barely spoke to one another. Unwisely, the Prime Minister instead preferred to work around Clegg – maintaining links with his party via back channels. Andrew Adonis, himself a former Liberal Democrat, advised the Prime Minister and kept his own contacts warm.

It would, however, be wrong to put all the difficulties of creating a solid platform for Labour to negotiate with the Liberal Democrats simply down to Gordon Brown's relationship with Nick Clegg or the party's concerns about electoral reform. There was also deep-seated dislike of the Liberal Democrats within the Labour Party that reached the highest levels.

One Labour member of the Cabinet said: 'I would much rather have done a deal with David Cameron than I would with Clegg. I've always had a problem with the Liberal Democrats, you largely know where you stand with the Tory and Labour brands, but with the Liberals what they say not only differs constituency to constituency, but ward to ward, street to street and house to house. They are scavengers.' Another said: 'The problem with Nick, and the Tories have reason to know this, is that he resorts to some of the lowest politics imaginable.' Many members of the Labour Party would have been deeply unhappy about any deal, and not just because of the parliamentary arithmetic. It was simply that they had experienced Liberal Democrat campaigning methods, and found that they stuck very firmly in the throat.

Gordon Brown felt that his personal friendships would bear fruit. He was close to former Lib Dem leader Menzies Campbell, for example – a friendship born in Scotland. Like leaders David Steel and Charles Kennedy before him, Campbell came from an environment in which alliance with the Tories was unthinkable. In the smaller political village north of the border, Labour and Liberal Democrat MPs had shared friendships as well as political common ground. Campbell had been extremely close to the former Labour leader John Smith, and became friendly in turn with Smith's protégé Gordon Brown. On one of Smith's hill-walking trips, the two peeled off the main group and strode down the mountain together for four hours. In their background and their outlook they found much in common. An ongoing friendship with Brown gave Campbell a perspective different from some of his party colleagues who had little love for the Labour Prime Minister.

The other friendship the Prime Minister had cultivated was with Vince Cable, the Lib Dem spokesman on economic matters. It was not a close friendship, but they 'got on reasonably well', trusted each other, and met at frequent intervals to discuss events, particularly the economic crisis. The meetings became supplemented by phone calls, Brown increasingly seeing Cable as an intermediary with his party. During the economic crisis through 2008 and 2009, for example, Brown was keen that the Liberal Democrats supported the Government position against the Conservatives.

Andrew Adonis was later to describe this Labour negotiating strategy to the BBC: 'It's like a patchwork quilt where all of us were seeking to create this great quilt but all of us were working on different bits at different times and then trying to sew the whole thing together.' Friendships with former senior members of the Liberal Democrats were all well and good, but none had sufficient influence on the current leadership. A patchwork quilt of back-channel negotiators was never likely to end up sewn together.

Indeed, so far as the Liberal Democrat leadership was concerned, it only added to the frustration at Labour's tactics to know that they were attempting to go behind their back, to pull strings and to influence party grandees. This method of operation by Brown and his team caused tensions and resentment.

Peter Mandelson has said of his party's preparations: 'You may be surprised given that this was the opening gambit of a negotiation for the future of a coalition government but no, we didn't have a document, a paper, an agreement, a negotiating position. I mean we were flying blind in that sense.'

One member of Labour's Cabinet blames Mandelson, at least in part, for the lack of preparation and the failure of Labour during the general election campaign to get its message across. 'Peter spent far too much of his time screening contact with Gordon rather than getting on with the job,' he said.

Whatever the reason, in May 2010 the Labour team was underprepared. In advance of formal negotiations beginning on Monday evening following the general election, it was the Liberal Democrats who supplied the document around which the discussions were based.

Ed Balls' experience of Labour's preparations for a hung parliament, or lack of them, is perhaps the most instructive. The first that Balls, one of Brown's closest and most long-standing allies, heard of the fact that a Labour negotiating team would hold talks with the Liberal Democrats – and that he was part of the team – was when Brown called him late on Saturday morning, with the meeting due at 3pm. It was only on the drive down to London from Yorkshire that Balls found out who else was in the negotiating team and then he spoke to Adonis, Mandelson and Brown about the meeting on his mobile phone. The pre-meeting briefing with Mandelson consisted of a conversation as Balls bought a cup of tea in Portcullis House and the pair walked to the lifts to get to the third-floor meeting room. This lack of any formal preparation towards staying in power was frankly astonishing.

Gordon Brown's character

Brown's character flaws were at the heart of the failure of his government, the failure of his general election campaign and the failure of his negotiations over the five-day period described in this book. I was present in the Commons when Tony Blair famously described Brown as 'a clunking fist' and the picture painted immediately resonated across the chamber – a phrase that was superficially a compliment but which was, in its underlying suggestion and message, anything but.

Mandelson's description of Brown as a 'snowplough' was also apt. Brown was a man whose political style involved assuming a posture and resolutely maintaining it against all opposition; certainly not a man with the sinewy guile to fashion a way forward in a coalition situation.

Brown's verdict of himself was somewhat at odds with these descriptions, he saw himself more as a romantic hero – he once, to general bemusement, drew the parallel with Emily Brontë's Heathcliff. One could certainly characterise Brown's view of himself as akin to the romanticism of the medieval knights – with the characteristics of strength, boldness, courage, passion and fighting for others, but heavily armoured and carrying a big sword.

Of course, many around Brown saw him very differently, with little to admire. He was difficult, touchy, even prickly, insensitive and unable to make even the most basic of decisions. A number of his former Cabinet ministers volunteered privately that they didn't like him.

Unfortunately for Brown, politics, like warfare, moves on quickly. The new politics wasn't about the old heavily armoured medieval knights, but the young, lightly armoured, fast-moving generals with a rapier thrust. Cameron was a hard target for a heavy sword or a clunking fist, and Brown therefore was always unable to deliver a fatal blow.

However, had he been able to forge any form of personal rapport or relationship with Clegg, Brown may have been able to extend his longevity.

The Liberal Democrats

Paddy Ashdown wrote in his autobiography *A Fortunate Life* that every leader of Britain's 'liberal third force will, if they are successful, sooner or later have to face the dilemma of choosing between purity and power'. The circumstances and the choices would always be different but 'in the end', Ashdown concluded, 'the consequences of success in growing the party and its support are that th[e] hand [dealt to the party leader by the British political system] must eventually be played and cannot be avoided'.

Not only had the political circumstances changed a great deal since Ashdown was leader, but the Liberal Democrats themselves had changed significantly. The election of Nick Clegg as the Liberal Democrats' latest leader in December 2007 marked the ascendancy of a new generation within the party. More pragmatic and market-friendly than idealistic activists, talented and ambitious politicians such as Clegg, David Laws, Chris Huhne and Danny Alexander were driven by – as James Crabtree put it in *Prospect* magazine in July 2010 – 'the need for change, frustration with their current leadership, and a hunger for power'.

As Menzies Campbell told me, this new generation were 'very professional … they had made enormous sacrifices to get in [to Parliament], they had not come in to forever sign Early Day Motions – they had come in with a clear feeling that they wanted to make progress and they wanted to make government progress.'

Many of the new generation of Lib Dems – including Nick Clegg, Chris Huhne, Ed Davey, Mark Oaten and Vince Cable (though most did not immediately associate Cable with this group) – had contributed to *The Orange Book*, edited by David Laws and Paul Marshall and published in 2004, which presented a collection of essays proclaiming that the new political outlook was more pragmatic, less misty-eyed and more market-friendly than that of either the 'bearded civil libertarians' of common stereotype or the left-wing refugees that had turned to the party out of dissatisfaction with Tony Blair and New Labour.

Crucially, in the eyes of one elder statesman, the 'young turks' appeared to have a more 'open-minded' attitude to the Conservatives (perhaps as a consequence of spending their parliamentary careers in opposition to a Labour government), rather than the 'visceral antipathy' of previous generations of Liberal Democrats.

When in November 2009 the *Observer* reported an Ipsos MORI opinion poll showing the Conservative lead down to six points, down from twenty points six months earlier and the lowest figure in any poll since Gordon Brown was being hailed for his handling of the economic crisis, Danny Alexander, Clegg's 37-year-old chief of staff (and a first-term MP), wrote in the *Observer* on 23 November that the Liberal Democrats were now having to 'look very closely and seriously' at what would happen if they became the 'kingmakers' in the event of a hung parliament.

However, the party's preparations for a hung parliament were little advanced by this point. A combination of successive Labour landslide election victories, followed by polls consistently giving the Conservatives a clear lead since the autumn of 2007, led the party to take the prospect of a hung parliament somewhat less seriously than in the run-up to the general elections of the 1990s. The high turnover rate of the Liberal Democrat leadership in recent years had not helped matters either: planning exercises that had taken place under Sir Menzies Campbell, including an 'away day' at the Henley Business School and even contact with Buckingham Palace, do not seem to have been taken forward under Clegg. One senior Liberal Democrat observed that the frequent changes of leadership inevitably affected the 'corporate memory' at the centre of the party.

In late 2009, Clegg had quietly selected four MPs to prepare for, and act as the party's official negotiators in the event of a hung parliament. Sensitive to the inferences that would be drawn about the party's positioning in a hung parliament, the existence of the group largely remained a secret. The first that one Liberal Democrat frontbench spokesman knew of the composition of his party's negotiating team in 2010 was on the morning of the Saturday after polling day.

The chosen MPs were Danny Alexander, Chris Huhne, David Laws and Andrew Stunell. Alexander was leading work on the party's manifesto, which was deliberately developed in co-ordination with the work of the negotiation group. Huhne, a former leadership candidate, had negotiating experience from his career in the City, as did David Laws.

Laws, the party's former Director of Policy, also had direct experience of parliamentary coalition negotiations. When Paddy Ashdown had been leader of the Liberal Democrats, he had sent Laws north to negotiate the first coalition in Scotland. It had given Laws an early understanding of the intricacies and challenges of building a coalition government, leading one witness to the negotiations to describe him as the Liberal Democrats' 'star negotiator' during the post-election period.

The group was completed by Andrew Stunell, a former Chief Whip of the Parliamentary Party and a vastly experienced negotiator at local government level. The appointment of Stunell was to be popular within the Liberal Democrat Parliamentary Party, and Danny Alexander believes that Stunell played an 'absolutely crucial role in developing the negotiating role because he had an awful lot of experience'. Stunell had written a book entitled *In the Balance* on hung councils and how to handle the meetings and plan out your negotiating strategy, 'where you hang tough and where you give in, how they should be handled'. Alexander considers this to have been 'absolutely invaluable' to the preparations.

There were notable absences from the Liberal Democrat team. Although Stunell was a reassuring presence to many in the party (at least in part because he was not seen as close to Clegg) and Huhne had appealed to the party's left during his bid for the leadership, none of the prominent figures from the left were included in the negotiating team. More significant was the absence of Vince Cable.

Cable's absence from the eventual hung parliament negotiations (although he was a member of Clegg's 'reference group', to which the negotiating team reported and which met to advise the party leader on key strategic decisions both before the general election and in its immediate aftermath), came as a surprise even to members of the Liberal Democrats' own 'shadow Cabinet', and mystified both the Conservatives and Labour.

The Conservative negotiating team assumed after the first meeting with their Liberal Democrat counterparts that Cable's absence from the negotiations meant that he was simultaneously conducting a separate formal negotiating channel with Labour.

On the Labour side, this would lead to a more serious misunderstanding. With the Liberal Democrat 'shadow Chancellor' not part of the negotiating team, there was also no Labour Chancellor, Alistair

Darling, in their team. Darling's absence may well have been due to Cable's absence, but could equally be because he did not believe his party should hang on to power. Labour's assumption was that when it came to the finer details of the negotiations, such as costings and spending commitments, there would need to be separate bilateral economic negotiations between Cable and Darling. The two parties apparently never reached an understanding on this point of procedure, with Labour's unwillingness to agree to spending commitments in Darling's absence proving a major source of frustration to the Liberal Democrats.

While Clegg had appointed his main negotiating team in the Autumn of 2009, the negotiators' discussions about the party's strategy in a hung parliament did not get going in earnest until February. As might have been expected of the party for whom a hung parliament constituted the best hope of political influence and even government, the Liberal Democrats began to prepare extremely thoroughly.

A series of meetings followed with papers tabled and minutes taken. This preparation took place, however, away from the main party life at Westminster and was not publicised among party members. The 'shadow Cabinet' and wider Parliamentary Party were not included or consulted about either the appointments or the wider discussions that took place.

The papers and minutes of meetings demonstrate a level of professionalism and thoroughness that isn't normally associated with, for example, Liberal Democrat policy-making. While these documents do not necessarily give a detailed blow-by-blow account of what was argued by each of those present, a clear picture does emerge of the party's thinking and planning before the election result was known.

Senior Liberal Democrat MPs knew that in the event of a hung parliament, the eyes of the nation would be focused on their actions. The party had long worried about the public's perception of its fitness to govern at the national level (the so-called 'credibility gap'). Senior figures knew that such judgements by the public would be made on the basis of the speed and clarity of its decision-making in the hours and days after polling day.

More perhaps than either of the other parties, the Liberal Democrats were conscious that they would suffer in the popular estimation from a messy and protracted negotiating process. There was also another consideration: a drawn-out or acrimonious period of uncertainty might be damaging to the cause of electoral reform which was so dear to Liberal Democrat hearts. Opponents of proportional representation would undoubtedly point to this as an example of the sort of prolonged and chaotic bartering behind closed doors which inevitably went with PR as a system.

However, by the time they held the first of a series of secret meetings in the House of Commons, Clegg had already set out the party's 'public line' on its approach to a hung parliament. When a hung parliament had first emerged as a serious prospect the previous November, Clegg had told the Andrew Marr programme on BBC television that 'whichever party has got the strongest mandate from the British people will have the first right to seek to govern'. This could be 'either on its own or with others'.

Amid growing media speculation early in the New Year, on 5 January 2010 Clegg wrote an article for *The Times* in which he ruled out any 'backroom deals or under-the-counter "understandings" with either of the other two parties'. Clegg repeated the party's mantra that the party with the 'strongest mandate' should have the 'moral right' to govern, although he did not clarify what he meant by 'strongest mandate'.

Since Clegg had opened up the possibility of working with either of the two main parties in a hung parliament, the principal dilemma facing the negotiators was how to deal with a situation in which the Conservatives were clearly the largest party in a hung parliament. In an e-mail circulated to the other three negotiators prior to the second meeting on 24 February 2010, David Laws presciently envisaged a 'very early offer of co-operation or coalition' from the Conservatives in the event of a hung parliament, or even if the Conservatives had a small majority.

The offer would be based around 'the importance of economic stability and addressing the budget deficit'; 'the importance of calming financial markets'; 'shared policy aspirations', including reform of politics, education, the environment; fiscal oversight and civil liberties; and 'the importance of working beyond party boundaries'. However, the purpose of such an offer, Laws reckoned, would be at least in part a cynical attempt to make Cameron's Conservatives appear 'inclusive and constructive' while wrong-footing the Liberal Democrats into appearing 'divided, indecisive and partisan'. He concluded that it was 'incredibly important' that the party responded in a 'swift and professional' way.

The negotiating group's initial instinct was to let the Conservatives form a minority government. While the party would offer some support and adopt a generally constructive approach to a Conservative minority government (in order to avoid an early second election and a major squeeze on its vote), it would remain at arm's length (to steer clear of guilt by association for the unpopular decisions that the government would have to take). Laws's initial suggestion had been for some sort of agreement from opposition with the aim of securing a 'second election after a period of time, at an appropriate moment, without being blamed for the breakdown'.

When the group met on 24 February, the agreed preference was for a deal that involved the Liberal Democrats remaining on the Opposition benches, from where they would offer 'some co-operation, but would fall short either of full coalition or of making a formal "Stability and Reform Agreement"'. The implications of this approach, Laws considered, could mean the party abstaining on the Queen's Speech (unless it had been designed to secure Liberal Democrat support); supporting most elements of the Emergency Budget, but perhaps abstaining on controversial items such as a rise in VAT; and not seeking a mechanism formally to advance a common policy agenda or seeking pre-consultation on new policies or legislation.

The Liberal Democrats would make an early offer, perhaps on the day after polling day, of co-operation on a 'Growth and Deficit Reduction' strategy, in order to appear on the front foot and to neutralise any criticism in relation to market instability. But otherwise the strategy would be to give mild support until they felt there were major policies they could not accept, at which point there might need to be a second election.

Most of the group were sceptical about whether a full-scale coalition with the Conservatives could be achieved, owing to a lack of support in the party and basic differences over policies and values. Laws had rehearsed the facts in his note: many Liberal Democrats are 'deeply anti-Conservative'; many MPs would have just finished fighting 'very vicious local campaigns against Tories'; the party hoped to win seats in Labour areas, 'where people may not appreciate a "deal" with the Tories'; Labour would 'clean up on the "anti" vote as the government became less popular'.

However, Chris Huhne has recalled being the one member of the group to dissent from this view. Huhne, who prior to entering the

House of Commons had founded a ratings agency, argued that there was no precedent anywhere in the developed world for a minority administration with or without support delivering the large and sustained budget consolidation that the financial markets would demand.

The Liberal Democrats had to recognise that there was a trade-off between political ease of arrangement and economic risk. A stronger deal with the Conservatives would be more politically difficult, but a weak deal could ultimately lead to a bond market or sterling sell-off. 'Financial crises', Huhne warned his colleagues in a note, 'are catastrophic for the political parties that are blamed, and we should avoid this at all costs.'

Not only did Huhne believe in the merits of a coalition over a 'low trust' confidence and supply deal – an agreement involving some co-operation but well short of a formal coalition – he also reckoned that in the event of a hung parliament, the Conservative offer would be 'quite good', including movement on constitutional reform. Huhne's reasoning was that if the Conservatives failed to secure a majority, David Cameron would be under strong pressure from within the Conservative Party to get into Downing Street. If he didn't, Huhne thought, Cameron would be 'dead'.

The Liberal Democrats too would be more amenable to a deal than people thought. From his experiences around the country, Huhne believed that the party's activists were far more realistic and mature than many people gave them credit for, partly because of the experience of local government – running real budgets, taking tough decisions, and doing the things that were necessary to make coalitions work at local level.

This view was backed up by evidence from a brief note from Andrew Stunell. Far from being unpalatable to the Liberal Democrats' local councillor base (a key component of the party's activist base), the party already *was* sharing power with the Conservatives in fourteen councils across the country, in places such as Birmingham, Leeds, St Helens and Warrington. Stunell noted that 'the initial condition in nearly all the above was that two opposition parties came together to deny an out-going Labour administration office.'

Had Huhne's arguments for a stronger deal with a possible minority Conservative government been widely known at the time, they would have caused widespread surprise to many. Huhne had based his second leadership campaign around an appeal to the party's left, and in public around the time of these planning meetings was making vocal and trenchant attacks on the Conservatives over the tax affairs of Lord Ashcroft.

By the time the group's conclusions were presented to a meeting in mid-March of the party leader's 'reference group', consisting of Clegg himself, Cable, party president Baroness Ros Scott, and Paul Burstow, the Chief Whip, there was a new emphasis on securing stability. In the event of a Conservative minority government, the party would 'seek to negotiate a formal agreement to allow it to function stably for a fixed period in return for delivery of key Liberal Democrat policy objectives', including, 'as a minimum fixed-term parliaments and an electoral reform referendum'. The Liberal Democrats would remain on the opposition benches under such an arrangement, but support the government on the Queen's Speech, and confidence and supply measures, subject to the 'Stability and Reform Agreement' being adhered to. All legislation and major announcements would be pre-agreed through a Stability and Reform Committee of senior Liberal Democrats and Conservatives. Although the party would have lost some of its freedom of manoeuvre, the negotiators hoped it would be 'clear which governmental actions were as a consequence of Liberal Democrat involvement and which were not'.

This marked an important step towards closer and stronger co-operation with the Conservatives in the event of a hung parliament, although a 'blue-yellow' coalition was still not on the cards. Alexander summarised the group's discussions in a memorandum, dated 16 March 2010, and in the light of subsequent history, its conclusion is striking: 'It is clear that there is a substantial gulf between the values of the Conservatives and those of the Liberal Democrats …This would make it all but impossible for a coalition to be sustainable if it were formed, and extremely difficult to form without splitting the party.'

The Liberal Democrats also needed a strategy to deal with Labour in a hung parliament. It seemed to the Liberal Democrat discussion team that negotiations with Labour might offer a significantly greater range of possibilities – including a greater likelihood of working towards a full coalition arrangement.

The negotiating team recognised that this was the party's preferred option. In a paper submitted shortly before the elections, the group concluded that there were 'fewer in principle barriers' and the party could probably be persuaded to support a deal with Labour. There would almost certainly be widespread hostility on the Liberal Democrat benches to a close collaboration with the Conservative Party.

However, somewhat ominously for the prospects of the Liberal Democrats' eventual post-election negotiations with Labour, the party's negotiators agreed to 'set the bar for such an agreement very high.' They would demand parity of esteem in any negotiations, based on the rationale that 'they need us more than we need them.'

A coalition with Labour would need to be 'fresh', a demonstrably new government, 'different', requiring a new set of policies including all of the party's 'four steps to a fairer Britain', and a clear and agreed deficit-reduction plan as the new government's first action. Significantly however, the group concluded that the party should not use valuable political capital pushing for the abolition of tuition fees. One of the Lib Dems' flagship policies would be ruthlessly sacrificed in any coalition negotiations: 'On tuition fees we should seek agreement on part time students and leave the rest. We will have clear yellow water with the other [parties] on raising the tuition fee cap, so let us not cause ourselves more headaches.'

A final consideration was the role of Gordon Brown in any coalition. While it was 'clearly the case that a government without Gordon Brown would be greatly preferable', Brown's continued tenure as Prime Minister was not entirely ruled out.

At the meeting of the reference group on 16 March, with the general election approaching, the negotiating group recommended that in the event of a hung parliament in which a deal with either the Conservatives or Labour remained possible, the party respect the public line it had set out by entering into negotiations with the party with the 'strongest mandate' first. (During the election campaign Clegg would indicate that by 'strongest mandate' he meant the party with the most votes *and* the most seats.) While private channels would be kept open with the other party, the group recognised the importance of being seen to attempt in good faith to deliver what they had promised. Above all, the Liberal Democrats would have two objectives: 'maximum stability' and 'maximum Lib Dem policy delivery'.

After the 16 March meeting, further preparatory work was commissioned. Laws was tasked with writing a 'Draft Programme for Government', Huhne with preparing a deficit-reduction strategy, and Stunell was to work with Jim Wallace, who had negotiated the party into coalition at Holyrood between 1999 and 2007, to draft a negotiating strategy and set out the internal processes for two parties to successfully co-operate under any of the deals discussed. Alexander and Paul Burstow discussed internal communications arrangements within the Parliamentary Party during the post-election period.

By the time the hung parliament negotiations actually took place, the 'Group of Four' had been working as a team for several weeks and knew each other's thinking well. The Liberal Democrats had thoroughly considered their strategy, policy demands and internal and external communications. As we have seen, this would turn out to be in marked contrast with the Labour team they would face.

Conservative preparations

The Conservatives had for several years operated a strategy to woo Liberal Democrat voters, part of a general attempt made by David Cameron to detach the party's image from its own right wing and to shift it onto the moderate middle ground. In the spring of 2007 Cameron publicly called on Liberal Democrat sympathisers to recognise that there was 'a home for them in the modern, moderate Conservative Party'. High-profile campaigns (and photo-shoots with huskies) emphasised the party's 'progressive' thinking on environmental policy and on issues of social justice. In a speech in Bath, Cameron summoned Liberal and Conservative voters to 'rally together behind an alternative government-in-waiting'. In words that seem now uncannily prescient, he declared that the time was right for a 'new Liberal–Conservative consensus' which would combine individual freedom and social responsibility.

His ambitious aim was to achieve a shift in the way in which the relationships between the three main parties were analysed: from the conventional view of a centre-right Tory party on the one hand, confronting centre-left Labour and Liberal Democrat parties on the other, to a view in which the fundamental divide was between a 'statist' Labour Party whose answer to problems was invariably more government intervention, and 'liberal' Conservative and Liberal Democrat parties, which both sought to encourage 'social responsibility' at an individual and community level and to buttress individual liberties against the encroachment of the state.

What the Conservatives quite astutely noticed and were keen to exploit was an emerging division within Liberal Democrat ranks, between those such as Nick Clegg, David Laws and others who fundamentally accepted the wisdom of free-market economics and who sought to develop policy ideas in this context, and those more traditional Liberal Democrats who could often be – as Andrew Adonis points out – more left wing than many on the Labour benches, and who would recoil at the very thought of collaboration with the Conservatives. The former group had acquired an identity associated with *The Orange Book*, and Cameron was quick to point to this gulf publicly. 'There is a question mark', he stated, 'over the future direction of the Lib Dems, between the Orange Book Liberals and what we might call the Brown Book Liberals – those who look forward to a coalition government with Gordon.'

Cameron's senior adviser Steve Hilton had convinced him that there were close ties between the two opposition parties in important areas of philosophy and policy – not something that many Conservative MPs had realised. Hilton stressed that the things that divided the parties, such as Europe, were much smaller than the things they agreed about, particularly the philosophical scepticism of big government. For several years before the election Hilton made sure that leading Conservatives peppered their speeches with the things they had in common with Liberal Democrats – green politics, school reforms, identity cards, and decentralisation of power from the centre to people and communities.

The decision had been taken not to bludgeon Liberal Democrat voters into agreement with the Conservative Party, but to respect them and demonstrate their shared values. This gave any Liberal Democrat voter the option that, if they wanted to get rid of Gordon Brown and Labour (and many did), they could vote for a Conservative Party that had changed to one that shared their values.

The 'Big Society' was to be part of the intellectual underpinning of the package being sold to Liberal Democrat voters. The concept became muddled in the general election campaign and formed a focus for criticism: it became folklore that one of the reasons the party failed to deliver a clear and consistent message was because nobody understood the Big Society.

In fact the leadership had started to use the theme well before the general election campaign, although few inside or outside the party took any notice. The Big Society was supposed to be one powerful answer to the question that had dogged David Cameron and the Conservative Party for years: What do you stand for?

The Big Society was to become a big issue for many Conservative MPs fighting the election because they felt it was a concept rolled out too late in the day: the widely held view was that it simply didn't resonate on the doorstep. Hilton believes that this is due to a misunderstanding of what the concept was and is. It was never developed to be a doorstep message, rather it was an overarching message of what the party believed in. As always in elections, both internal and external communication are muddied.

It is interesting to note though that at grass roots level the Big Society concept soon became something people respond to. In communities all across the UK people and communities are talking about it and trying to give it life.

Of course, as far as the Conservatives were concerned, the first priority was to try to win an overall majority. Francis Maude – then shadow Cabinet Office Minister – had been specifically tasked to get the party ready for government. Cameron had moved Maude in mid-2007 from Party chairman and asked him, initially, to be ready for an autumn general election. The short timescale meant the work undertaken was 'rough and ready'. When the election didn't take place, Maude appointed Nick Boles (who was to enter the House in the 2010 general election) to head an implementation team, which was gathered together over the following twelve months and made up of members seconded from major consulting firms and people who would work for little or nothing (or 'begged, steal and borrowed' as Boles put it).

The team worked through policy areas, using green papers as the starting point. Schools, welfare reform and justice were part of the early reform programme that was developed. From early January 2009, the implementation team had access to Permanent Secretaries in the Departments, which allowed briefing packs for shadow ministers to be fully developed.

Training seminars, papers that helped shadow ministers understand their department and a whole host of other activities, evolved into a plan for a wholesale reform of government. All shadow Secretaries of State were asked to produce a draft business plan for their department, which then became the basis for the structural reform plan by late 2009. It forced the shadow Cabinet to think policy delivery through in a disciplined, systematic and chronological way.

Most of these department-by-department plans would be handed to Sir Gus O'Donnell – head of the Civil Service – and departmental permanent secretaries either just before or at the outset of the election campaign, and largely remained intact. Most senior civil servants engaged enthusiastically, relieved that one potential incoming government had a plan and would seemingly be capable of making decisions.

Nevertheless, for all the hope of a large workable majority, there was awareness that Brown's slide in the polls always stopped short of an irreversible slump; circumstances would allow him to appear the man for a crisis and he would stage a mini-revival. George Osborne, shadow Chancellor of the Exchequer, had become increasingly concerned that a hung parliament was likely. Whereas others would look at the party's poll rating and translate that into seats, he and Cameron would occasionally (using all available evidence) work through the list of constituencies, giving their own instinctive assessments of the likelihood of winning in each. It was as basic a process as, 'We've won that one, we might have won that one, we haven't won that one.'

Having done this, the feeling generally was that everything had to go well: destroying Labour in the south and Midlands, doing well in the north-west, west Yorkshire and Wales and making progress in Scotland. Even in the best scenarios, this method only delivered the Conservative Party a small majority of up to ten seats. To hope for anything more was simply unrealistic.

As time passed, it became increasingly obvious that a spectacular election result was needed just to win a majority, and this became part of the message to the Conservative Party at large. The language of 'we have a mountain to climb', 'we need a bigger swing than Margaret Thatcher' became increasingly common right up to the election. The party hoped that a combination of its marginal seats programme and a late swing on the night would be just enough to win.

But Osborne believed that the mountain was higher to climb than it should have been. The 2001 result was explicable, as Blair and Brown made a stronger transition to government than anyone could have imagined, the economy continued growing and Blair, in particular, caught the mood of the time and proved a popular Prime Minister. Osborne thought it was 'a bit of miracle we held on to what we'd got'. But in 2005, after the Iraq War and eight years in government, Labour's popularity had slumped, as had Tony Blair's personally. At the election the Labour vote share fell to 36%. But even in this advantageous circumstance, the Conservative Party barely increased its vote share, which made the option of one final push to victory extremely difficult to achieve.

In the event the problems were compounded by the outcome of the first leaders' television debate, because Clegg's acclaimed performance suddenly presented the danger that the Conservative Party might actually lose seats to the Liberal Democrats rather than make gains. Until the first debate, the Conservatives had anticipated cutting a swathe through the Lib Dems' 62 seats, particularly across the south and south-west. The pain was eased by Brown's poor performance through most of the campaign, but the loss of the Liberal Democrat battleground in the middle of the campaign made a hung parliament much more likely. Cameron's decision to agree to televised leader debates in which Nick Clegg would have an equal billing became openly questioned in the Conservative Party, where some felt that it had been a major and possibly decisive strategic blunder.

For months Cameron had insisted that he himself had no desire to be distracted from the task of pressing for a Tory majority. Osborne too had taken the view that the Conservative Party could not do a huge amount of internal work on planning. First, because it would leak (which meant that nothing was ever written down) and that might have been catastrophic for the party's prospects. Second, there had been a long-term strategy in place, led by Party chairman Eric Pickles, to 'love bomb' Liberal Democrat voters and demonstrate that the Conservatives were reasonable people occupying the centre ground of British politics.

But with Clegg riding high after the first television debate, and the strategy to absorb large sections of the Liberal Democrat vote seemingly in tatters, Osborne realised it was sensible to recognise where all the signs pointed. He saw the imperative to be prepared for all potential election outcomes. Around two weeks before the general election, Osborne approached Cameron and asked if he could begin preparation work.

Osborne had been at Cameron's house before the second leaders' debate to discuss how to handle it, following the difficult first outing. Once they had finished discussing the television debates specifically, their talk, as might be expected, turned to the election campaign more generally and the prospect of a hung parliament. Cameron was convinced by Osborne that there was a need to do a more thorough job of planning ahead. He agreed to let a small but high-powered team, consisting of Osborne himself, Oliver Letwin, Ed Llewellyn and William Hague, work through all the likely scenarios, and to consider the responses that each might trigger.

It was done covertly, with Osborne selecting a team that would have needed to know what had been agreed with Cameron: Letwin, because he was head of policy, Llewellyn as Cameron's representative on the group and Hague as de facto deputy leader and an ex-leader well aware of all the sensitivities involved – and a wise head to boot.

Planning for a hung parliament therefore began half way through the general election campaign itself and was approved by the party leader. On one thing, though, Cameron was adamant: he as leader must be kept at arm's length from any preparations for a hung parliament. He was firm that his focus should and must remain the winning of an outright majority, and that any sense that he was resigned to failing in this objective might prove disastrous to his and his party's prospects. Among other things, Cameron was concerned that he was involved in a punishing eighteen- to twenty-hour a day election treadmill. The last thing he wanted was his election message distracted and diluted by information blurted out unplanned in an interview. Don't report back to me, was his firm message to Osborne, unless specific decisions are urgently required – the less he knew the better.

'There was some planning going on', Cameron remembered later, 'but it didn't distract me for a second. I don't think I spent any time on planning scenarios.' This was not simply because he thought it would be wise to remain focused on an outright victory. He still genuinely believed that a coalition government was a very unlikely outcome. Even in the event of the Conservatives (or any other party) failing to win an outright majority, what seemed likely to transpire was a minority government. This seemed to be the lesson of British post-war history, so different from the political culture of the Continent: 'I always believed, as it turned out wrongly, that almost all scenarios short of a majority would end up with a minority government. I felt it was the way we do things in Britain,' Cameron said.

The team met twice, both times on Sundays – at Osborne's house, where they had dinner – and analysed what the Liberal Democrat leader had said in speeches and television interviews about his approach to a hung parliament: what he would want and his key policy demands.

Oliver Letwin in particular pored over the Liberal Democrat manifesto and policy documents, looking for areas of overlap or likely deadlock. For Letwin this was, in any case, a hobby as much as a duty (it would become a running joke among the Liberal Democrat negotiators that Letwin knew their policies and manifesto better than they did). Later during negotiations Letwin was teased about being a policy 'geek', which he took in good spirit, and it helped cement him as the favourite Tory among the Liberal Democrat negotiating team.

Hague, Osborne, Letwin and Llewellyn met again on the Sunday before the election at Osborne's house to go through their latest thinking and Oliver Letwin's work on the synergies between the two parties' policies. The meetings focused heavily, William Hague told me, on 'what we could do as a minority government to get a supply and confidence agreement'. By the end of the second meeting Letwin had a firm outline of the agreements and disagreements between the two parties that would be the ultimate source of the coalition agreement – although at the time it was developed, it seemed likely to be used for the purposes of a minority Conservative government wishing to have a confidence and supply arrangement.

In their planning and consideration of what Clegg and his colleagues had said, the Conservative team took the Liberal Democrats at their word. If this was going to work, it had to be done on the basis of trust and grown-up politics. The Conservative calculation was that if they had most votes they were in with a chance, but if they had fewer votes than Labour, the election was certainly lost – any 'moral' claim to precedence in forming a government would be fatally undermined. More votes than Labour but fewer seats gave them an outside chance of claiming they had won, but this, it was agreed, was an unlikely contingency. Win more votes and more seats than Labour, and it did seem likely that the Liberal Democrats would agree to a confidence and supply arrangement. It would not be a very stable government, not easy to manage, but it was on this basis that the document was drawn up.

Unlike Brown, Cameron had tried to establish a good working relationship with Nick Clegg – with some success, in the sense that he felt there was a feeling of mutual trust that each could be relied upon to be open and honourable in their dealings, but with little genuine bonding of any personal nature. When Nick Clegg became leader of his party, Cameron invited him and his wife to dinner in the hope of establishing a strong peer-to-peer relationship. He saw it as a way of cutting to the chase on the big issues that would arise, such as constitutional reform and MPs' expenses. The invitation was made in such a way that refusal did not bring embarrassment, and when Clegg declined, there was none. Clegg also declined a further invitation to dinner, seeing it as important to resist these offers, as maintaining his distance from other party leaders helped to protect his independence and room for manoeuvre.

It is claimed that a 45-minute meeting between Clegg and Cameron at the Supreme Court, while waiting for the Queen and Prime Minister, was important in their personal relationship. Cameron said that it helped him realise that Clegg was a reasonable person who was in politics for the right reasons. In addition, they met at state dinners, commemoration services and other such formal occasions. But there were also times when working together proved to be confidence-building on both sides.

Clegg and Cameron collaborated on a Liberal Democrat opposition day motion in the Commons to support the Gurkhas' residency rights. Whipped Conservative votes delivered victory, but Cameron was relaxed about Clegg taking the spotlight for a campaign that the

Liberal Democrat leader had pioneered. There was also the less well known co-operation on MPs' expenses and setting up of the Independent Parliamentary Standards Authority (IPSA) where the two teamed up again, winning a vote against the government and 'both sticking to the deal'. These measures built the confidence that each would deliver on what they promised. Yet despite all this, it would be wrong to claim the two men knew each other well or would be ready to jump into government as a partnership.

The Civil Service takes control

Arguably the most prepared for a hung parliament was the Civil Service – although this had not been achieved without considerable difficulties. Behind the scenes it had been burning the midnight oil for approximately a year, worrying about how to manage a smooth transition of power (should that be necessary) – not least because it liked to be in control of events. In the final weeks of the general election, it had even gone to the trouble of preparing four draft legislative programmes and Queen's Speeches based on a close study of the party manifestos.

But it was back in the autumn of 2009 that the planning became deadly serious, with a range of scenarios war-gamed. The main options were a Conservative majority, a continuing Labour majority, or a variant of each with the Conservatives or Labour dependent on Liberal Democrat support. There was also planning for alliances with minor parties, such as the Unionists (as John Major's government had depended heavily on their support).

Civil servants believed that there would be no difficulties for them resulting from a continuing Labour majority government, nor a Conservative majority. There were plenty of people within the service who had experience of both. There was also some precedent for a major party being dependent on a minor one, thanks to the Lib–Lab Pact of the mid-1970s. And there was the new experience to be drawn from Scotland, where the Civil Service had supported coalition formation in 1999 and 2003.

With all the covert work being undertaken within the Civil Service, Gus O'Donnell felt it would be important to have all the constitutional ground rules published so that political parties could understand the process and refer to the rules that existed. The Civil Service work was already being compiled into a Cabinet manual, 'A Compendium of the Laws, Conventions and Constitutional Underpinning of the UK System of Government'. It was to have ten chapters and chapter 6 was to focus on the formation of government. The final version was to have eleven chapters.

Gus O'Donnell wanted the chapter on 'How Governments are Formed' published in draft form to start to build a consensus around what should happen in the event that there was no clear result, to avoid disputes and ensure there was clarity in areas where perhaps members of the public may not understand the constitutional position.

There was, however, a huge challenge for those wanting to ensure a smooth handover, and bring the Civil Service's covert preparations into the public domain. The Conservative Party leadership did not want to give any impression whatsoever that it thought a hung parliament was likely to happen. The Prime Minister and the Labour Party were also reluctant, as the incumbent government, to give any sign that it thought events were on the turn.

On the recommendation of Peter Riddell (best known as a *Times* political commentator) and the leading constitutional authority Robert Hazell, the Institute of Government was used as the cover for Civil

Service activity and preparation. To that end, in November 2009 the Institute of Government held a seminar at Ditchley Park in Oxfordshire with a number of academics, civil servants and politicians in attendance.

Suma Chakrabarti, permanent secretary at the Ministry of Justice, was present, along with his predecessor Alex Allan, now chairman of the joint intelligence committee. He had been appointed in September to co-ordinate an orderly transition of power, mainly due to his experience in handling the changeover to the Blair Government in 1997. The senior Conservatives Francis Maude and Dominic Grieve, then shadow Secretary of State for Justice were also there.

As a result, the Commons Public Administration Committee chaired by Dr Tony Wright MP was approached to help investigate the matter and put together a report, but Dr Wright declined on the basis that he felt it would divide his committee. However the Ministry of Justice Select Committee, under the chairmanship of Sir Alan Beith MP were only too willing to step in. The 'Draft Cabinet Manual Chapter on Elections and Government Formation' was presented by the Cabinet Secretary to Beith's select committee on 23 February. Although Sir Gus O'Donnell had been concerned for some time that the rules in the case of a hung parliament needed to be clear, Buckingham Palace was even more anxious to have the matter sorted out well before polling day, as it did not want the Queen to become embroiled in a constitutional crisis.

So the document set about clarifying a number of important issues. It stated that it was 'open to the Prime Minister to ask the Cabinet Secretary to support the government's discussions with opposition or minority parties on the formation of a government. If opposition parties request similar support for their discussions with each other or with the government, this can be provided by the Cabinet Office with the authorisation of the Prime Minister.'

It confirmed constitutional acceptance that the incumbent remains Prime Minister until a clear successor is found, that the Queen should not be involved in any way, although her Private Secretary will talk to all parties. But as nothing like this had happened since 1974, it answered some questions that were still open. For example, how should the Civil Service behave, and would the general election 'purdah' period be extended (when contracts could not be signed and appointments made)?

The Ministry of Justice Select Committee reached its conclusions and published its report covering all such matters, and its findings were widely welcomed. Crucially both Cameron and Clegg accepted in late February the 'caretaker convention', which codified that the Prime Minister (in this case Gordon Brown) continued after a general election until such time as a clear successor was found. The Civil Service, rather covertly, had got what it wanted: a set of rules that it administered and therefore controlled.

DAY 1

– Friday 7 May –

The Labour Party

As polls closed – to scenes of uproar and protest in several constituencies where people had been unable to cast their vote – the mood at the centre of each of the three parties varied. Brown, it emerged, had spent the evening hammering out drafts of speeches to meet a variety of eventualities. He then dined with his wife on lamb stew – or so the attendant press were notified – before retiring for a doze: a scene of domestic contentment at odds perhaps with the mood among his closest confidants.

If the Labour campaign had salvaged some momentum after the horrors of 'Bigotgate' – when Gordon Brown, campaigning in Rochdale, had been caught referring to Labour loyalist Gillian Duffy as 'that bigoted woman' – it was nevertheless viewed as a disappointment by those who ran it. 'We had never really seemed to be able to set the campaign agenda', Peter Mandelson admitted in his memoirs *The Third Man*. Given the low ratings of the party and of Gordon Brown personally before the campaign starting gun was fired, there were few Labour MPs who did not worry about their employment status on 7 May. The Conservative lead in the polls had remained narrow enough to inspire hope of avoiding a meltdown, but a heavy defeat remained on the cards. Where his first campaign in charge in 1987 had seemed 'a brilliant defeat', this one, Mandelson lamented, had been less distinguished: 'I was now certain it would end in defeat, but brilliant it wasn't.'

Gordon Brown was briefed to expect a poor result. For all that many around him took a realistic view of their prospects, however,

Brown retained hope that even a loss would not be so comprehensive as necessarily to mean the end of government either for the Labour Party or for him personally as Prime Minister. Brown had been 28 years old when Margaret Thatcher came to power, and it was at Thatcher's second general election triumph in 1983 (when Brown was 32) that he first became an MP. Only two years later he became an opposition spokesman for trade and industry, in the year that the miners' strike finally came to an end. Some of his formative political years, in other words, occurred during the most divisive period of Thatcherite government, which left a lasting imprint on most of the politicians who worked through it. Brown might as Prime Minister have invited Mrs Thatcher to Downing Street for tea and photos, but he never managed – as his early political room-mate Tony Blair so conspicuously did – to shake off the tribal attitudes of those years. The desire to keep the Conservatives out of government at all costs remained deeply entrenched in his being. For Brown there was a simple and fundamental division in the House of Commons: while Labour and the Liberal Democrats were *progressive* parties, the Conservatives were *regressive*. They would undo at great cost to the country some of the work which he and his party had achieved – and by the same token they would not do the further work which he believed remained to be done. The country was not out of economic peril, and Brown sincerely felt that he, and only he, could provide the solutions the country needed.

He had met a group of his trusted allies – including Sue Nye, Iain Bundred, Christina Hyde, Justin Forsyth, Nicola Burdett and Kirsty MacNeill – at his house near Edinburgh before going to his count at Kirkcaldy. Listening to his words at the count, David Dimbleby thought they had the ring of a valedictory speech. This perhaps was read into it by one who assumed – as most assumed – that Brown was resigned to defeat and to the end of his premiership. But in fact, according to close aides, he had aimed to hit the right note of being 'both humble and proud' while trying to keep all options open. Which is why he said that the 'result was not yet known. My duty to the country, coming out of the election, is to play my part in Britain having a strong, stable and principled government – able to lead Britain into sustained economic recovery and able to implement our commitments to far-reaching reforms to our political system upon which there is a growing consensus in our country.'

It is quite clear with the benefit of hindsight that this message, with its talk of far-reaching reforms to our political system, was an early opening bid to the Liberal Democrats, should there be any chance of forming a government with Brown at its head. The night ahead would be one in which Brown's expectations, hopes and moods would rise and plunge with exhausting regularity – influenced not only by the increasing flow of results, but also by the public reactions (often infuriatingly off-message) of senior members of his own party. Just as Brown was flying south, for instance, his mood was darkened by an interview that David Blunkett gave on television in which he effectively conceded defeat, long before the final state of play was known. 'In a democracy', Blunkett declared, 'you don't just win, you also sometimes have to concede defeat. That's the essence of a living democracy and it involves us being mature in how we handle that and being prepared to rebuild and fight back.' It would seem that those who knew Brown best were well aware that he would seek to cling on at all costs – and that some of them actively sought to make it impossible, or as difficult as possible, for him to do so. There is no doubt that the call for 'maturity' and a concession of defeat was directed at one man. Nor, to Brown's fury, would this be Blunkett's last unhelpful intervention.

But in fact the news from around the country began to appear better than Labour or Brown himself had anticipated. Certain seats that were expected to fall to the Conservatives did not, and when Labour retook Dunfermline and West Fife, Brown was seen clenching his fist and crying 'Yes!' During his flight from Edinburgh back to London the Prime Minister took the opportunity to move to the back of the plane to talk to the media pack. There he spoke to the BBC's veteran World Affairs Editor John Simpson, who duly reported that Brown felt it his 'duty' to establish a stable government. 'Brown insisted there would not be a quick settlement,' Simpson said. Brown's initial calculation was that the longer he remained in position overseeing the gestation of a stable government which could operate in a hung parliament, the harder it would be for anyone to oust him. (David Cameron's fear was that he was right – which goes far towards explaining the profound sense of urgency which drove the Conservative leader over the ensuing days.)

When Brown landed in London he was greeted by further good news: Rochdale (a seat which had acquired unforeseen significance after the embarrassment of 'Bigotgate' had taken place there only a week or so earlier) had also fallen to Labour, in spite of Gillian Duffy's understandable vow to tear up her postal vote. Slight boundary changes meant that the seat was in fact notionally a Labour seat; but even so, the overall result suddenly began to look less dire than had been predicted or expected.

When Brown arrived at his party's HQ in Victoria Street the mood – as described later by some of those who were there – was 'defiant and upbeat'. Brown made a speech to party workers which went down well: he continued to 'find his voice' that he had discovered too late during the general election campaign itself. It was clear that Labour, in the midst of a terrible economic recession, was probably going to deny the charismatic young Conservative leader a clear majority – and for members of a party who had at many points during the preceding months feared a catastrophic meltdown of the sort that hit the Conservatives in 1997, this seemed almost as good as a victory. After sitting down with two of his key strategists, David Muir and Greg Cook, Brown felt reassured that neither he nor Labour were necessarily 'out of the game' as had been so widely anticipated, and he was understandably buoyed by the news.

Brown then disappeared into a private room with his two Lords, Adonis and Mandelson, to discuss the likely scenarios and possibilities thrown up by the results. By this time Andrew Adonis had already texted Danny Alexander, Nick Clegg's chief of staff, to say: 'Is it time for us talk?' – but Alexander was in no rush as the Liberal Democrats were still reeling from a much poorer than expected showing and needed time to regroup and reappraise recent plans that had been made in expectation of a markedly stronger performance. Besides, he still had his own count to complete. Adonis, perhaps as much as Brown, had a powerful desire to bring about during the ensuing hours and days an effective Lib–Lab Government. As much as anyone on the Labour side, he had a track record of working for what he describes as 'Lib–Labbery'. He had himself moved from the Liberal Democrat side to Labour and retained many friendships within his former party. He had played an important role in the ultimately unsuccessful move to forge closer Lib–Lab co-operation in 1997, and admits now that he had been advising Brown 'for some time' on relations with the Liberal Democrats (though this was 'not a big thing as I had a ministerial job to perform').

Although Adonis did not know personally the Liberal Democrat chief negotiator Danny Alexander, he did know David Laws, originally

from their joint part in negotiations over the first coalition government in Scotland, and subsequently from their shared interest in
education as their parties' spokesmen in this area. He had friendships
with Paddy Ashdown, Ming Campbell and many others. The Holy
Grail of constitutional reform, held so dear by Liberal Democrats, was
also core to his beliefs. Adonis had no doubt whatsoever that a deal
could be done. He felt indeed a strong sense of mission, of destiny
calling: history demanded that a deal should be done! It is obvious
from the slightly embittered articles Adonis wrote in the aftermath of
the resulting Conservative–Liberal Democrat deal the extent to which
he had felt an emotional stake in securing a Lib–Lab arrangement, and
the extent to which he felt angered and dejected that this (as it seemed
to him) natural resolution had been stymied by a lack of will on the
Liberal Democrat side.

At their meeting, Brown confirmed that, if it was at all possible to
do so, a Lib-Lab 'majority' would be put together. Peter Mandelson
describes in his memoirs how Adonis and Gordon Brown competed
with each 'in their excited calculation of how we could make what
Gordon called "an arrangement with the Liberals" happen'. Adonis
felt that this would be the natural conclusion to Brown's wooing if
the Liberal Democrats, which had begun within a month of his assuming the premiership, with his constitutional reform speech and
appointment of Liberal Democrat advisers. At the general election the
Labour Party had been the only party that expressly stipulated a desire
to introduce a referendum on AV.

From the outset Mandelson was less hopeful. 'We were heading', he remembers, 'for a result that put us at under 30 per cent of
the vote … Any way you juggled the figures, we lost the election.'
Brown, however, supported by Adonis, believed that the opportunity

to promote electoral reform was the key to successfully negotiating a coalition deal: a new voting system was far and away the Liberal Democrats' main priority – only more so now that their dispiriting electoral showing had confirmed once again the extent to which the existing system seemed stacked against them. Any concerns that they might have about entering a government with a chastened Labour Party could be overcome by holding out to them a serious prospect of achieving their long-desired prize.

Calculating how Clegg might be hooked, Brown was already shaping in his mind a much more extensive constitutional offering than merely a referendum on AV. When Adonis did finally make a call to Alexander, there was a sense of hope that progress was possible. It was in the event a fairly brief conversation: Adonis informed Alexander that Mandelson would be leading any negotiations for Labour; Alexander played a straight bat, suggesting that Nick Clegg would be a making statement outlining their position shortly.

Brown certainly did not lack for those wishing to offer him their advice. Within the Labour Party everybody in any position of authority, past or present, had an opinion on what Brown should do next. There were a number of very senior figures in the party, such as Tony Blair, who counselled strongly against doing a deal with the Liberal Democrats. Blair regarded the election as lost and felt the Labour Party would be punished if it tried to hang on. Left to make the best of an unconvincing victory, the Tories, Blair thought, would have to form a minority government which would be weak and which ultimately would be relatively short-lived. Blair's direct influence in the Labour Party and in government circles had waned considerably since his resignation as Prime Minister. (It is rather difficult to imagine him ever occupying a position as an honoured grandee within the party, which is a curious situation when one considers that he led them to an unprecedented hat-trick of general election victories).

Nevertheless, Blair did reflect a strain of opinion that was strong, becoming stronger by the hour, and – to Brown's frustration – increasingly hard to suppress on Labour's back benches. As the final positions began to firm up, David Blunkett continued to express himself freely: 'We have lost the general election. We should be proud of what we have done.' Talk of a Lib–Lab coalition, he stated baldly, was 'nonsense'.

Labour MP and blogger Tom Harris, 'having watched Brown over a number of years', was quite clear about what the Prime Minister's reaction would be after the election result: 'He would try to put together a deal with the Liberals. But there was no mechanism for it to be approved. I got the impression that Gordon would do a deal with Clegg and put a "fait accompli" to the PLP.' Harris did not like it, and representing a wider group of Labour MPs, contacted PLP chairman Tony Lloyd to tell him categorically that any deal with the Liberal Democrats would 'be decided by the Parliamentary Party and we will let Gordon Brown know what our decision is'.

It was intended to be a warning shot for Brown about negotiations with Clegg. The Labour Party had been and continued to be in a sulphurous mood. When Brown said, during negotiations, 'I can handle my party', he was perhaps overly confident, even boastful, considering there had been three unsuccessful coups in three years against him involving senior members of his Cabinet which he had barely survived.

Through the Friday morning Brown was focused on making calls to influential senior Liberal Democrats with whom he had had close associations: Menzies Campbell, Paddy Ashdown, Charles Kennedy and Vince Cable. The task he set himself was to sow in the minds of important figures the seeds of what he might be able to deliver as part of a Lib–Lab deal – particularly, of course, in the area of constitutional reform. Finally, he emphasised and (as is Brown's way) re-emphasised, the fundamental realignment of the left in British politics for which they had all at one time worked was within their grasp. He hoped he could count on their support in securing a deal which would make possible the fulfilment of a long-cherished ambition. He believed that the influence of these major figures in the Liberal Democrat party would help him less in the long run – when the situation would be in his own hands – than in getting to the negotiating table in the first place with the Lib Dem team in a frame of mind to collaborate. As Andrew Adonis put it: 'Gordon Brown was a master of power, par excellence ... We saw this as a straight and very important competition for power between us and the Conservatives.' Perhaps this is one of the few things that Cameron and Brown wholeheartedly agreed on.

Aides close to Brown say that when Clegg announced that he would talk to the Conservatives first, he was 'disappointed' – or, according to Mandelson's memoirs, 'visibly deflated'.

It was true, of course, that Clegg had stated in advance his view that the Liberal Democrats should talk first to the largest party – that the one with the most seats would have a 'moral right' or 'moral mandate' to try to form a government. Labour figures like Adonis and Mandelson pointed out in the immediate aftermath of the result that, from a constitutional point of view, this position of Clegg's was fundamentally misconceived. 'The constitutional conventions', Mandelson stated, 'are very clear': 'The rules are that if it's a hung parliament, it's not the party with the largest number of seats that has first go – it's the sitting government.' Adonis made the same point: 'The constitution is clear that Gordon Brown has the first opportunity to form that government.' In so far as anything is concrete in our unwritten constitution, Mandelson and Adonis were correct: the constitutional principle is that in the event of a hung parliament it is the sitting Prime Minister who has the first right to seek to form a government, precisely because he remains the Prime Minister until such time as it becomes clear that he is unable to form a government, and resigns. There was little, however, that Brown could do other than bide his time and try gracefully (or with some outward semblance of grace) to accept that the Lib Dems would in public at least open their discussions with the Tories.

There were certainly many who felt that in laying out his position so definitely in advance – both in terms of talking first to the largest party and in terms of refusing to sustain in office a Prime Minister who had clearly been rejected by the British public – Clegg had made a major strategic error, limiting his and his party's options unnecessarily. It is true, of course, that Clegg had only promised to talk to the largest party *first*. He had never said that the process would necessarily work out in favour of the largest party. Nevertheless, his talk of the largest party having a 'moral right' must surely come back to haunt him in the event of an ultimate Lib–Lab deal which left the largest party – the Conservatives – on the sidelines, tearing into what they could too easily paint as a coalition of the defeated. Likewise regarding Brown himself: it was all very well to cast such doubt on Brown's mandate to remain in office (and one can see why it seemed necessary in advance of the election to appeal to Conservative-minded voters put off the Lib Dems by any thought that they would hand the keys of No. 10 back to Brown), but what was the alternative in the event of a Lib–Lab deal? How could any hypothetical coalition of the left justify replacing Brown with a new leader – and Prime Minister – who, like Brown before him (or her), had no personal electoral mandate whatsoever? Did Clegg dare to think that, if the Lib Dems succeeded (as for a while they looked like doing) in displacing Labour from second place, that he – Nick Clegg – might rightfully claim precedence as a tenant of No. 10? There are suggestions from inside the Clegg camp that at the height of 'Cleggmania' this was tentatively mooted.

In any event, Danny Alexander was careful to ring Andrew Adonis to ensure that Labour continued to be encouraged that there was still a chance for them. Adonis confirmed that Alexander was clear that this was merely Clegg confirming what he had promised during the general election, that the party with the most seats and votes would have the first opportunity to form a government. But it was not to be taken as a message that the Liberal Democrats were 'only interested' in going with the Conservatives. Brown was cheered and pressed on with phone calls and now, encouraged by Mandelson, put out a statement welcoming Clegg's decision.

The calculation was purely a cynical one. There was little Brown could do, and he was already being treated by the media as a 'sort of squatter' in Downing Street. Brown needed to be seen to be helpful, proactive, shaping events rather than responding to them. Power was dribbling away as each hour passed, and taking initiatives, however small, was important, and if nothing else boosted morale. Advised by Alastair Campbell, Mandelson and Adonis, Brown agreed that rushing out a statement before David Cameron could respond to Clegg was important.

As the drafting began, Mandelson was already torn about what to do about the problem of 'personnel' – by which of course he meant one person in particular. Back-channel conversations with senior Liberal Democrats during the election period had confirmed for

Mandelson what he had been inclined to suspect, that Clegg supporting Brown as Prime Minister would be at best problematic, and probably a deal-breaker. The actual result had significantly increased these difficulties. Publicly Mandelson continued to show concern and loyalty for the man who brought him back into British politics, and privately he could not dismiss outright Brown's increasingly fevered schemes to cling to office. But internally he knew from the beginning that Brown would have to go.

Mandelson had been convinced of this from the early hours of Friday morning – not only because of the poor relationship with Clegg, the open dislike of Brown by a good number of his own MPs and ministers, but because Brown had fundamentally lost the general election. Mandelson knew privately it would largely fall to him to assist with Brown's removal, albeit in the most dignified way possible – he would do what he could (anything else would appear disloyal) but the fight for Brown's survival, he knew privately, was already lost.

As such, it was not the Liberal Democrats who forced the early pace on the issue of 'personnel', it was Mandelson. He knew it was a key issue that would stop an early formation of a Lib–Lab government, and for it to be discussed openly he had to get it on the agenda and sorted out. To that end, as he recounts in his memoirs, 'I texted Danny shortly after noon: "Between us (pl protect) ask Nick how big an obstacle is GB for the LDs".'

What he doesn't say in in *The Third Man* is that Alexander didn't respond to that text, and when they spoke later in the afternoon Alexander put 'personnel' on the backburner. He told Mandelson that they (the Liberal Democrats) meant what they had said about the process; were not in any way going through the motions with Conservatives; were ready to talk about policies; had reservations about Labour with regard to the parliamentary numbers and to do with their attitudes; but were not going to discuss personnel issues for the moment. As Mandelson saw it, this was a clear and unambiguous reference to 'the GB issue'. Publicly, Mandelson would continue to be loyal to Brown. Privately, though, he knew that the sooner the Prime Minister went, the better Labour's slim chance of forming a government would be.

Meanwhile Gordon Brown continued with his pre-empting operation in a statement outside Downing Street, that was originally to be made later in the afternoon. The Prime Minister's statement aimed to demonstrate that the government, if not quite conducting business as usual, was still governing by suggesting Alistair Darling was taking part that weekend in a European discussion about Greece and the growing European financial crisis.

Perhaps in reminding people that the financial crisis was ongoing Brown hoped to reinforce in the popular mind the notion that he was the steady, experienced pair of hands the nation needed on the tiller. Too late to alter the electoral result, of course: but in the event of him leading a Lib–Lab coalition, he would need the public to accept this outcome.

Brown's statement, while largely self-serving, was also prime ministerial. What he was very conscious of, of course, was that any statement would be analysed not only by the public and the press, but by the Liberal Democrats in particular, and with this in mind he thought carefully about the message he wanted to convey to them. He did sincerely believe that he had powerful cards to play: there were two key issues – the economy and constitutional reform – in which he believed that Labour would have a distinct advantage over the Conservatives in any negotiations. He might have no choice but to let the Liberal Democrat and the Conservative negotiating teams talk first – but he could keep this message in the forefront of Lib Dem minds. His message to the Liberal Democrat party, and to Clegg in particular, was clear: 'You will get a better deal from me.'

Within No. 10 the Prime Minister and his closest aides and allies then gathered around the television to watch Cameron in turn make a public statement. Interestingly, the majority opinion – to Brown's gratification – was that Cameron had made a significant strategic blunder. In gunning openly for a compromise deal with the Liberal Democrats, it was felt, he had shown weakness at a time when the public was looking particularly for strength from its leaders. In difficult economic times, the assembled Labour figures reassured themselves, people wanted strength rather than fudge and compromise. But not everybody was quite so sure. Peter Mandelson, for one, was secretly rather impressed: Cameron's speech showed, he felt, 'an openness to the new sort of politics' for which so many had apparently voted and which had been such an important theme during the general election campaign. Andrew Adonis was another who reluctantly admired the Tory leader's stance: 'David Cameron's strategy from the viewpoint of the Conservatives was brilliant because what he essentially decided on the Friday was he would do what it took to get the Conservatives into government.' Adonis was certainly right about Conservative thinking.

It was late Friday afternoon, at 5pm, when Brown spoke to Clegg directly for the first time (only an hour, as we will see, after Clegg had spoken with Cameron). As far as Brown was concerned, a deal between Labour and the Liberal Democrats was the natural and obvious outcome from the point of view of policy and ideals; the only question then became whether it was practically viable in terms of pinning down a sustainable parliamentary majority. It was this, therefore, that Brown sought particularly to discuss. In the account of the conversation given in his memoirs, Peter Mandelson quotes Brown as saying: 'Nick, the only issue is a majority of seats in the Commons.' Brown felt that, provided that the two parties could make the numbers add up, they could do a deal – and one that would be totally legitimate. 'Nick, if we agree on public expenditure and economic recovery everything else will fall into place.' By 'everything else', close aides confirm, Brown intended primarily to imply electoral reform, not – an elephant in the room that the short-sighted Prime Minister wasn't easily able to identify – his own continued position as Prime Minister.

This phone conversation, held strictly in private, would become one of those key set-pieces over which competing accounts would be traded in public in an effort to shape popular perceptions.

According to Clegg: 'The conversation was very much Gordon constantly trying to impress on me that, yes he accepted there had to be talks with the Conservatives, but it would be a disaster to do anything with them. He reminded me then and in every subsequent conversation that it would be a complete disaster for the country and that we were progressives together and there was so much that we could do together. We could do more on constitutional reform and more on the economy, the Conservatives were completely wrong and he was completely right on the deficit. It was as much a conversation distinguished by vindication rather than the successful art of persuasion if that is a delicate way of putting it.'

Brown had slightly misjudged the tone of the call. As was his wont, he spoke too much and listened too little, failing to give Nick Clegg enough space to get his own message across. However, that evening and the following morning the media was awash with accounts of a disastrous and highly acrimonious conversation.

Guided by the Lib Dem top team, Paddy Ashdown had put it about to the media that the Prime Minister had been 'threatening in his approach to Nick Clegg' and that the conversation had gone particularly badly with Brown delivering 'a diatribe and a rant'.

This was a caricature at best, untrue at worst, certainly not a fair reflection of what had happened. Clegg himself now accepts this, and that although the conversation was 'a bit one-sided, Gordon, to be fair to him, was trying to get his foot in the door of a process where I'd been quite open that I would speak to the Tories first'. But as an example of the tendentious public portrayal of private discussions, it set the tone for the contacts between Labour and the Liberal Democrats in the days that followed.

Andrew Adonis believes the Liberal Democrats were determined at every stage to produce a narrative, essentially for their own party purposes, to the effect that it had been impossible to get a deal with Labour, in spite of good will and the best intentions on the Liberal Democrat side – the need for this narrative being the predominant expectation and desire among Liberal Democrat MPs that a deal with Labour would be the preferred choice for the party. 'I think what was happening', Adonis now reflects, 'were two things: in principle Clegg and his chief negotiators, for a whole set of reasons, had decided that they wanted, if possible, to go with the Conservatives, but there were two requirements they had to fulfil. The first is they had to get a reasonable deal from the Conservatives which they could justify and the second is they had to persuade their MPs that it wasn't possible to get a satisfactory deal with Labour. Part of that process was this constant narrative that all contacts with Labour were unsatisfactory and so we had the briefing [to Jon Sopel of the BBC] of the first Gordon Brown call as having been a terrible call. It wasn't a terrible call, it was a perfectly satisfactory call.'

Despite much huffing and puffing in the media, the Conservatives had failed to get the removal men into Downing Street. Gordon Brown had made it through the day, when perhaps many commentators believed he would have gone. More than one member of Brown's Cabinet was certainly of that view. One story tells how Jack Straw was informed that he must be back in London by mid-afternoon on Friday 'without fail'.

One of the quirky requirements in our democracy is that the Lord Chancellor must go to the Palace and hand back the Great Seal of the Realm. (The Great Seal is attached to the official documents of state that require the authorisation of the monarch to implement the advice of the government.) To ensure that a new cabinet could be appointed in a timely fashion, Straw was informed that he must be ready to go to the Palace on Friday before the Courts close. Clearly officials did not believe the existing government would be continuing.

The Conservatives

Cameron had spent the first part of polling day with his closest advisers at Steve Hilton's house, a short drive from his own Witney constituency home, where a meeting began at 10am with George Osborne, Ed Llewellyn, Patrick McLoughlin, Stephen Gilbert, the party's director of field operations, and Hilton present, along with Andy Coulson, Director of Communications and Catherine Fall, Cameron's deputy chief of staff. Cameron joined the meeting having been to vote, and the team went through a wide-ranging agenda that included appointments to Cabinet in the event of victory, actions in the first few days, and all the possible scenarios that the election might throw at them. It was decided that if the Conservatives won 300-310 seats, Cameron would 'claim victory'. A little over 24 hours later the plan would be swiftly dropped when the reality of the result hit home.

The team, including Cameron, took lunch at Hilton's. George Osborne then left for his own Tatton constituency in Cheshire. Cameron left for his nearby constituency home at around 2.30pm, with the others following in the later afternoon, remaining there until the early hours when they accompanied their leader to his count. Cameron's aides let it be known that he had whiled away the afternoon chopping logs – inviting comments about his facility at wielding an axe, or perhaps seeking to impress Liberal Democrats with his irresistible Gladstonian energy. Supper for the Cameron team was another meaty, no-nonsense, getting-to-work-on-the-deficit sort of dish: a chilli con carne prepared by his wife Samantha.

Conservative expectations had been mixed. At campaign headquarters on Millbank, activists stuck stoutly to their belief that the party would outperform the polls. Many genuinely felt that the marginal seats programme, under the stewardship of Lord Ashcroft, would deliver a return beyond that being measured by the pollsters. (And Labour MPs and ministers had long feared they were right, agonising over the impact of 'the Ashcroft money'.) Polling in the marginal seats close to the election had suggested the programme's impact might not be as marked as first thought. But this did little to shake what had become an entrenched assumption among the politicians of both main parties.

Within Cameron's inner circle, however, the mood was more uncertain. While Party chairman Eric Pickles hoped for the best and believed a single-figure majority still likely, those like Oliver Letwin who had spent time poring over the polls and the likely outcomes believed that a hung parliament was overwhelmingly the most likely result. The average of all the polls seemed to suggest this beyond doubt. The final estimates of nine polling organisations put the Conservative lead at between four and nine points: they all said hung.

This, Letwin had judged for some time, was 'the rational best measure of what is likely to happen.' He for one had doubted the impact of even a well run campaign. From the moment the battle commenced, he remarked to party colleagues, 'We all fire huge amounts of am- munition at each other and end up broadly where we started.' On this assumption, the huge swing the Conservatives required for an overall majority seemed likely to be beyond them – a view that was shared by a surprising number of senior members of the party. Certainly no one, one of Cameron's chief aides now stresses, imagined they could sweep back to Downing Street with a majority of 40 or 50: 'The mantra that we trotted out in the months leading up to the election was believed internally very strongly; that to win this election everything would have to go right. It required a phenomenal swing; it required gaining 116 seats, and nobody had ever done that before. It was a bloody big ask.' There was some optimism that, just like 1992, a last-minute consolidation would see the party scrape home with a majority of 5 to 10: 'That was never impossible at all. It was quite possible that we would notch up another point or two in the last few days.' And as the polls closed, rumours from within the Conservative camp did begin to circulate that a late swing had set up the Conservatives to do better than expected. But no one was in any doubt that this was going to be a mighty close call.

A Conservative press release was soon rushed out, trying to set the mood music, hailing what was provisionally a 'historic result': the most seats gained by Conservatives since 1931, the biggest swing to the Conservatives since the same year, a basis to govern: 'Labour can't possibly expect to continue in government after this humiliating rejec- tion.' In the cold light of dawn, a different emphasis was adopted from what had seemed advisable 24 hours earlier, when a claim of victory was thought to be more provident. What this reflected was a revised reading of the public mood, which was that while Labour had clearly lost, the Conservatives could not realistically claim to have won.

Early results did little to clarify the picture. The first three, all from Sunderland, showed Tory swings of between 4.8 and 11.5%. But the local variation was too great to provide a meaningful indication. Accurate as the polls would prove in terms of the overall picture, at local level, in individual constituencies, surprising anomalies could and did occur. Particular results left party chairman Eric Pickles scratching his head. 'For the life of me', he later remarked, 'I'll never understand how we took Sherwood but never took the adjoining seat. It was remarkable.'

With Cameron, Hague, Letwin and Osborne strung out across the country waiting for their counts to make progress, it was difficult to get a co-ordinated view with all the uncertainty from the early results and the exit poll. Osborne, waiting at his secretary's house, which was closer to the count, held the initial view that 'we've done it, we haven't got a majority but we've clearly got more votes and seats, I think we're in.' He believed the party would have the political and moral momentum which would drive Brown out of Downing Street and carry Cameron in.

Both Cameron and Osborne had been tipped off slightly early about the result of the exit poll and spoke at around 10.15pm. Watching the early election coverage, both felt it was drifting towards a view of 'the Tories haven't done it' and that somebody needed to make the point that Labour had lost the election and give the statistics, only 29% of the vote, the worst result since Michael Foot, and so on. Osborne was not going to head to his count at Macclesfield leisure centre until after 1am, but it was agreed that he should go early and get his leader's message out sooner rather than later.

Theresa May had been in the television studio, but without direct connection to the leader was not aware of what was now required. So from 11pm, Osborne was on air putting the official Conservative message out on national television that Labour had lost and could not possibly continue in government.

Osborne's early arrival at the leisure centre meant he was stuck in the café passing the time of day with reporters from ITV, Sky and the BBC – not quite what he had planned. His mood swung from at one point worrying his party may not reach 300 seats, to feeling the wind was in the party's sails. As soon as his count was over he went by helicopter to London, arriving shortly after 6am and having had no sleep.

This small episode demonstrates something that has become accepted throughout the Westminster village – the extremely close relationship between Cameron and Osborne. It is a partnership built on mutual respect and closely corresponding political views. They are not just political friends but personal friends, godparents to each others' children. Some commentators have made the mistake of believing this close friendship was forged before both men became MPs. This would not be true as, although they had been acquaintances before they both were elected in 2001, it became a strong friendship only after they became MPs, and was assisted by a large number of mutual friends and similar views across a range of subjects.

As two youthful MPs they never dreamed of becoming Prime Minister and Chancellor. However, they did spend time thinking about what changes were required to bring their party back to power. As Osborne said: 'We were fed up with the party being a debating club and a *Telegraph* editorial instead of a party that wins elections and gains seats.' Both men were dismayed by what had happened to the Conservative Party, and the desire to modernise bound the two men together.

There was also a lack of competition between the two men. Osborne never really saw himself as party leader, so there was never any prospect of the rivalry that dominated the Blair–Brown years. When Michael Howard made Osborne shadow Chancellor, commentators speculated that this was a precursor to his running for the leadership, but it had not even crossed Osborne's mind – he was even surprised to be made shadow Chancellor at the time. There could never be the same feelings that existed between Brown and Blair as Osborne could never feel he was cheated out of becoming party leader and Prime Minister.

However, the two men do have robust arguments about issues, although never falling out, as Prime Ministers are wont to do with their Chancellors. The two men also work hard at keeping their relationship close, ensuring trust does not break down. Neither Cameron nor Osborne will gossip or brief about the other, as this is usually the source of conflict between senior members of any Cabinet. This has created the basis of an extremely strong working relationship in government. With the pressures mounting on a modern day Prime Minister, having a close and trusted team nearby to provide support is an essential part of government.

The early plan on the morning of Friday 7 May was to get Brown to go by putting him under enormous moral and political pressure. The Conservative plan was still to form a minority administration and to get into government as soon as possible, but first Brown had to be ripped out of Downing Street so that Cameron could get into the building. Osborne was convinced that once the party was through the front door at Downing Street, the rules of the game changed (echoing Brown's earlier view to Mandelson that 'once the Tories get their hands on the levers of power we'll never get them off'). However, the Civil Service-designed rules, recently accepted by the parties, re-emphasised that Brown had the authority to remain in place. The Conservatives had not fully anticipated that the now written convention, that the Prime Minister stays until an alternative is found to form a government, would give Brown the necessary political cover to stay on.

Osborne said: 'The rules were not unreasonable, but I don't think anybody had thought through the implication, which was that Brown was determined to stay. You could argue another Prime Minister might have said "Look, I've lost", and obviously some people in his party were telling him that. It only became clear later in the day that there wasn't going to be a quick resolution. It wasn't going to be all over by Friday evening.' The game of chess that ensued over the following days was essentially due to the formal codification of rules pushed for by the Civil Service.

Shortly after 12.30am on the Friday morning, the Cameron inner circle accompanied their man to his count, stopping off for a non-alcoholic drink at the New Inn in Witney, whose landlord chaired the local Conservative Association. After dropping him at the leisure centre which was hosting the count, most of his team motored off to London to be at party HQ as the flow of results started to pick up pace. Cameron himself had to wait until moments before 3am for his result to be announced. As he took to the stage, the electoral fog had barely lifted. In his acceptance speech the Tory leader warned of the dangers of prolonged uncertainty, promising to put the national interest first 'in the hours ahead and perhaps longer than the hours ahead.' The one thing that seemed clear, he affirmed, was that the Labour government had 'lost its mandate to govern this country'.

For Cameron, the journey back to London was spent – inevitably – on the phone. He spoke at length to his chief political ally George

Osborne, as well as to his chief of staff, Ed Llewellyn. The latter, having already reached Tory HQ, had the surreal experience of talking to
his boss while watching the progress of his car, beamed via helicopter
camera to the live news channel. While discussing key policy decisions
Llewellyn was able to relay Cameron's journey to him as he moved
from traffic light to traffic light.

By now the electoral signals were equally clear. A hung parliament
would indeed be the outcome: the Conservatives 'were not going to
cross the wire'. The analysis from Conservative head office remained
consistent: the party was looking at between 303 and 308 seats, 310
at the outside.

Osborne and Cameron were not yet of one mind. Cameron's
instinct was strong that an early call should be made to the Liberal
Democrats. Osborne had his doubts, feeling that the Liberal Democrats were unlikely to join with the Conservatives and that the party
should tread carefully – his view was that their whole focus should
be on getting Brown out of Downing Street. Cameron was calm but
determined, aides remember, and was clear that the time had come.
From the car he declared, 'You should get hold of Danny, now!'

In all their minds was the knowledge that a political bidding war,
a struggle for power, would soon commence, in which the early moves
would be critical in shaping the outcome: 'We needed to get onto [the
Liberal Democrats]. We were very conscious that Labour would be
doing the same.'

Cameron now knew he was involved in a struggle where time
was of the essence, and he was determined to take the initiative and
force the pace. Already, his strategy to take power was becoming well
developed in his own mind.

(Where the seed for Cameron's determination to make a 'bold

invitation' to the Liberal Democrats came from is not entirely clear. It was certainly there in the campaign, as he first mentioned it at the meeting to plan for the second leaders' debate at Osborne's house. Interestingly, members of his party recall a Conservative parliamentary 'away day' in 2006, the year after Cameron became leader. Former Labour MP and broadcaster Brian Walden had been invited to address the assembled Parliamentary Party, and his contribution is remembered as quite outstanding, both intellectually and in terms of his oratory. The section of his talk that now recalled itself to the minds of those who heard it was a discussion of the Conservative response to a hung parliament scenario. Walden believed that in a hung parliament the best option for the Conservatives would be to make concessions to the Liberal Democrats and bring them into government. The likely outcome, he argued, would be the absorption of a considerable part of the Liberal Democrats over a period of time.)

Early on the Friday morning, Ed Llewellyn – an absolutely key player in the drama, particularly over the first 24 hours – contacted Alexander as the internal debate continued, and around 4am, with over 250 results in, showing a hung parliament swing of just under 5%, the first link was made. Llewellyn texted Alexander just as the latter was awaiting his count in Inverness, and quickly received a response: 'I'll call you back as soon as my count is over.' Shortly afterwards the two spoke. Little of substance needed to be said that was not already clear to both; they agreed they would need to speak again later in the morning. But the first symbolic bridge had been crossed.

Cameron arrived back at Tory HQ and immediately headed for the command centre to talk to key aides and get the latest assessment. He then went to the gathering being held in Millbank Tower for an assortment of party workers and donors, all the while thinking about his next move. The mood was downbeat, but Cameron spoke and raised spirits, albeit briefly. One senior Conservative told me that some at this party were 'the worse for wear. One or two were complaining loudly that we had thrown it away, and a few who were really quite nasty! I was glad to leave.'

There followed a short meeting in Cameron's office, which he was sharing for the duration of the election with George Osborne, the pair having wrestled it from Andrew Feldman. At that early morning meeting Andy Coulson was worried. Gordon Brown, he felt, was appearing prime ministerial, and there was a danger that he might succeed in developing 'the initiative and momentum to take the government'.

It was, according to one who witnessed it, a tense meeting. There was 'a lot of argument, I suppose creative tension, between Steve [Hilton] and George [Osborne] about what to do next. George thought the Liberals [sic] would go with Labour and they would be difficult to get some kind of decision from. It was the first time for a long time he wasn't quite certain. He'd always given decisive leadership through the campaign. But we were all bloody tired.'

Cameron decided to draw a line under it and said, 'Enough – I'm going to my hotel', which would give everyone the opportunity to get some rest. He left for the Westminster Plaza Hotel just after 6am, ordering his team to reconvene at 10am in his hotel suite. Party chairman Eric Pickles, Chief Whip Patrick McLoughlin, shadow Education Secretary Michael Gove and Tom Strathclyde, Conservative leader in the House of Lords, would also join the meeting. William Hague, shadow Foreign Secretary and de facto deputy leader, was driving back from his count and joined the meeting by telephone at key moments.

The unsurprising disarray and chaos of early Friday morning is demonstrated by the experience of McLoughlin and Hague. Mc-Cloughlin, highly regarded by the Parliamentary Party, was once described by a parliamentary sketch-writer as resembling Butch, the dog from Tom and Jerry. The resemblance is notable, as when on the front bench he appears to be guarding his team and even when he is seemingly uninterested, at the slightest discordant noise an eye will open to survey the horizon.

After his count McLoughlin headed to London from Derby station, arriving at 8.30am. He headed straight to Conservative HQ, expecting a hive of activity around the leader. There was nobody there. He went to his Opposition Whips' office, and there was nobody there either. Not quite what he had expected, so he rang Ed Llewellyn, who told him to head across to their hotel. On arrival, he rang Llewellyn again to ask which room – to discover that unfortunately he was in the wrong hotel …

He finally made it to the Westminster Plaza and headed up to Cameron's suite on the twelfth floor (senior Conservative aides had demanded to be moved from their original allocation of the 'unlucky' thirteenth floor to more cramped quarters on the twelfth, to the irritation of the leadership). Suddenly his route was blocked by two burly men who demanded to know who he was and where he was going? He explained he was the Opposition Chief Whip, here to see the Leader of the Opposition, and after the appropriate checks he finally made it to Cameron's room. It was indeed the Leader of the Opposition he had come to call on. However, as John Prescott might have noted, the presence of the security men told their own story: the 'tectonic plates' of UK politics were shifting.

Hague also had a chaotic start to Friday. At key points in the intense conversations at the Westminster Plaza, he would have to call into motorway services in search of a decent phone signal that would allow him to join in discussion of the issues at hand. There were three separate conference calls with a group of people, initially Cameron, Osborne and Hague, which grew as they spoke to people like Ken Clarke and Liam Fox, whose approval was important to a potential coalition agreement. It ended up with the shadow Cabinet on a conference call!

For those on the road it was all rather surreal. 'It sticks in my memory', Hague recalls, '[that] we were deciding the potential future government of the country while I was at some curious places like a Little Chef and a McDonald's car park, where we'd had a quick burger. It was certainly one of the longest journeys from Yorkshire to London I'd ever had as we set out around 10am and didn't arrive until late afternoon!'

At the hotel, as one of those present remembers, Cameron was on impressive form in spite of the long night. He 'was firing on all cylinders. He accepted what he had to do and how he had to go about it. He was completely in command.' The path he wanted to take forward was now clearly mapped out in his mind: he was absolutely clear that he was going to make a very bold and generous offer to the Liberal Democrats.

Cameron had had the seed of an idea about coalition in his mind for several weeks, but was focused on victory. The exact mathematics of the result, having discussed pursuing a minority government with his team only 24 hours earlier, made him focus. The result had left the prospect of a non-Conservative government as a reality and he determined that for both the political and national interest he must not allow it to happen.

Therefore before he slept he had been turning the option of coalition in his mind, and when he awoke he had decided the best thing to do was to aim high, as he said, 'to pitch for a partnership government'. It was, he felt, a twin-track approach, because if a formal coalition proved impossible to construct, then he hoped for a minority government. But either way it would give the Conservative Party the moral high ground.

Discussions with George Osborne about this strategy confirmed Cameron's view, and as one who witnessed events said: 'After a bit of sleep, George was back as the old George. He said we needed to make a generous offer, we needed to offer "the top price for the Turkish carpet".' Osborne had a new focus and determination, and a very firm sense of purpose. It was his job, he now believed, Cameron told me: 'to get us out of opposition and into government. He was going to drive that chariot as fast as he could leaving the leader of the party to make the final decision on whether the deal was the right one.'

When Letwin began describing to the assembled team the policy issues and the overlaps, he did it from a basis of painstaking preparation. Going through issue after issue, he described the detailed positions of each side: close on environment, but there was the nuclear issue; clear overlap on education; George could deal with the affordable parts of the Liberal Democrats' tax plan; and so it went on. Meanwhile Coulson had reappraised his early-morning view on Brown – or at least he noted, with gratification, that his own view that Brown was appearing prime ministerial was not one shared by the media. The press, he observed, were 'now treating Brown like a squatter'.

As the discussions continued, Ed Llewellyn kept in regular touch by phone and text with Danny Alexander, who was ensuring that Cameron broadly knew what Clegg was expected to say in his statement outside party headquarters in Cowley Street at 10.30am. Neither team appeared to want any surprises, so it appeared as if the Liberal Democrat and Conservative pronouncements were almost choreographed.

The Conservative team continued working and while Clegg made his live TV appearance, one Cameron aide told me: 'We expected Clegg to honour his commitment to the largest party and we were the largest party in the number of MPs and votes cast, but obviously we needed public confirmation.' As soon as Clegg's public reassurance of this had been given, Cameron's team 'got weaving very quickly as to what David would actually say'.

As a result of Clegg's statement Osborne made it clear: 'We are going to treat it seriously, treat them like grown-ups, and we're going to behave like grown-ups.'

The view on the twelfth floor of the Westminster Plaza, particularly from Steve Hilton, was that Cameron needed to get his response out rapidly. There was a view that Cameron should meet or talk with Clegg before he made his response, but Clegg was clear (as relayed via Alexander) that a conversation should only take place after the Conservative position had been clearly laid out. It was therefore agreed that the two leaders would speak at 4pm.

The activity was now focused on drafting Cameron's response to Clegg. Cameron's clarity of thought proved inspirational, setting out what he wanted to say. Steve Hilton retired to a separate room (aided by Kate Marley) to draft what Cameron wanted. Hilton's draft took longer than expected as sheer tiredness kicked in, and anxiety started to rise. His first draft was rejected as too stark in its offer of a coalition: George Osborne felt that it tried to do everything in one leap. The very word 'coalition' was dotted throughout the draft, and Osborne in particular was concerned that the intention was too blunt and might stir unnecessary hostility within the Parliamentary Party. Hilton retired to peace and quiet to put together several further versions as Osborne, Ed Llewellyn and Andy Coulson made suggestions. Letwin also reviewed a late draft. 'Cameron is always very clear in these situations about what he wants to say, but obviously we discussed what the key elements of it should be,' is how one of those in the room described it.

With events now moving quickly and Cameron about to make his opening 'forward leaning' bid, it was important that the shadow Cabinet and senior members of the party were on board. From 11am a frantic series of phone calls ensued with Sir John Major, Iain Duncan Smith, Michael Howard, David Davis, and others called by Cameron, in addition to senior members of the shadow Cabinet such as Liam Fox and Ken Clarke. At this stage, there was little resistance to the plan, although it is reported that Pickles, calling members of the party board, apparently did run into some resistance from individuals who were firm in wanting a Conservative minority government and no agreement with the Liberal Democrats.

While the call-rounds continued and the statement was drafted and mulled over, the wheels were set in motion for a full shadow Cabinet conference call for 1.45pm. Much to the Conservative leader's chagrin, Prime Minister Gordon Brown suddenly brought forward the time of his statement to pre-empt the Leader of the Opposition. Brown was doing what he could to try to remain the person dictating events – to be ahead of the Conservatives in the race to woo the Liberal Democrats. Cameron was all too aware what Brown was up to and was mildly irritated to be pre-empted. From the very early morning he had been pressing his team on the importance of setting the pace and driving the agenda.

As one of Cameron's close associates told me: 'We heard about Brown's statement quite close to the wire. It was a typical Brown pre-empting operation which was slightly frustrating and annoying and we thought, "Maybe we should have got this out there sooner," but we did need to get our ducks properly in a row.'

As it turned out, the Conservatives were in no position to respond to Brown's pre-emptive strike. They had booked St Stephen's Club in Westminster, a regular venue for Cameron's press conferences, because it 'was a very good backdrop and created the right sort of impression', but it simply wasn't available any earlier. It was also true to say the final statement wasn't ready, as the final version was 'shoved into David's hand as he left the hotel. I remember cursing the printer to hurry up. David hadn't even read the final version at that stage,' said a senior aide.

By the time most of the shadow Cabinet had logged into the conference call it was almost 1.45pm and the press conference was looming large. According to a member of the shadow Cabinet who was on that call: 'David briefly set out what was about to happen at 2.30: "this is what I'm going to do and I'm letting you know in advance." It was one of those moments where I genuinely don't think you could have a real discussion with twenty to twenty-five people over a phone about the strategy. A few people spoke, but I don't believe there was any significant dissent because it was primarily about opening discussions.'

The work that Hilton and others put into getting the Cameron statement right paid off handsomely – the statement, as one Labour MP reluctantly admitted, 'was a blinder, hitting all the right notes.' His implicit message was that the Conservatives had effectively won the election and that Labour had lost – the moral right to govern was with the Conservatives (implicitly Osborne's message to Brown to go). He sought to respond to the desire for a new politics which had permeated the election campaign, emphasising his intention to rise above the bickering and manoeuvring of routine party politics to deliver what the country urgently needed: a strong and stable government.

He spoke to the nation. But also, perhaps more importantly, he spoke to the Liberal Democrat leadership, whom he knew with certainty would be scrutinising his every word. It was important to thank Clegg for his earlier statement as that had opened the door for what Cameron was now able to say about compromise and considering 'alternative options' for a more collaborative government. The message to the Liberal Democrats was clear: they could be in no doubt that the 'big, open and comprehensive offer' which Cameron promised entailed him proposing a coalition government in which they would play a full and equal part. Both parties together could repair the enormous damage wrought by Brown's Labour government. There were more areas of agreement between the two parties than disagreement, and a deal could be done. Much work remained, of course, to deliver a workable programme for a coalition government that both parties could sign up to. But the important thing was that in a few well-worded lines the tenor of the Conservative–Liberal Democrat negotiations had been set.

Once again, Cameron had pulled out a big performance when he needed it, as he had done during his leadership campaign and at his party conference in 2009 over the expenses scandal. It was another defining moment for Cameron, a big speech given in circumstances where nothing less than the future direction of the country rode on the outcome – yet with as little as three hours' sleep in the past 48 hours. In the circumstances it was an extraordinary performance.

The Liberal Democrat response was immediately warm. Danny Alexander has commented: 'David Cameron's speech set up the good feeling for the negotiations because it was clear from what he said that he was very interested, and indeed excited, by the prospect of a coalition. He was prepared to have proper negotiations in key areas of interest to the Liberal Democrats.'

Andrew Stunell, an expert on negotiating power-sharing deals, remembered: 'I was in our leader's office when David Cameron made his wholehearted offer to the Liberal Democrats. I remember saying: "Oh shit, we're in trouble now," because I could see a pre-emptive offer had been put on the table, which it was going to take a lot of ingenuity to avoid taking very seriously. The first meeting with the Conservatives I was waiting to see what the catch was, but events showed that my attitude was overly cynical.'

Similarly impressed was a man who had a keen ear for the nuance of political statements. Watching with Gordon Brown and his team, Peter Mandelson recalls that both the Prime Minister and some of his advisers felt that Cameron's bid 'was a mistaken show of weakness, given that the Tories had won the largest number of seats.' But 'to me', he writes in his memoirs, 'it sounded like the new politics.' And while there were those in the Conservative party fiercely opposed to any coalition deal, this very fact illustrated its advantage to Cameron as he sought further to decontaminate the Conservative brand by distancing it from its right-wing element. Mandelson saw that a deal, should Cameron secure one, offered 'a renewed prospect of delivering a changed perception of his party'. As a central architect of 'New' Labour, who shaped an electable party from the stricken and serially defeated Labour Party of the 1980s and early 1990s, this was something about which Mandelson was qualified to talk.

Looking back on the events of the five-day period, it was Cameron's bold speech that unlocked the real possibility of a Conservative-led coalition government being formed with the Liberal Democrats.

Cameron, urged on by Osborne, had done what was necessary to bring power within his reach.

Cameron went back to Central Office with his close aides and spent almost an hour with Steve Hilton, Ed Llewellyn and others looking at a map of constituencies, trying to analyse and understand what had happened. Then it was time to call Nick Clegg.

The Liberal Democrats

The countdown to 10pm was all about the exit poll, announced on the BBC moments after voting closed. Tense groups of politicians, advisers, staff and volunteers gathered round their screens to await the verdict, while key party spokesmen stood poised to provide an instant on-message reaction. The Conservatives, the poll projected, would win 307 seats, nineteen short of an overall majority – a figure that was shortly afterwards revised down to only 305 (up 95 on the 2005 general election). Labour were predicted to win 255 (down 94) and the Liberal Democrats 61 (down 1). It was a result which brought no great cheer to any of the three parties.

But across the spectrum the exit forecast was greeted inwardly as well as outwardly with surprise and scepticism. It was not that the overall picture of a hung parliament was unexpected. The prediction of a Liberal Democrat downturn, however, seemed wildly at odds with the anticipated surge. Where was the much-heralded breakthrough for the third party provided by the game-changing television debates? Where was the 'Clegg effect'? 'Cleggmania', to be sure, had moderated since the first debate had launched the Lib Dem leader to a prime-time audience. But almost no one in Lib Dem headquarters or outside it doubted that vastly increased media coverage would show in the electoral arithmetic.

The pollsters themselves were under pressure. In 2005 the exit poll had been remarkably accurate, nailing Labour's eventual majority exactly. But no one had yet forgotten the egregious error of 1992, when the nation went to bed to predictions of a hung parliament, and woke to a Conservative majority government. It was a memory which fortified those caught off guard now.

Simon Hughes, Deputy Leader of the Liberal Democrats, was quick to draw the comparison: 'In 1992 when it was very tight', he remarked, the exit polls were 'wildly out'. Clegg's closest ally Danny Alexander also went on air to dismiss exit polls as 'notoriously unreliable'. Indeed, Alexander was so confident the pollsters had blundered that he offered to join Conservative blogger Iain Dale in a naked sprint down Whitehall if the prediction of fewer Lib Dem seats proved accurate. (To date the Chief Secretary's diary commitments have got in the way of this particular coalition photo-op.) At any rate, as Alexander told me, rather tongue in cheek: 'That was a commitment made before we were in government and is not in the coalition agreement.'

Nick Clegg himself was in a deep gloom – 'crestfallen', as one witness described him. He could not quite believe the exit poll, and how his seemingly extraordinary popularity after the first television debate had translated into fewer seats. The result was almost a humiliation. He remembers now very honestly the depression he felt that Thursday night: 'I felt bruised, disappointed on all sorts of levels. Bitterly disappointed not just for myself but for a good friend of mine, Paul Scriven, who was the candidate in Sheffield Central next to me, and had worked really hard. I worked really hard to try and help him get elected and he just missed it. We were at the count together in Sheffield in the big sports centre there. After all the hype of the leaders' debates, to see the exit polls put us right back down where we started and the realisation as the night wore on that we'd lost valued colleagues and friends and we didn't win a string of seats (particularly in the north), and an awareness as the night wore on that it was just all so ridiculously close, left me frustrated. I now know that ... if we'd have had 4,000 extra votes we'd have won eleven extra seats. I mean it was astonishing – just pipped at the post. I knew we were being squeezed ruthlessly in the last two days of the election contest and I could feel it wherever I went – so yeah, I was disappointed.'

Because of the problems in Sheffield with people being unable to cast their votes late in the day, Clegg's count did not finish until after 6.30am. He had not slept properly for several days and was feeling the pressure that the disappointment brought. If the Liberal Democrats could not make a breakthrough now, when could they?

Clegg was in close contact with Danny Alexander right through polling day itself and, as the results came in, through the night, and as the position became clear, the two men spoke of their disappointment. The paradoxical situation, though, was that in the midst of their greatest disappointment as Liberal Democrat politicians, they recognised also their greatest opportunity, because of the larger parliamentary arithmetic which left neither of the established parties with an overall majority.

Clegg and Alexander discussed what the former should say in his statement at Cowley Street and what they thought the reaction might be. Alexander was also reporting back his conversations with a variety of early-morning contacts from both big parties.

Alexander was to prove an adept and loyal lieutenant to Clegg over the next five days. The two had developed a very close working relationship, although not quite the so-called unbreakable friendship said to exist between George Osborne and David Cameron. They had entered

Westminster in 2005 with desks next to each other, displayed a similar sense of humour and worked closely, often attending events together.

A close confidant of both Lib Dem men characterised their friendship: 'It's not really a social relationship, although it is sociable. They are good friends but not godfathers to each others' children. They are both pro-Europeans and have similar views across a range of topics, but the friendship and trust is rooted in Danny's loyal service, for example in running Nick's leadership bid and then subsequently in Parliament as Nick's chief of staff. So they are good and loyal friends.'

The other politician particularly close to Clegg was former Liberal Democrat leader Paddy Ashdown. It was Ashdown, his long-standing mentor, to whom Clegg turned to when at his most gloomy. The no-nonsense ex-soldier was frank and told him to focus on the job at hand, not what might have been. 'Elections are bastards,' he said: 'The important thing is to pick yourself up, dust yourself down and focus on the positive in the new situation.'

The Liberal Democrats looked like holding the balance of power between Labour and the Tories, a result former party leaders like Ashdown himself would have killed for. For Ashdown, who had himself come close to entering a power-sharing arrangement with Tony Blair, the opportunities and also the difficulties of the present situation were all too manifest. He was one of many older-generation Liberal Democrats for whom the natural reaction in a hung parliament was to look towards an arrangement with the Labour Party. But, as he recognised, the agony of this result was that it was precisely this path which was narrowly rendered impassable. As he told the BBC's Nick Robinson, the electorate had contrived to come up with 'an instrument of excruciating torture for the Liberal Democrats, where our hearts and emotions went one way but the mathematics the other', a description which he reprised on that Friday morning's *Today Programme* on Radio 4.

Clegg also spoke to his press secretary Lena Pietsch, to his Head of Communications Jonny Oates, and to John Sharkey, chairman of the general election campaign: his was a small and loyal team that had worked together closely and under pressure for several years. Clegg's mind began to clear as he got on the train from Sheffield to London in the early hours. 'The great thing about the train trip between Sheffield and London,' he said, 'is that there's almost no reliable telephone connection, so it's the one time your phone doesn't go and you can sit and think. Actually the main thing I was preoccupied about was to just say my piece to the cameras as soon as possible because I was very preoccupied with, maybe unduly with hindsight, the principles on which I operated before the election. Which was to be quite public and open about what I thought should happen if there was no decisive outcome; namely that it was the party with the most votes, the most seats, that had the first right to try [to form a government]. I also wanted to be consistent about not having a double game of what you say publicly and privately.'

While Clegg was preparing to make his statement of intent, and with the exit poll (and the results that were already in) pointing clearly to a hung parliament, spokesmen from all three parties moved to position themselves for the resultant horse-trading. Lord Mandelson affirmed on the *Today Programme* that if no party won a majority Gordon Brown would be entitled to try to form a government (on which score the constitutional experts agreed). Shortly afterwards Mandelson was explicit: if the poll was accurate, he said, Brown would try to form a 'stable' government with the Liberal Democrats. Michael Gove fended off reminders of Edward Heath in February 1974. Things had changed, he argued, in the modern world of 24-hour news, and Brown might find himself pressured into resigning immediately.

The Liberal Democrats closeted inside Cowley Street (including Paddy Ashdown, who had been doing the media rounds at the request of party officials) had come to an early conclusion: 'It was unanimous. We simply did not want a Tory coalition.' Whether it was tiredness or simply a knee-jerk reaction, this failed to take account of one overwhelming reality that would return time and again, the numbers simply didn't stack up for a deal with Labour.

When Clegg arrived at Cowley Street at around 10.30am he was ready to meet the waiting press hounds, who were anxious to know which way he would jump. Nick Clegg publicly reaffirmed his pre-election promise to give the party with the most seats and votes the first opportunity. He couldn't conceal his obvious disappointment, gave the Conservative Party the signal to get moving, and made his bid for electoral reform. It was short, honest and clear.

Meanwhile, Alexander and Llewellyn had been keeping in touch. Alexander was aware of what Cameron's offer was likely to contain, which allowed the two Chiefs of Staff to arrange the leaders' first telephone conversation for 4pm. Alison Suttie, Clegg's deputy chief of staff and later Special Adviser, was despatched by taxi from Liberal Democrat HQ in Cowley Street to his Putney home to act as a note-taker.

At 4pm Nick Clegg took the first call from David Cameron. During a short conversation described by Clegg's aides as 'business-like, efficient and warm', Cameron said: 'I am serious about the nature of the offer I am making – it is real and I really want to try to make it work.' Cameron also acknowledged the positive statement made by Clegg that morning. Clegg made the point, which he would make consistently in the early phase of exchanges: 'What is really important is that this is a policy-based negotiation. What matters is getting it right, and that depends on policy rather than personalities.' (Interestingly, Clegg was making exactly the opposite point in his conversations with Gordon Brown!)

The Cameron–Clegg call went extremely well, lasting around fifteen minutes. As Clegg later said, 'I knew I could do business with him.' Cameron was keen to force the pace as he had been from the very early hours of the day, saying, 'I think our negotiating teams should meet today.'

The names of the two negotiating teams were swapped and Clegg agreed that talks should be put promptly in motion, and that the two teams would meet at 7.30pm that evening. That was more of a problem than anyone anticipated, as by Friday afternoon everyone was tired after a fraught night without sleep, and the trusted election-night cocktail of coffee and adrenalin had lost its punch. With the Liberal Democrats' 'shadow Cabinet' and Parliamentary Party due to meet the following morning to approve talks, the four Liberal Democrats chosen to form a negotiating team had retreated to their London homes, or hastily booked hotels, in hope of some sleep.

But the respite was to prove brief. It was Alison Suttie who had the unenviable task of rousing a drowsy and rather disgruntled Liberal Democrat team from their slumber. All their pre-election planning had led them to expect to regroup for a first encounter on Sunday, because they believed they would need a mandate from the shadow Cabinet, Parliamentary Party and Federal Executive to authorise negotiations to begin. 'It was our clear objective from that phone call to get negotiations started that night and not let them drift to the weekend and we secured our objective,' said a close Cameron aide.

The two teams met at 7.30 that evening at 70 Whitehall. On 5 May, the eve of polling day, the Conservative team had been offered a range of meeting venues in addition to 70 Whitehall or the Cabinet Office by Sir Gus O'Donnell. George Osborne decided that it was 'psychologically important' to meet in a building overlooking No. 10, and therefore declined Portcullis House and Admiralty House. 'It was important to establish almost literally a bridgehead to No. 10 from the off – it gave the right message about our intention,' said a top Conservative aide.

Osborne wanted to be at the heart of government, putting pressure on the man who had lost the election but was still occupying Downing Street. He remained insistent throughout the process: 'Get the guy out, get your foot in the door – the first thing you have to do is get into office.' Even though the Conservatives were about to enter a negotiation, Osborne was not prepared to compromise on matters of principle – for example, the action required on public expenditure. However, he does acknowledge there were alternative approaches that could have been taken.

Some argue that the Conservative team should have called the Liberal Democrats' bluff and taken the line: 'We won the election; you come to us, and if you want try to put together a Liberal–Labour deal, just see what the public think of that.' Osborne believed the outcome would have been completely unpredictable: 'It might have paid off with a majority after a second autumn election, but equally the Conservative Party could have been out of office for a further five years because we were not controlling events. Harold Wilson's government in 1974 lasted five years and everyone thought John Major's government would fall apart in the mid-1990s and didn't. I am in no doubt that if Brown managed to stay on, in the narrative he would very quickly have become the "Comeback Kid", the man who pulled it off. The Conservatives would be useless Conservatives, having a massive internal war, while the Labour Party announces its new programme.'

Osborne thought that the moment the Conservatives were in office the rules would change. Suddenly the party was the party of government, its leader the Prime Minister, in control of the agenda, implementing policies, delivering commitments, while other parties would be characterised as having internal rows. Osborne wanted the authority of incumbency so that the political landscape of politics was fundamentally altered with the change of office.

The first negotiating session would be a short introductory meeting and would last a little over an hour. The content has been variously characterised by aides as 'talks about talks' or 'a ground-clearing exercise to set the parameters' for the negotiations to follow. The decision to meet early turned out – as the Conservative leader had hoped – to be beneficial to both sides, as it allowed the leadership teams to set the pace, well ahead of their own parties. The discontented were left behind the blistering pace and were never able to catch up. The atmosphere between the teams was also 'immediately very positive'.

The Conservatives arrived first and were greeted by the Cabinet Secretary Gus O'Donnell. William Hague, Oliver Letwin, George Osborne and Ed Llewellyn were chatting amiably when the Liberal Democrat team arrived after a rushed preparatory conversation at the National Liberal Club.

Neither group was sure what to expect. The teams did not know each other well. In fact, and to a degree which surprised the Liberal contingent, the atmosphere was immediately warm, even at times jovial. Alexander thought the chemistry was 'really excellent and William Hague is someone with a really warm personality, very easy to do business with'.

Gus O'Donnell helped with introductions (although none were required) and every combination of Liberal–Conservative handshake was duly completed. When the two teams took their places at the negotiating table, Letwin, Hague and Osborne faced Laws, Alexander, Huhne and Stunell, with Ed Llewellyn at one end and Alison Suttie, the Liberal Democrat note-taker, at the other. Peter Campbell took notes for the Conservatives and each session, over the following days, would have relevant party policy researchers present to offer support and advice.

The role of the Civil Service

There have been suggestions that civil servants were actively seeking a change of government during the five-day period. There is little doubt that very senior civil servants were worried that one of the outcomes over the five days might see the UK enveloped in 'the perfect storm', essentially a weak government (or even no government) overrun by the markets.

There had been concerns for some time in the Civil Service that the government had been putting off decisions. But worse, the way that Gordon Brown worked as Prime Minister had caused a near crisis in government, as at one stage the Civil Service found him paralysed, almost unable to make decisions at the rate required. He had a desire for more briefings and reviews, coupled with endless questions. It is said that he was the disastrous combination of being a control freak who could not make decisions.

A senior civil servant tells of a period in the Brown premiership when they were instructed to avoid passing anything up to the Prime Minister for decision unless it was absolutely critical. The way Downing

Street worked had to be restructured radically to suit the way the Prime Minister functioned (or did not function, as the case may be), with people being brought in and shuffled out as a series of 'solutions' failed to deal with the basic problem – the Prime Minister's personality.

There is little doubt that there were civil servants who had become eager for change, particularly in the Treasury and the Bank of England. The Governor of the Bank of England, Mervyn King, had told the Conservatives he was worried about the size of the deficit and government overspending, and he had also been enthusiastic about Conservative plans for fiscal responsibility. Indeed, the Conservatives had listened carefully to what the Governor was telling them at a number of meetings held at the Bank, and drew up their plans accordingly. A strong and close working relationship had developed.

Senior officials at the Treasury also realised that the Labour government had not had the necessary will to take key decisions about deficit reduction before the election and would be too weak to do so after the election in some sort of rainbow coalition. William Hague described it in this way: 'They [the Civil Service] were very professional. They were willing it to be sorted out one way or the other and perhaps they could see there was only one way where you arithmetically would get a strong government, a Conservative–Liberal Coalition.'

Over the next five days, the Civil Service did act as a support to the negotiations, arranging meeting places and administrative help, standing ready to provide advice on constitutional issues and processes and factual information in policy areas. All these were provided on request, so each team had a nominated civil servant specifically attached to their party so that each party's requirements could be channelled through a named individual.

The Prime Minister had announced earlier in the day that he had asked the Cabinet Secretary to 'arrange for the Civil Service to support on request to parties engaged in discussions on the formation of a government'. Brown was effectively putting in motion the Cabinet manual chapter 'Elections and Government Formation' that all parties had agreed before the general election. This set the rules of engagement for the next five days that all three political parties adhered to.

The offer of support, set out in the Prime Minister's statement, was taken up by Conservative, Labour, Liberal Democrat, DUP, Plaid Cymru and Scottish National parties. As expected, the nature of the support was governed by strict rules laid out in detailed Civil Service papers. It was the Civil Service that had taken the preparation for the event of a hung parliament most seriously to try to ensure there was a smooth transition of power, but more importantly that it was largely in control of such a transition.

But the politicians were not necessarily keen to play ball. 'They [the civil servants] were very helpful,' says William Hague: 'They had a strong sense of urgency about them which they tried to impress on everybody. But in fact we didn't need a sense of urgency because we really were trying to get a coalition or minority government nailed down as fast as possible.'

However, one thing the negotiating teams quickly agreed upon was a desire to be free of civil servants, even though they were, concluded Hague, 'eager beavers … Having war-gamed all the scenarios, I think they were slightly miffed when we said we didn't want them.'

But not before O'Donnell had impressed upon those around the table the need for a sense of urgency. He was particularly anxious about the opening of the markets on Monday morning – worried that they would be bound to respond negatively to a weak, unstable government in the UK. The problems which had recently been afflicting European countries like Greece and Spain were all too fresh in people's minds, along with a clear awareness that the size of the UK's deficit meant it was not immune from a similar crisis. He told the BBC: 'A minority government wouldn't have had the strength in Parliament to pass the tough measures to get us through the problem.' O'Donnell felt that if this was the outcome of negotiations, the markets 'would really make us pay a price on Monday morning by selling our debt and that would have been a real problem for the country'.

So O'Donnell's offer of support in the taking of minutes was turned down, with Hague (who chaired proceedings from the Conservative side) light-heartedly suggesting that this would keep prying eyes at bay: 'That way', he remarked, 'we don't have to worry about anyone putting in a Freedom of Information request for the minutes of the meeting!' In fact, O'Donnell smoothly responded, dodging such requests was straightforward enough: the minutes could simply be categorised in a different way, a sleight of hand whose apparent ease amused both sides of the table. By Monday a number of FOI requests had already arrived for details of the meetings.

Before he departed, O'Donnell – like any good host – found another way to lighten the atmosphere and to bring the groups together. He offered them immediate briefings from the Governor of the Bank of England and the Head of the Security Services, whose doom-laden surveys of the horizon were intended, no doubt, to impress the urgency of an early conclusion to talks and of a credible deficit reduction plan. After 36 hours or more without sleep, the prospect of cheerless lectures on the national finances or counter-terrorism caused little in the way of eager anticipation. But the opportunity to reject unanimously the offer got the talks off to a harmonious start. (The Civil Service was not to be shaken off so easily; by Sunday they had, it seemed, found another, altogether more devious method of gaining access to the meeting. The room's radiators were jammed on full and if the atmosphere, metaphorically, was warmer than some expected, the same was also literally true. Those present recall that the only civil servants who were admitted were summoned in desperation to open some of the windows.)

When the room was clear, talks began on the negotiation process; there were no detailed policy discussions at this first session. The economy was the most detailed policy area of conversation and the Conservatives had thought, even after rejecting Gus O'Donnell's initial offer, they would need independent corroboration of the facts regarding the state of the country's finances and the markets from the Treasury and the Bank of England. The Liberal Democrat team insisted that it wasn't necessary, and during Sunday's negotiations it quickly became clear why: the third party had already changed its mind quite radically on the economic policies on which it had been fighting an election during the preceding weeks.

What immediately emerged was a marked difference in party culture. The Liberal Democrats – surprised to be there on Friday evening at all, without clearance from its party bodies – were firm that Saturday would be occupied by party consultation.

Chris Huhne gave the Conservative team a long-winded description of the triple-lock system the Liberal Democrats would have to go through on Saturday before proper negotiations began. Hague explained the Conservative process: 'We inform the leader and then he decides what we do.' The juxtaposition of the two approaches caused great amusement to all present. However, a Conservative aide noted there was 'a certain degree of incredulity that they would have to spend all of Saturday doing internal processes'. At least, Oliver Letwin joked, a day off negotiations would give his team more time to prepare.

To a Liberal Democrat aide, it was the immediate ease and good humour, the 'instant sense of camaraderie', which was most striking and which she admits that she found 'slightly surprising'. In fact, however, though the teams did not know each other well, a series of significant contacts had taken place which, crucially, had established a foundation for mutual liking and respect.

Early in 2006, for example, George Osborne – then shadow Chancellor – had paid a visit to the office of David Laws at One Parliament Street. The two of them had sat together at the circular table in Laws's office and Osborne, apparently out of the blue with little or no preamble, had invited him to join the Conservative Party and take on a significant role, an offer made with the full knowledge and blessing of David Cameron. Though Laws later turned the offer down, he was naturally flattered by the approach, a sign of the high regard in which he was held by the Conservative leadership. He in turn, Laws admits, had considerable respect for Osborne as a political strategist: 'The first shadow chancellor to really get the better of Gordon Brown, which is no small achievement.' He also knew and liked Oliver Letwin, who was a neighbouring MP – not quite in spitting range, but 'over a couple of hills'. Chris Huhne had shared City interests; and Ed Llewellyn had worked as a political adviser to Paddy Ashdown in Bosnia.

Perhaps more importantly, beyond the immediately personal contacts the two parties shared a common experience of opposition to Gordon Brown's government. Though their lines of attack had not always coincided, in certain key areas they did – most strikingly, perhaps, in Home Affairs in the period while David Davis was the Tory spokesman. Davis might be surprised to hear himself described as a midwife to the coalition government – and perhaps such a description stretches the point – but he certainly played a significant role in engineering better understanding and closer co-operation between the two parties.

As shadow Home Affairs spokesman, Davis had developed close working relationships with Liberal Democrat Home Affairs spokesmen Mark Oaten, Nick Clegg and Chris Huhne over a range of issues, but particularly in his passionate commitment to civil liberties. Davis had moved the Conservative Party onto new and unfamiliar territory which made possible the close co-operation that would spread to educational and environmental issues. After 2005, the well-known right-winger had managed to change the perception, at least in Parliament, of the Conservative Party. Davis, a libertarian by nature, had a natural affinity with many aspects of liberalism and turned it into Conservative Party policy, cutting a path through the undergrowth that David Cameron was pleased to follow.

At local level, as Chris Huhne and Andrew Stunell pointed out, a culture of co-operation had been established in key regions – Oxfordshire, Leeds, Birmingham – which boded well for similar co-operation at the centre. There was already a pragmatism within both parties about the potential for co-operation.

Since Cameron became leader, the Conservatives had developed a strategy of 'love-bombing' Liberal Democrat voters in the country. Its main public advocate was Party chairman Eric Pickles, who consistently pushed the party's campaigning in to less traditional Tory areas, preferring to appeal to a broader base of support. It underpinned a new strategy of reaching out beyond the party's traditional support base and at the same time continued the job of 'decontaminating' the Tory brand.

For the two teams who sat opposite each other that Friday evening, therefore, there was an all-important sense which some of their predecessors would scarcely have recognised that a combined Conservative–Liberal Democrat platform was at least possible.

After the meeting, both sides returned to their leaders to report. The Liberal Democrat team and reference group met for a report-back session on the day's events, which proved to be a key moment, because it was here that Nick Clegg decided that it was impossible to make a deal with the Labour Party and Brown work. They sat in front of a whiteboard looking at the parliamentary arithmetic, because Clegg 'was rubbish at it'. Clegg went over and over the figures, even though after one look he had arrived at the view that, 'It's a joke, we can't do anything with a *smorgasbord* of minor parties.' It became a regular refrain at the telephone conversations and meetings between Clegg and Brown that whatever Brown said, Clegg would respond by drawing attention to 'the sheer unforgiving political reality' of the figures.

Vince Cable confirms this view: 'On the first evening we all met at Cowley Street and had a discussion of the basic options. We looked at the numbers and I think it was fairly clear that there wasn't much prospect of working with the outgoing Labour government … It was widely accepted that we needed to talk to the Conservatives.' The only way a government would have been viable would have been if the Scottish and Welsh nationalists were on side. Those gathered could see immediately the problem of the Scottish and Welsh nationalists demanding more money every time there was a tight vote in the Commons. Even with the nationalists, any workable coalition would still need the Northern Irish MPs, which meant any rainbow coalition would have to be very brightly coloured.

Cable knew the intention of the leadership of his party, and his focus over the next few days would be 'offstage', as he termed it. Cable had met Gordon Brown in 1975 when, as a Labour councillor in

Glasgow, he wrote an essay in *The Red Paper on Scotland*, which Brown had edited. Cable would perhaps like to forget his closing assertion that 'Scotland could, in all probability, expect in the 1980s to be more prosperous as an independent country'.

But this contact had started a relationship with Brown that had developed over the years, and Cable was aware that he could use this relationship to pull the Liberal Democrats towards Labour, by offering timely advice and support to Brown. Cable was determined that this negotiation process would not be a shoo-in for the Tories: he had spent too long fighting them for that to happen.

When Nick Clegg went to bed on the Friday night, he felt he was faced with what he described as a series of 'invidious and extraordinary choices'. On the one hand, he felt it was 'highly unlikely' that he could do a deal with the Labour Party: the politics wouldn't stack up partly because of Brown and partly because of the arithmetic. But on the other, Clegg also felt the traditional antagonism felt by the Liberal Democrats to the Conservatives meant a deal would be difficult to get through his party's complicated internal approval processes. However, he already knew in whose direction he would rather go.

DAY 2

– Saturday 8 May –

The public was intrigued but, as yet, not unnerved by what was happening. Unlike large parts of Europe, this country was not accustomed to having a government that was negotiated between political parties rather than directly and straightforwardly elected. Given the consistent indications provided by opinion polls during the preceding weeks, of course, a hung parliament was scarcely a surprise, and the public mood seemed patient and hopeful that the parties might be able to act for the good of the country. A sense existed, nevertheless, of a serious national event which would require an urgent and conscientious response from political leaders if the markets were not to take fright when business reopened the following week.

Any such sense would have seemed confusing in many European countries, where coalition governments are so frequent as not to constitute any sort of abnormality, let alone any kind of crisis. The very terminology used in Britain – a 'hung parliament' – with its sinister undertones of some sort of revolutionary bloodletting, has no real equivalent on the Continent, where a parliament without an overall majority for one party is, very simply, a parliament. In fact, in having had no coalition government since 1945, it is the UK that is the European peculiarity. In Luxembourg, the Netherlands, Germany, Belgium, France, Finland, Italy, Austria, Ireland and others, coalition governments have been routine. In one of the UK's closest neighbours, the Republic of Ireland, no single party has governed since 1989.

Commentators in Britain opposed to coalition government often point to the chaos and frequent regime changes in countries like Italy and Belgium. But it is only fair to point out that Belgium (whose last government took a remarkable nine months to put together) is plagued by a deep cultural division between Flemish and French speakers, and that major northern European states like Germany and the Netherlands treat coalition government as the norm rather than the exception, and their administration is not, as a rule, chaotic as a result. Helmut Kohl and Gerhard Schröder's governments were coalitions, as was CDU leader Angela Merkel's first government after 2005. After the 2009 German general election, Merkel managed to put together a new coalition which took around three weeks – which was considered to be unusually fast as on average it takes approximately five weeks.

Even in the UK, coalitions outside Westminster are now not unusual. The electoral systems in Scotland, Wales and Northern Ireland gravitate against one party having an outright majority. Coalitions are therefore likely to be the norm, even though the SNP currently runs a minority government in Scotland. At local government level, furthermore, coalition is a common experience: after the local elections in 2010 over a quarter of councils were in no overall control and many had formal or informal coalitions.

Nor, for all the talk in Britain about Labour being the Liberal Democrats' natural partners as opposed to the Conservatives, are coalitions between centre-right and liberal parties at all unusual when one looks beyond our borders. Indeed some ten countries in the EU – including France, Germany, Denmark and Sweden – are now governed by precisely such partnerships.

It would not, of course, be right to give the impression that coalition government has been an unmitigated success or that it does not have disadvantages. While some coalitions in Europe have lasted for many years, others have disintegrated quickly, providing unstable and unsuccessful government. And it is not just the length of time the coalition as a whole lasts that is important; it is also the length of time that a particular coalition cabinet lasts. Even in the more stable countries like Germany, the average duration of a coalition cabinet is just two years.

In Germany, the new Coalition between the CDU and Liberals was seen as a 'dream' coalition after the previous 'grand' coalition with the Social Democrats. Many German commentators are suggesting that the problems besetting Merkel's government are a result of the excessive speed with which the government was put together! Merkel has suggested that when you get what you want, things later turn bumpy. Indeed, a recent poll in Germany suggested that the Liberals in Germany's coalition may suffer the same fate as the Liberal Democrats in the UK. A poll at the end of July suggested that while Merkel is doing well, the Liberals' vote share is now 4%, below the minimum threshold to sit in the Bundestag.

*

In the wake of the UK general election in 2010, for many of those involved in preparing for the party negotiations, Friday night and Saturday morning merged into one. Texts, phone calls, e-mails and meetings continued late into Friday night, but at least some of the key players had managed to get a decent rest.

Peter Mandelson informs us in his memoirs that he began his working day on the Saturday by reading the many texts on his mobile phone and calling Danny Alexander at around 8.30am. Danny Alexander confirms the conversation reported by Mandelson was indeed accurate. The Liberal Democrats were keen to encourage the Labour Party, despite their own reservations about any likely outcome, because as one Liberal Democrat negotiator put it: 'Although the mathematics were, to say the least, tricky, we still didn't know where this process would finally end up.' In fact, keeping the Labour Party in the game would remain a key part of the Liberal Democrat strategy right to the very end on Tuesday.

Alexander told Mandelson that Labour was a more natural bedfellow for the Liberal Democrats, but that the Tories at their first meeting with them on the Friday evening had been constructive and open-minded. The men arranged talks later in the day, but Alexander insisted that they should be kept strictly secret – the Liberal Democrats did not inform the Conservatives, either before or after the event, that a meeting with Labour had taken place. The Labour Party agreed to secrecy and acted in good faith; it was not for some time that details of the meeting would become common knowledge. Had the meeting got back to the Conservatives it would have been met with real disappointment and possibly cries of bad faith – particularly within the Parliamentary Party. Nick Clegg had, after all, made significant play of the fact that the party with the largest number of seats would have the moral right to make the first bid at creating a government. Fortunately for the new coalition, it did not.

Immediately the Liberal Democrats began to test the outer parameters of what they might be able to extract. As they now admit, leading Liberal Democrats had decided before the election that they would push Labour hard, 'setting the bar high' in terms of the price of their collaboration. Just how high they set it has only recently begun to emerge. Peter Mandelson tells us in his memoirs that Alexander asked about the possibility of Labour implementing the alternative vote system without the manifesto-promised referendum. And, crucially, this would be considered as merely a first step on the journey towards a fully proportional system.

As we will see, this would be the first of many occasions over the next four days when the Liberal Democrats raised the prospect of a fundamental change to the constitution of the country without recourse to the people. As far as the Liberal Democrats were concerned, an agreement with Labour simply to hold a referendum on AV as part of a coalition deal would be worthless. The referendum would be bound to be lost. The public would regard it as some kind of stitch-up by the election losers. The Conservatives would campaign strongly against the change on precisely this basis. And the chance for reform would be lost for a considerable period. All in all, the Liberal Democrats thought, it would be better not to have one.

At 10 Downing Street Gordon Brown (as ever) had not slept much, according to a close aide. He was in overdrive, agitated about how to force his way into the political process. It was not in his nature to sit back and wait. He made and received a number of phone calls, and phone and text contact pinged between members of the Cabinet. John Denham, Peter Hain and Ben Bradshaw (supporters of electoral reform and of a deal with the Liberal Democrats) speculated: 'It looks as though there might be some hope of keeping those bastard Tories out,' one said. They called Sue Nye, Brown's gatekeeper, to lobby for a deal and were called back by Mandelson. Their message, they told him, was unequivocal: 'You must go for this.'

Media coverage continued to be largely unfavourable to Labour. On Saturday morning the BBC carried a report suggesting that the phone conversation between Brown and Clegg the night before had degenerated into an ill-tempered slanging match, in which Clegg had told Brown in no uncertain terms that no deal would be possible in which he remained as Prime Minister. The reports were not true, but they undermined Brown's position within his Cabinet, even with potential supporters, who quickly believed that Brown could be the price paid for a deal.

The print media quickly picked up on the story and Labour sources were frantically pushed out to issue denials. Less of a surprise, but damaging nonetheless, was the beginning of a campaign by the right-wing tabloids to prevent Brown clinging on as Prime Minister. The *Sun*'s front page on Friday had declared 'Britain Rejects Brown', and on Saturday the paper led with 'Whitehall Property Scandal: Squatter Holed Up in No 10': 'The squatter, named as a Mr Gordon Brown from Scotland, was refusing to budge from the Georgian townhouse in Downing Street, central London – denying entry to its rightful tenant.' The paper despatched to Downing Street a van emblazoned with 'Brown & Brown Removals'.

In reality, of course, Brown did remain Prime Minister, and it was to emphasise this fact that his aides let it be known that he had been conducting phone conversations on Saturday morning with Nicholas Sarkozy and José Zapatero about the eurozone crisis. He was certainly perfectly entitled to remain in No. 10 until the identity of the next government was resolved. For all that recent Prime Ministers have adopted a presidential style (Tony Blair being a conspicuous example), the British electorate does not elect a Prime Minister as other countries elect a President. A general election is simply the election of a parliament. Only once a new House of Commons has been chosen does the monarch (on the basis of a majority decision among MPs) summon a party leader and invite him or her to be Prime Minister. Such constitutional niceties, however, were largely lost on a blood-thirsty media who sensed, rightly enough, that Brown was looking for a way to postpone his change of address. Holed up in Downing Street, Brown's mood swung wildly: from unexpected hope that a narrow defeat might still leave him room to lead a coalition government, to despair as prominent voices (including a number on his own side) dismissed any notion of his remaining in office.

Late morning, Brown called his long-standing ally, Ed Balls, at his home in Yorkshire. Balls, as usual, was direct with his advice: 'You must leave Downing Street and go home to Scotland because the appearance of hanging around in Downing Street while the Tories and Liberals [are] talking is a problem.' Brown reluctantly agreed, but told Balls: 'You must be at the meeting planned at 3pm in Portcullis House to talk to the Liberals.' Brown was in a hurry because he had to be at the Cenotaph for the 65th anniversary of VE Day: all the party leaders would be present and he hoped to talk to Clegg.

Brown was privately criticised by his own MPs for going to Scotland. One said: 'I thought he was barmy doing that at a time of constitutional crisis. I thought: "What's the point of staying in No. 10 and not resigning if you are actually going to leave it and not physically be there?"'

On his return from the Cenotaph, Brown saw Mandelson. Brown was worried by the crowd reaction to him at the Cenotaph and his failure to discuss anything substantial with Clegg, and still agitated about the Liberal Democrat talks with the Conservatives. On the positive side, at least talks with his own team were now scheduled for 3pm that afternoon – albeit billed as simply a 'preliminary session'. His spirits did rise sufficiently for him to start speculating feverishly about which Liberal Democrats would be in his new Cabinet: Vince Cable, Paddy Ashdown, David Laws, Chris Huhne, Nick Clegg. Brown was still focused on doing all within his power to remain in Downing Street, and if that meant giving a large number of Liberal Democrats a place in Cabinet, so be it. This idea was to grow over the following 24 hours as the Prime Minister, faraway in Scotland, mulled over events in London. As he did so his desperation to hang on and to keep the Tories out of power only grew.

The Liberal Democrats

Each day began the same way for the Liberal Democrat team, with a 7.30am meeting of the 'reference team' at Cowley Street. Saturday was to be the first proper meeting, so a text whizzed out shortly after 7am asking selected people to call Danny Alexander. Some people, such as Jim Wallace, were on standby and as yet were not clear whether they would be required. So the early morning text and subsequent phone conversation served as confirmation that they were to have an important advisory role.

The Liberal Democrat reference team had a core to it of the party leader, his deputy, the party president and chief executive, and the negotiating team. However, the team was effectively larger with senior advisers such as Alison Suttie, Polly Mackenzie, Chris Saunders, Jim Wallace and one or two others regularly in attendance.

When the meeting began at 8am, Clegg's reference group discussed what had happened the previous night with the Tories. One of those present at this first gathering proper was later to say: 'My abiding memory of that first time was the positive response to the meeting the night before with the Conservatives.' It had been a pleasant surprise – both the warmth of the meeting and the fact that the Conservatives had taken the Liberal Democrats extremely seriously. The meeting also discussed how to handle each of the day's other meetings, which included a 'shadow Cabinet', followed by a Parliamentary Party meeting and finally a Federal Executive meeting. Saturday was a day of Liberal Democrat consultation and party democracy in action.

The first democratic decision arrived even before the first meeting began. After a summons had gone out on the Friday from the Chief Whip for the 'shadow Cabinet' to assemble at Local Government House at 8am sharp, howls of protest ensued at the early start, and the meeting had to be moved back until 10.30am, before finally being moved back further to around 12 noon, owing to Clegg's attendance at the VE day remembrance service at the Cenotaph.

Clegg left at around 10.30am to get to the Cenotaph before the ceremony at 11 o' clock. He joined other dignitaries milling around in a Foreign Office ante-room to wait for the ceremony to start. When Brown arrived, 'he immediately made a beeline for Clegg' and engaged him in a short conversation – but nothing of substance was discussed. The ceremony itself was remarkable for the circumstances in which it took place: all three leaders together at a national com-memoration, while the watching world studied them closely for hints or body language which might offer clues as to the negotiations ahead. The existing plan was for the Prince of Wales to lay a wreath, followed by the Prime Minister, but in light of the indecisive election result a compromise was agreed whereby all three party leaders would lay wreaths together. Though still officially Prime Minister, Brown was denied the customary precedence. In one much reproduced photograph of the occasion Cameron stands in the middle of the three, reaching into his jacket pocket, while Brown to his left looks pointedly away, chin raised disdainfully.

Afterwards all the leaders had been invited to attend a reception for veterans nearby on Horse Guards Parade, but Clegg had to return to the LGA for his first Parliamentary Party meeting. Brown and Cameron did go, and the reception given to both men as they walked past a big crowd pressed up against railings by St James's Park was instructive. One observer said: 'David got a very enthusiastic welcome when he came out through the back of the Foreign Office. There was a lot of "well done, congratulations", and several called him Prime Minister' – it was quite a moment. There was something in the air.' As Brown went by there was no reaction, no cheers and no calls of support. It was instructive of the public mood, of what was happening in the country, depressing for Brown and a huge boost to Cameron.

When the shadow Cabinet meeting eventually commenced, those gathered in the packed room heard feedback on how the election had gone and were told that a negotiating team had been appointed. An initial report was given of the Friday evening meeting with the Conservatives.

It was the first that most of the senior Liberal Democrats had heard about a negotiating team. The meetings and papers that formed the main part of preparations in the pre-election period had been kept secret from the party and even from the 'shadow Cabinet'. The composition of the team caused some surprise – both positive and negative. The presence of Clegg's key allies, like David Laws and Danny Alexander, was wholly predictable. Like Clegg himself they were seen as belonging to the economically liberal 'right' of the party, and their central role now only bolstered the cynicism of those on the left who felt that their values had been shunted aside under Clegg's leadership. (Although David Laws did have experience of coalition negotiations in Scotland, where he had advised Jim Wallace.)

The inclusion of Andrew Stunell, however, was for many a genuine surprise, and one that was widely welcomed; Stunell was highly respected among Liberal Democrats of all hues for his years of work out of the limelight at local government level, not least (and hence his inclusion now) in negotiating local coalitions. Unlike Laws and Alexander, he was not associated with a particular wing of the party

– and, unlike them, he was not regarded as in any way Clegg's man: no fly-by-night apparatchik, as he puts it himself, but someone with 'bottom' in the party. For those on the left, however, gratification at Stunell's surprising inclusion was offset by an equally surprising exclusion. Where was Vince Cable?

Both within the Liberal Democrats, and among their Conservative and Labour counterparts, it was assumed that Cable would play a decisive role in any negotiation. The argument made by Chris Huhne that as deputy leader Cable had 'his hands full' scarcely rings true.

Clegg laid out at the meeting the size of the challenge the party faced. He described how this negotiation and any agreement would be 'the biggest risk that he and everyone in the party would take with the Liberal Democrat legacy in their political lifetime'. But there was, he emphasised, no easy option – no path of least resistance. Whichever way it went it was, he said, 'an enormous risk both with their personal political careers and the future of their party.' Clegg then let everybody around the table have their say one by one, with the consensus being that the strategy was right: talk to the Conservatives, but the Labour option must be kept open. It would be fair to say that Liberal Democrat memories are divided in that some remember the Labour option as substantially favoured by the 'shadow Cabinet' at this stage, (even though all accepted that the numbers were a sizeable obstacle to overcome) while others suggest opinion was more evenly divided.

The former Liberal Democrat leaders

As events unfolded and the Liberal Democrat MPs had their chance to input their views, a succession of former leaders found it impossible to resist making their opinions heard. Here, at last, was the chance to shape events of which they all had dreamed – the chance, in all seriousness, to prepare for government. Old muscles twitched instinctively, though not all welcomed the contribution. To one senior Liberal Democrat, now a minister, the ex-leaders limbering up and flexing on the sidelines seemed 'like Dads at a prize-giving who were jealous of their sons'.

These ex-leaders had some influence in the party and Clegg knew that any of them could be troublesome, particularly where the agreement more likely to be made was with the Conservative Party. If the Liberal Democrats were to make an agreement involving their bitter enemy, it would be important to muster from the former leaders either their support or their acquiescence.

At their Saturday morning meeting, therefore, it was a substantial surprise among the 'shadow Cabinet' that Vince Cable was not included in the negotiating team, because he had wanted to be part of it. One said: 'I still don't know why he wasn't, but it is a suspicion that Vince was to the left of the party and perhaps the negotiating team weren't.'

There is clearly a school of thought both within the Liberal Democrats and elsewhere that the leadership set up the negotiations with the task of arriving at the answers it wanted. It wanted control over information and strategy. Vince Cable, extremely highly regarded by his parliamentary colleagues after a successful spell as stand-in leader, would have been difficult to control inside the negotiating team. For example, Andrew Adonis believes (although does not know) that Vince Cable would not have changed his view on deficit reduction, as Clegg did before negotiations began, or gone for further and faster reduction.

Labour negotiator Adonis said: 'I don't think he [Clegg] wanted him. The fact is that he wasn't on the team and since he was the deputy leader of the party, that's quite a big thing. Our deputy leader was on [the team], the Conservative deputy leader was on.'

The initial Conservative reaction to Cable's non-appointment was also one of surprise. However, they arrived at a completely different conclusion from Adonis. One member of the negotiating team said: 'Our thought after the first meeting was "Why is Vince Cable not on this delegation?" Our assumption was that he was conducting a separate negotiation channel with Labour. Which to some extent he was; he was having those phone conversations with Brown, although not an equivalent negotiation.'

Of the two views, Adonis is probably closer to the truth. Cable was, as he later described himself, 'detached from the process', an astonishing admission from the 'shadow Chancellor' of the party when many of the key decisions were economic. It was decided by the leadership team, apparently on the Friday night, that Cable should step back from the negotiating process and not become embroiled in it, helping to set basic strategy and 'giving overall guidance'. Although Cable had at best mixed feelings about his role, he agreed to go along with it.

Cable spent his time holding discussions with the senior Treasury officials and attending an array of meetings, including reference group meetings. The advice from the mandarins was that an incoming government would have to act early to deal with the growing crisis and Cable accepted that something would have to be done. However, he was not keeping pace with his own negotiating team, who were pushing Labour for an agreement to an emergency budget, in-year cuts and a faster deficit reduction. His own negotiating team had effectively signed up for the Conservative economic plan lock, stock and barrel, from fairly early on and were pushing Labour for a similar commitment in negotiations. This was *not* something that Cable was discussing or negotiating with Alistair Darling or Gordon Brown, for example. It is therefore extremely likely that he did not sanction or know how far the Liberal Democrat negotiating team were pushing forward on economic matters within the negotiations, until after the event. A point made by members of the negotiating team on many occasions was that they (unlike their Labour counterparts, they said) had the authority to negotiate, while Labour wanted to keep deferring to the Chancellor.

Clegg's relationship with Cable was known to be complex and at times difficult. Cable comes from a Labour Party background, having stood as a Labour candidate, though he was in the Liberal Club at University and joined the SDP when that party was created in 1982, and as a result is sometimes portrayed as being on the left of the Liberal Democrat spectrum. In terms of detailed policy, this may be overstated, but there is no doubt that faced with a choice between Labour and Conservative, Cable's emotional allegiance tended firmly towards the former. Clegg on the other hand has a background of working for Conservatives, and of having free-market 'Liberal Conservative' views (though he professed 'no memory' that would cast light on the appearance of an 'N. Clegg' in the records of the Cambridge University Conservative Association). Ken Clarke often said that Liberal Democrats such as David Laws and Nick Clegg would most likely have been members of the Conservative Party in another era.

Cable's emergence as a major player in the public consciousness as well as the Liberal Democrat Party after his brilliant performance as temporary leader – laced with memorable Commons lines such as his characterisation of Gordon Brown as having transformed in a matter of weeks 'from Stalin to Mr Bean' – was a mixed blessing for the man who took over from Menzies Campbell. As party economics spokesman, Cable maintained a high profile, thanks largely to the banking crisis, during which he launched calculated and well-publicised assaults on government policy as well as on the stance taken by the Conservative opposition. Having warned about levels of personal debt for some time, Cable was one of very few politicians in a position to say, 'I told you so'.

As Cable's profile and popularity with the general public soared (the most popular politician in Britain, the media was fond of calling him), Clegg himself seemed by comparison callow and inexperienced. He struggled to make an impression with either the media or the public. In an edition of the satirical television news quiz *Have I Got News For You?* early in the election campaign, the script read by guest presenter Alexander Armstrong made repeated jokes about Clegg's anonymity, referring to Brown, Cameron and 'the other one'. More uncomfortably for the Liberal Democrat leader, Cable's status was made plain to Clegg in planning the election campaign: Clegg was obliged to accept that strategy would be planned around both men rather than only him, because Cable outshone him and was considered the greater asset with the public. Where the Conservative poster campaign used (allegedly airbrushed) photographs of David Cameron, the Liberal Democrat campaign bus went into battle bearing pictures of Clegg and Cable together, in the hope that some of the latter's popularity would rub off on the leader and his party generally.

Privately this was a source of intense annoyance and frustration for Clegg, and it gave Cable a greater influence than Clegg would have liked. With an appearance on the three-way televised leaders' debates looming as an opportunity that could not be wasted, the pressure only became more intense within the party when the preliminary Chancellors' debate saw Cable put in another assured performance, marginally getting the better of both George Osborne and Alistair Darling in the eyes of most commentators as well as with viewers who voted during the broadcast.

But if he was feeling the pressure, Clegg did not let it show. In a dramatic role reversal, his assured performance in the first leaders' debate thrust Clegg into the media stratosphere. Capitalising on the sense of disillusionment with politicians generally in the wake of the parliamentary expenses scandal, Clegg contrasted himself and his party with Labour and the Tories. 'The more they attack each other', he remarked of Brown and Cameron (who were concentrating their fire on each other), 'the more they sound exactly the same.' He went on to tell the audience: 'Don't let anyone tell you that the only choice is old politics. We can do something new.' Viewers responded strongly to a man many had seen little of – in ITV's instant poll 43% gave the debate to Clegg, 26% to Cameron and 20% to Brown. The media was quick to capitalise on an exciting new storyline: 'Cleggmania' was born, with some commentators describing his new profile as Obama-esque. It was something quite new for a British politician.

Suddenly Cable looked tired and old – Britain's favourite uncle rather than a man of action – and his views were no longer sought so readily. Cable now began for the first time to play second fiddle to the younger man, and he was concerned his influence would wane further.

Many of the senior Liberal Democrats either hint or are explicit that Cable was conducting a separate line of communication and negotiation with Labour, separate from the main team. It is extremely unlikely that this had Clegg's full blessing, particularly as Paddy Ashdown (Clegg's close confidant) was operating, as he has said himself, as the Liberal Democrat's 'official unofficial' channel to Labour, but separate from the main negotiating team. Ashdown's actions were communicated to and approved at the top of the party; Cable's apparently were not. Although

Cable was part of the elite 'reference group' which met both prior to and during the negotiations to provide Clegg with strategic advice, he cut a more peripheral figure in relation to the crucial negotiations than might have been expected.

Notably outspoken was the last person to lead the party at a general election, Charles Kennedy. 'Chat Show Charlie' had always been at ease on the airwaves and discovered no hidden streak of shyness now. Proclaiming the lessons of the 'history book' over the 'crystal ball', he summoned the ghosts of coalitions past, so chilling to Liberal Democrats present – in particular the spectre of Joe Chamberlain, who 'split the political family' (Churchill's 'splendid piebald' – 'first fiery red, then true blue'). The Liberals, Kennedy warned, had 'never prospered when they got into bed with the Conservatives'.

For Kennedy and others the direction of events was disorientating. 'For some of us at least,' he confessed, 'our political compass currently feels confused.' To cohabit with the Conservatives was 'to drive a strategic coach and horses through the long-nurtured "realignment of the centre-left" to which leaders in the Liberal tradition, this one included, have all subscribed since the Jo Grimond era'. He baldly continued: 'I would not have formed a coalition with the Conservatives had I been leader' – though, he did reluctantly admit, 'My alternative [a centre-left Labour–Liberal alliance wouldn't have worked either.'

Late on the Tuesday night, as Liberal Democrat MPs put the coalition deal to a final vote, Kennedy abstained, and made his reservations clear in his only open contribution to the debate within the Parliamentary Party. He later specified that he had voted against the deal, though the official record of the meeting records a 50 to 0 result. Does this obvious rewriting of history have a purpose?

Kennedy's furious reaction to the budget and the VAT rise marked him out as a potential rebel leader or even defector to Labour (although the latter was highly unlikely). If in the early months of the coalition he refrained from blowing the trumpet of outright rebellion, faint praise and unconvincing gestures towards neutrality – 'I wouldn't like to start a row' – have bracketed him firmly among the disgruntled. While nodding towards the attractions of government ('This party has been out of power for seventy years so I think people will be pinching themselves by the time the party conference comes around'), Kennedy was brooding about troubles ahead. 'There is an inevitable combustion about politics,' he warned darkly: 'Splits, tensions, it would not be politics if that did not happen.' Little wonder that he was seen by some of his colleagues as biding his time, waiting for the shine to wear off the coalition, before launching an offensive.

At the time of the coalition discussions, Kennedy was privately still smarting at the way he was removed from the party leadership: a wound that must have stung all the more for knowing that it could have been him in May 2010 holding the political balance of power. Nor has the perceived disloyalty of those MPs who called on him to step down been forgotten. It is telling that the rebellion against him was manned, disproportionately, by that new generation of MPs – many of them comprising a forward-thinking, market-oriented tendency within the party associated with *The Orange Book* – who were the leading actors in forging the Liberal–Conservative coalition. It was this younger group, one former leader observed, who 'would not tolerate Charles' style' – his political style or his lifestyle – and it was these same people for whom the coalition represented a 'logical outcome'.

For Menzies Campbell the emotions were less raw. A victim, like Kennedy, of his party's new-found lust for regicide, he was able to accept that the irresistible tide had moved on. Cameron's arrival, he acknowledged, had shifted the game and Campbell's party also needed to jump a generation. Nick Clegg, he felt bound to admit, 'looked like the new politics'. And in the party as a whole, a new intake in 2001 and 2005 had altered the mood. Whether or not this group had, as Campbell imagines, 'given up sex, drugs and rock and roll to get in' (the whiff of bohemianism is a little faint among some), they had no doubt made sacrifices as full-time candidates and aspired to rapid progress and government.

If Campbell was willing to accept this as 'legitimate ambition', he – like Kennedy – made no secret of his own sense of disorientation. At the meeting of MPs on the Saturday he made known his 'shock' at the turn events were taking: 'I was making the point even then this was something for which I had no natural sympathy.' Coalition with the Conservatives, he says now, 'goes right against the grain – you have to understand that.' Like others of his generation he had long dreamed of a realignment of the left, and this, he could only think in exasperation, 'is not a realignment of the left.'

Campbell, though, is happy to acknowledge a generational shift. Regardless of their taste in music or narcotics, what the new intake did not share with the older guard was the experience of being MPs during the Thatcher years. Their formative parliamentary experiences were spent in opposition to Labour and alongside the Tories, not the other way around. They had, as Campbell admits, 'less of an anti-Tory bias than people like me.' They did not have the same inhibitions. (And, he has been prepared to concede, the Conservative Party was changing).

Gordon Brown was a prodigious caller over those five days; from early in the morning until late into the night colleagues and friends would have their views sought or their ears bashed. Campbell was on the receiving end of a number of phone calls from the Downing Street bunker as the party negotiations advanced – the last time at noon on the day that Brown resigned.

Until late in the day, Campbell recalls, Brown was defiantly optimistic that a Labour–Liberal Democrat deal could be done. Campbell was sympathetic, and offered his encouragement. But at the same time he was aware that Labour were being outbid. It was essential, he urged Brown, that he 'put more eggs in the cake'.

'If this is going to fly,' Menzies Campbell told Brown (now imagining a kite, one assumes, rather than a cake), 'it needs to have more substance because the Tories appear much more up for it.' This was a message echoed by a close Brown aide, believed to be Alastair Campbell, who similarly urged the PM to do all he could to keep a Labour–Liberal Democrat deal on the table.

Lord Ashdown was also in the thick of it from the beginning, but like Campbell dreaming of a 'realignment of the left'. Paddy Ashdown was and is close to Nick Clegg. They talk regularly and e-mail often. Ashdown says that he identified Clegg as a future leader of the Liberal Democrats when he was working for the then Conservative European Commissioner, Sir Leon Brittan. They talk about each other with fondness, admire each other, and for over a decade they have helped one another politically as and when it has been necessary.

However, with whom their party should now govern the country was one issue on which these friends fundamentally disagreed. Ashdown was clear he wanted a realignment of the left and he had spent much of his political life trying to achieve it. Clegg was drawn to the Conservatives. Ashdown, though, placed his loyalty and service at the behest of his leader. It suited Clegg to have Ashdown encouraging Labour to believe in a deal, because it meant that a better deal could be driven with the Conservatives. Ashdown encouraged it, because he believed in it and thought it would be the better outcome for the Liberal Democrats.

From the first moment to the last, Ashdown was in the thick of the action, talking to both Conservative and Labour aides, giving 'unofficial official' feedback, advising his leader and briefing the press. It must have seemed nostalgic as the Liberal Democrats' very own veteran action hero was brought back for one last blockbuster outing. Ashdown was in his element: he loved every minute of it, and also proved useful to his leader.

David Steel was probably the ex-leader who had most experience of negotiating an agreement, albeit not a coalition, with another party leader. After the February 1974 general election, Edward Heath remained Prime Minister for a few days while he tried to form a government. The general election had been, as usual, on the Thursday, but Heath only resigned as Prime Minister on the following Monday. With 297 seats, Heath tried to put together a government involving the fourteen Liberal MPs and most of the Ulster Unionists. The Liberals would only agree to support an agreed programme from outside government, and Heath therefore resigned as Prime Minister.

Harold Wilson became Prime Minister and ran a minority government for six months before holding another election in October. It won a majority of three, but with by-elections and defections it was gone by 1976. By March 1977 the Conservatives put down a motion of censure and Prime Minister James Callaghan needed the Liberals to survive. The Liberal leader David Steel held several meetings with Callaghan to try to stave off defeat. The two men agreed a plan and Steel's Liberals saved Callaghan's government from defeat and sustained it until 1978. Steel decided at that point that a period of separation was required to re-establish his party's own identity before a general election. Steel had always desired an exit strategy and a relationship that was close but that would not submerge his own party.

Clegg asked Steel for his advice as he had been part of the 1974–9 experience of talks and agreement. Steel's advice was unambiguous and based closely on his own experience. He told Clegg that he must have a fixed end to any agreement and an exit strategy. Whether Clegg took Steel's advice to mean a five-year fixed parliament is unclear, but this was not what Steel meant. Steel's advice was that Clegg must think how to get out of the coalition before a general election so that the party could reassert its own identity in plenty of time.

Steel, like all the former leaders, is no fan of a Conservative–Liberal Democrat deal. He describes it as the 'uncomfortable coalition', and has declared that it was 'bonkers' that the Liberal Democrats launched into coalition negotiations – particularly when everyone involved was so tired. The result, he believes, is that the Parliamentary Party in both the Lords and the Commons has elected more left-wing representatives to speak on their behalf, Simon Hughes in the Commons and Lord Alderdice as Liberal Democrat Convenor in the Lords.

During the five-day period, although Steel was treated by the media as 'the resident expert', he had little contact with his party's leader.

The Liberal Democrat Parliamentary Party meeting was a bittersweet affair, with many MPs seeing each other for the first time since the election. There was the happiness of welcoming new MPs, but not as many as was hoped, and also the sadness of friends no longer there. Nick Clegg and Danny Alexander reported back to MPs about the opening of negotiations with the Conservatives and said they had gone well. The Conservatives had been 'flexible and open-minded to a degree that was very encouraging', he was reported to have said.

Had Clegg decided the outcome of the negotiations at this point as he met his Parliamentary Party for the first time, or was he on a journey himself? Did he lead his party by the nose into a coalition with the Conservatives, as has been suggested by a number within the Labour Party?

It is likely that Clegg decided on the Friday evening that he was between a rock and a hard place, but that the best option was to go with the party that could deliver a long-term stable government. As long as Clegg could get his four main manifesto concessions plus movement on electoral reform, it is highly likely there would be only one outcome. But it could not be absolutely certain, and to make sure it happened his team needed to manage communications with both the Labour and Conservative parties, and indeed his own party. In this respect the professionalism and discipline of his negotiating team was outstanding. The control of what information made it outside the inner team was quite brilliant and a tribute to the extremely close-knit group that had developed. The people around Clegg – Alison Suttie, Jonny Oates, John Sharkey and Polly MacKenzie, plus the negotiating team itself – knew the high stakes being played for and were exceptionally loyal to the cause.

Ming Campbell was 'shocked' by what he heard at the parliamentary meeting and remembered thinking, 'This is not realignment.' But Campbell knew that his party had changed, particularly since 2005, when 'the new MPs who came in were much less anti-Tory than people like me'. Campbell spoke and made the point that it was important when selling your house that it's better to have more than one buyer – therefore Labour must have its opportunity and be treated seriously. Jeremy Browne MP spoke to say all options available were fairly bleak, but that allowing a Conservative minority government was probably least bleak. This was a view he would quickly move on from, but Browne had to be careful about what he said in party meetings. He was viewed with suspicion by some of his colleagues, seen as one of the foremost flag-carriers of right-wing views in the party.

There were strong voices raised against any form of deal with the Conservatives – John Leech and Stephen Williams, for example – but there were also pragmatists like Norman Baker and Mike Hancock, who knew the choice was not straightforward due to the parliamentary arithmetic. The overall mood was described as: 'If we can take another route, let's take it rather than going with the Tories.' There can be little doubt that many MPs' hearts were for the so-called progressive alliance with Labour, not least because it was easier to explain to the country. A policy alliance with the Tories was said to be 'getting into bed with our historic enemies'.

Many, like Jeremy Browne, felt it would be better to let the Conservatives go ahead into government on their own, and be one step removed and not be guilty by association. Some felt that this would be a way to have their cake and eat it, suggesting that they would be able to pick and choose what they voted for, thus putting a Conservative administration on a tight leash. It was felt it was also a way to demonstrate the party's parliamentary muscle.

But for all the 'talking big' that reverberated around the room, fear also stalked those present. The 'huge fear', as one senior Liberal Democrat told me, 'was that the Conservatives would lay a series of elephant traps for us and then pull the plug and call an election. An election we couldn't afford, and we would be smashed.' Many both inside and outside the party commented on the huge difficulty of Clegg's position: he found himself in a position of power and influence for which his party had long yearned, but at the same time all the routes open to him had the potential to cause great harm further down the line. An incoming government would be compelled by the economic situation to take highly unpopular decisions: why be associated with those? Past leaders and others were quick to point out the damage done to the party in the past by association with the Conservatives. But at the same time to be seen to prop up a tarnished Labour government – led either by an unpopular and arguably rejected leader in Gordon Brown, or by another unelected Prime Minister if Brown were to make way for a new Labour leader – carried its own grave risks and also brought with it the likelihood of a second, expensive general election.

The Conservatives had fought the election telling people that to get rid of Gordon Brown you had to vote Conservative, that a hung parliament would be unstable. If there were a short-term government and a new election it would confirm the Conservative message and it would mean 'Armageddon for the Lib Dems'. Although there was a lot of tough talk at the first parliamentary meeting from MPs, Clegg quickly realised that if he got the narrative right, fear of destruction would bring the party to heel.

While the meeting continued, a demonstration for voting reform which had assembled in Trafalgar Square took the opportunity to march to Smith Square, and as its numbers grew (some suggested to as many as a thousand, though watching BBC journalists guessed a couple of hundred) it attracted attention outside Liberal Democrat headquarters. Placards – many hastily sprayed – demanded 'Fair Votes Now' and summoned people to 'Take Back Parliament'. Lobby groups such as 'Unlock Democracy' and 'Power 2010' spoke to television crews, and presented a petition to the Liberal Democrat leader, whom they lured out to address the chanting crowd through a megaphone.

Never in his wildest imagination, Clegg said, did he expect to see

a thousand people protesting in London for proportional representation; reforming politics was the reason he had gone into politics.
(Pause for cheering.) Audible demands from the crowd not to 'sell
out' – referring, no one could have doubted, to the discussions under
way with the Tories – he waved away with an uncomfortable smile.

As an opportunity to illustrate to both main parties the pressure
he was under to get an agreement on AV or even full proportional
representation, the demonstration could scarcely have been more
convenient – so much so, indeed, that rumours have circulated ever
since about the moving forces behind the demonstration, though such
cynicism has never been substantiated.

Certainly if it was a set up, most of the Parliamentary Party knew
nothing about it. The meeting room at the LGA was at the back of the
building with a courtyard and no clear view of where the demonstra-
tors gathered. Although it was all over the news channels, MPs were
'oblivious to it'. Nevertheless, the demo did serve its purpose for the
Liberal Democrats simply because it was noticed by the two other
parties involved in what was already becoming a bidding war. As a
softening-up exercise for later negotiations to follow, it helped.

The secret meeting – Saturday 3pm

Less than 24 hours after meeting with the Conservatives in full media
glare, the same Liberal Democrat negotiating team met secretly with
Labour. The Labour team were horrendously unprepared and one of
its team, Deputy Leader Harriet Harman, did not attend. Alistair
Darling was not there either, having originally been scheduled to take
part. Andrew Adonis believes that Darling was not part of the team
because Cable was not, but that is short of the full story.

Darling believed early on in the process that a deal with the Liberal Democrats would not be in the best interests of the Labour Party, and he therefore did not wish to be part of the team negotiating such a deal. Darling apparently told Brown of his strong reservations and it was felt judicious to leave him out. Darling's relationship with Brown for the past eighteen months had in any case been an unhappy one. Darling famously blamed Brown for 'unleashing the forces of hell' on him after he gave an honest assessment of the country's economic position. Asked later whether he stood by the 'forces of hell' remark, Darling replied: 'Of course I do, and not just some of it, all of it.' Brown brusquely declined to concur with Darling's admission that the government shared some responsibility for allowing the City's culture of risk-taking to get out of control. The Prime Minister himself admitted in a newspaper interview to a 'difficult relationship' with his Chancellor. Darling has also spoken of the strained relationship, although he says they never stopped talking completely.

According to a senior Treasury official it is also believed that in a private meeting Darling advised Brown during the European election coup that he should resign because Labour could not win an election with him as leader. Darling did not have the stomach, the desire, to reach out to the Liberal Democrats and did not want to do so to keep the losers *in situ*. Rather like Vince Cable (although for entirely different reasons), he was a figure rather detached from the process.

Mandelson's opening remarks to the meeting are extremely significant, because they are a snapshot of Gordon Brown's evolving thought process. On the Saturday and Sunday, Brown was moving towards a position where he believed he could outflank the Conservative offer to the Liberal Democrats, whatever that offer might have been. Brown believed, along with Adonis, that the Conservatives would never be able to match the Labour offer across a whole range of issues because the Conservative Parliamentary Party would simply not stomach it. To an extent, they were right.

When Mandelson claimed that 'for any deal to have hope of political legitimacy we have to form a genuinely new Government ... it had to be, and it had to be seen as, a real departure', he was making a genuine offer that had come direct from Brown. The specifics had not fully gestated, but a range of offers would be floated by Brown in the following two days that were far better than the Liberal Democrats could have anticipated.

For the Liberal Democrats, Danny Alexander set out the negotiating process and their priorities, which were their four main manifesto commitments during the election – although with the added priority now of cutting the deficit. Certainly the Labour negotiator Andrew Adonis sensed a level of ambition that seemed to leave little room for principles: on constitutional reform in particular, he remarks: 'They just wanted as much as they could get and they basically wanted a Dutch auction game between Labour and the Conservatives and see who gives most.' (Peter Mandelson remembers feeling that Danny Alexander's shopping list of priorities did not seem outlandish, and that a compromise deal might indeed be possible.)

Conscious that the Liberal Democrats would feel that the parliamentary arithmetic would make any deal with Labour difficult, Labour representatives were keen to emphasise that talks with the Democratic Unionist Party in Ulster had already suggested that a rainbow coalition would be possible if the Liberal Democrats were willing to go for it, although Sammy Wilson of the DUP has since denied any such discussions with Labour.

Alexander formed the impression that Labour's negotiators were operating on the assumption that they were the government and they would co-opt the Liberal Democrats, but they weren't going to give much ground – a difference of perspective which, as we will see, would prove increasingly divisive as meetings between Labour and the Liberal Democrats continued on the Monday and Tuesday.

The Liberal Democrat negotiators again raised the issue of AV legislation, as Alexander had in his first conversation with Mandelson. Then he had proposed the introduction of AV without a referendum, but this had now moved to immediate legislation on AV, but accepting the need to hold a referendum. As this was a short opening meeting and a lot of issues had to be raced through, there was no depth to any of the discussions. That was fortunate, because the detailed proposals made by the Liberal Democrats during the second meeting with Labour took their breath away.

Balls, Adonis and Mandelson all agree in their separate accounts of the meeting that it was a good opening session, that there were no intractable policy issues and that the signs were good. Ed Balls commented: 'It was friendly. I started the meeting very sceptical about whether this could be done and I left feeling more positive.' Adonis added: 'The personal chemistry was fine, but it's not body language that determines negotiations; it's whether a panel can get an agreement.'

There was no briefing from this meeting, no comments about how the body language was bad, that people had rolled their eyes or had behaved badly, and the reason was that both sides needed the secrecy deal to be observed. Labour did not want to upset the chance of a potential deal by showing any bad faith. The Liberal Democrats also did not wish to upset their discussions with the Conservatives, for which they still had high hopes. (By Monday night the fundamental dynamics within the negotiations had changed and the briefings to the media were designed to relay a narrative that would destroy with the Liberal Democrat Parliamentary Party any chance of a deal with Labour.)

The meeting had lasted only an hour, as the meeting with the Conservatives had the day before. Liberal Democrats now headed to the Work Foundation in Palmer Street for the next of their marathon internal meetings, the Federal Executive.

The Conservatives

Party HQ was the focus of activity for the Conservatives throughout Saturday, as the important work of preparation for the next day's full negotiating session with the Liberal Democrats began. The Conservative team had wanted full-blown negotiations to begin on the Saturday, but the Liberal Democrats were busy with internal party meetings for most of the day. However, the delay allowed Oliver Letwin to focus on pulling a full negotiating paper together that covered the eleven key policy areas.

Letwin had not waited for Saturday to arrive before he began his work on getting together an appropriate negotiating document. After the first meeting with the Liberal Democrats on Friday night, Letwin continued to toil well into the night to ensure everything was as he wanted it. He realised the historical magnitude of what was being undertaken and was keen to ensure that failing to prepare properly would not be an issue.

Letwin finished late but was in early to CCHQ (Conservative Campaign Headquarters), where he worked with mainstays James O'Shaughnessy and Peter Campbell throughout Saturday, with William Hague, Ed Llewellyn, George Osborne and Steve Hilton engaging at different times. Hilton felt bad because he had a guilty secret:

he had overslept (arriving at around lunchtime) and missed the first sessions of putting together the negotiating papers.

The aim was to produce a negotiating paper that could be sent to the Liberal Democrats by Saturday evening as a basis for discussion at the scheduled Sunday talks. It would be fair to say that of the negotiating team, Letwin in particular has been the focus of some of the more barbed comments from Conservative backbenchers about the deal done with the Liberal Democrats.

Letwin's crucial role in preparing the papers, of reading the Liberal Democrats' policy papers, and his ongoing advice to the leadership was well known by senior Tories during this period, and the feeling developed that he was the main cheerleader and therefore culprit for a policy giveaway that would lead the party into coalition.

As one senior backbencher said: 'He was the one who let the burglar in his house in the middle of the night and that's what he did with this agreement.' Another said: 'I have worked with Oliver Letwin and he may have a great grasp of dialectic materialism, but in terms of hard core politics, he needs a post-it sticker with arse and elbow. I mean, the guy was outgunned by the Liberal Democrats!' Liberal Democrat negotiators were all extremely surprised and gratified by the document that would be put before them on the Sunday morning. One said: 'It was startling; they were conceding a whole range of issues to us from the off.'

One of Letwin's aides during drafting was Peter Campbell, who is highly regarded within the Conservative Party and particularly by the leadership. He is trusted and was for that reason the note-taker in all the negotiating sessions. But his role within the party is much greater: 'He's a fantastic guy, one of the unsung heroes of the Conservative Party. He's worked for the party for twenty years, he was in the research department; he worked for Michael Howard; he's now part of the PMQ prep team. He's extremely thorough and diligent and he was exactly who we needed to work alongside Oliver to produce these papers.'

Letwin, Llewellyn and Campbell met early at Conservative HQ on the Saturday morning. Letwin and Campbell did the legwork in terms of getting the papers ready, and William Hague and George Osborne met with Letwin and Llewellyn to approve them in the afternoon. The document needed careful reading by the Conservative leadership as it made a number of up-front concessions which would probably have scandalised the Conservative Parliamentary Party's right wing.

Divided into eleven overarching policy areas, the document had within the policy areas section headings and sub-divisions. Within the section headings, the trade-offs or compromises were mooted. One Liberal Democrat adviser described it thus: 'A pretty open document. For example, on tax it said: "We won't agree to the proposal for a mansion tax but we are prepared to consider increasing personal allowances." So it wasn't a question of here is what the Conservatives want; it was here is what we propose as the first set of concessions to see where we get to.' The document also set out what the Conservative Party's red lines would be, but the document had clearly been through the Liberal Democrat manifesto and policy papers in some detail.

David Cameron's Saturday had been fairly low key and relaxed, at one point exchanging absurd *Star Trek* texts with his PPS Des Swayne. He had arrived at party HQ through a back entrance early that evening to provide the final sign-off to the negotiating document before heading to meet Nick Clegg at Admiralty House. There hadn't been much contact with those around Clegg through the day, apart from arrangements for the meeting due at 7.30pm and the sending over of the negotiating paper for discussions the following morning.

Danny Alexander did hold a lengthy conversation on the Saturday evening with William Hague in preparation for the talks. Alexander wanted to be properly prepared and did not want any surprises – he also wanted the talks to get off to a positive start. He therefore spoke with Hague about how the subject matter would be divided up for discussion, deciding that they would begin with the political reform issues. This was always the issue that was most important to the Liberal Democrats throughout all their negotiations, and the one they would return to time after time.

It was felt best to deal with some of the trickier issues first, and as Alexander said: 'There were some areas of political controversy here as well as a lot of common ground' – which Conservatives understood to mean as reform of the Westminster voting system to one that the Liberal Democrats favoured. Hague and Alexander also agreed that Sunday would see them focus on the economy and wider economic issues. It was felt that these two rather big and potentially controversial issues may take up most of the time available on the agenda – but proper discussions on these two major issues were felt to be key.

Across the river from Westminster, Ashdown had gathered up senior Liberal Democrats at a loose end that evening and invited them to dinner at his house in Kennington. Don Foster, Michael Moore, Menzies Campbell, Norman Lamb, Alistair Carmichael and Chief Whip Paul Burstow were present.

Ashdown was keen to pursue a deal with Labour and wanted support from movers and shakers in his party. He had spoken during the afternoon with former Lib Dem chief executive Chris Rennard, who had said that 'although it would be very fragile, it's possible to do a deal with Labour, which would produce a minority government that would look like a majority in the House of Commons, because it would take a supreme effort to bring together an alliance against it.' It was felt the nationalist parties in Scotland and Wales, particularly with national elections next year, would not want to be seen as consorting with the Conservatives. There was the possibility that a Lib–Lab minority could effectively rule as Alex Salmond had in Scotland.

At their dinner they discussed this possibility around the table. After a number of bottles of wine, interrupted only by a call from the Prime Minister to Menzies Campbell and another from Alex Salmond to Alistair Carmichael, it was agreed that this was an extremely interesting proposal that should be pursued. The Liberal Democrats were feeling more than a little intoxicated, not just from the wine drunk, but by the proximity to power that had a Prime Minister of the United Kingdom and a First Minister of Scotland calling Liberal Democrat dinner parties.

Cameron meets Clegg

The first meeting between Clegg and Cameron was supposed to be a low-key affair, in that they did not want a media circus and that they wanted to set the tone (rather than the media) of how the meeting went. Clegg left his Federal Executive meeting early and Special Branch protection made sure that he arrived undetected having given the media the slip by changing cars in Marsham Street. Cameron was also able to leave Conservative HQ undetected via the underground car park, carefully chaperoned by Special Branch.

Clegg arrived first, accompanied by his ever-present aide Alison Suttie, shortly ahead of Cameron and Ed Llewellyn. When the two men met on their own in a small room but with comfortable chairs, Cameron was the more relaxed, in casual clothes having had a quiet day. For Clegg it had been a long day with endless meetings with his party, endless explanations and talking about scenarios; he was therefore dressed in his business suit.

Both men agree the meeting was 'very relaxed'. They were comfortable together as both men are by nature charming and good-natured. There was laughter as the two compared notes on their method of arrival and the absurdity of events.

There was a serious edge to their discussions, though. Clegg reported back that he was having a certain amount of difficulty with his party, as the leader had run the gauntlet of opinion within his party throughout the day. Ex-leaders, members of the 'shadow Cabinet', disgruntled and not-so-disgruntled MPs and the Federal Executive had taken their opportunity to 'advise' their leader. For Clegg, party democracy felt a heavy load on Saturday evening, when meeting a leader who had not had to go through the sheer scale and drudgery of consulting that he had.

The things Clegg wanted in any form of coalition deal rarely changed over the negotiation sessions ahead: the four areas of his manifesto. But Cameron was clear also about what he wanted and where he could not make compromises. Cameron felt that he was in the stronger position of the two men. Although the Conservatives had not won the election outright, the party had the moral mandate to govern of all the parties. The election had been a disappointment to Clegg, as despite the additional votes he had lost seats.

The two leaders were weighing each other up, but also weighing up whether a coalition could work or whether it would be better to look to a confidence and supply deal. Nick Clegg said: 'For me it was important to tell him in very unambiguous terms, and I think likewise for him, about what was possible and explain there were four big areas of the manifesto that were very, very important to me. I also wanted to explain how my party thought and explore the different options of supply and confidence and coalition.'

As the civil servants and party aides milled around outside, good progress was made in the talks. The personal chemistry was surprisingly good, even though the two men did not know each other that well. The meeting lasted slightly longer than it was scheduled to, which was a good sign to those outside. Cameron and Clegg emerged enthused, upbeat and positive, as Cameron said: 'A deal could be done, even though there was a lot of work to do.' Clegg summarised the meeting as: 'I think we were both trying to be sincere rather than just go through the motions.'

Both men had a great deal to gain from a positive meeting as both realised by now that the prize would be a coming together of the two parties. It was quite unlikely that, with so much to lose, the meeting would go badly. However, the fact that it was so businesslike and positive augured well for negotiations the next day. Perhaps it was just as well that Clegg did not tell Cameron about the Liberal Democrats' meeting with Labour only a few hours earlier, as most likely it would have upset proceedings.

Within fifteen minutes of the meeting ending, Clegg was on the phone to Gordon Brown, who was in Scotland with his family. Although Clegg had little time for Brown, at this stage it was important to keep him onside and eager to do business.

One of the Liberal Democrat negotiating team suggests that Brown's departure from No. 10 would always be a precondition of any deal with Labour – well before the result of the general election was known: 'Nick was certainly of that view and had for a long time believed we could not do a deal if Brown were still leader. He had said that and we had had discussions about that.'

The outspoken remarks that Clegg had made during the campaign, to the effect that it would be an outrage for Brown to continue 'squatting' in No. 10 in the event of a clear defeat for his party, did not strictly speaking tie his hands. The circumstance he had referred to was one in which Labour came third in the overall vote count – and in the event, Liberal Democrat hopes of displacing Labour from second place in the popular vote had proved wishful thinking. Nevertheless, the tone of his remarks scarcely laid the groundwork for a fruitful collaboration between the Liberal Democrats and a Labour Party that was still led by Brown as Prime Minister. Even if Labour finished as the largest party in terms of the number of seats, Clegg had stressed, a low vote share would make it impossible for him to remain: 'You can't have Gordon Brown squatting in No. 10 just because of the irrational idiosyncrasies of our electoral system.'

Not all members of the negotiating team felt Brown should be forced out, as there might be advantages to his continuing as Prime Minister. One view held by Chris Huhne, was that having a coalition partner with a rather unpopular leader could help the Liberal Democrats. Why waste political capital on removing another party's leader when it could be used for negotiating leverage on AV or full PR?

The call lasted approximately fifteen minutes and the discussion was cordial, with Brown persuasive about the option of doing a deal with Labour. Much has been made of Brown's inability to communicate, and it is true that in general it was poor. However, when focused and with the authority of the office of Prime Minister he could rise to the occasion. Clegg may well have ruled Labour out of the contest apart from in exceptional circumstances, but Brown was still up for the fight.

DAY 3

– Sunday 9 May –

Sunday began early for both the Conservative and Liberal Democrat negotiating teams – but also for Vince Cable. He was called from Scotland at breakfast time by a Prime Minister looking for information. Cable's relationship with Brown was largely in one direction: primarily he listened as Brown let off steam or talked about global issues. Cable offered Brown respect and often a thoughtful reinforcement of his position. During this conversation Brown 'confirmed that he was willing to consider the possibility of stepping down at some point in the future'.

To Brown's surprise, Cable's response was that vague promises would not be good enough for his colleagues, if he wanted formal negotiations to get under way soon. Brown still genuinely believed that there was a way to do a deal and he was still the man to deliver it – he was not about to give up. Cable had merely crystallised the size of the challenge for a man that believed he had, only eighteen months earlier, saved the world from financial collapse. This was not a moment for weakness.

Brown was determined to keep fighting for the position he had longed for and finally wrestled from Tony Blair three years earlier. It was now essential to meet Clegg face to face and, later in the day, he would have the opportunity to put his plan into action: he knew he could convince Clegg of the logic of a deal. His people were told to get the meeting firmly fixed for when he got back from Scotland.

With his mind elsewhere, Brown went to church with his family, but his real desire was to get back to Downing Street as soon as possible so that he could begin the business of persuading Clegg that he and Labour had more to offer in a 'progressive alliance' (by now the buzz phrase for all parties) than the Conservatives. Brown's plan was to make the deal irresistible to the Liberal Democrats: surely that would soothe any concerns about his own role, even if it meant a few of them holding their nose?

*

Oliver Letwin was also up early, working away on refining the Conservative position for the start of negotiations proper. He had put many hours into the preparation, toiling late into both Friday and Saturday nights. He was tired, and had drunk copious amounts of coffee to keep going, 'I don't think I ever drank so much coffee' he said. Letwin believes the extreme tiredness helped him 'in an odd kind of way'. It was simply impossible to focus on anything irrelevant as all of life's normal concerns seemed to drop away, 'because you don't have the emotional or intellectual energy to worry about them'.

Letwin described it like this: 'I've had the luck never to have been in a world war, but my impression is that when people are involved in very great events like wars, life sort of gets easier in one sense because it's so important that you lay to one side mortgages, debts, jobs – you just get on and fight the war and you're facing life and death so everything else seems trivial. Obviously what we were doing wasn't that, but on the other hand politically it kind of was and we could all tell, certainly I felt, that this was a momentous thing, that it mattered a lot what the outcome was, and therefore paying the bills didn't matter. I felt released from the ordinary cares of life.' Other negotiators simply admitted to being 'absolutely knackered' throughout the period.

Letwin's view of the negotiations was simple: 'The team would do its best, succeed or fail, and that they would do it in their own time without pressure from the media or civil servants.' But clearly one of the important elements would be trust. 'Our attitude then, and it was the right attitude and it had to be mutual, was that we should all shut up and that it [the negotiation] should be leak-proof. It was part of what created an atmosphere of trust, and the other effect was that the media literally got nothing. It was totally powerless and made us realise that if you want to you can keep your silence until you are ready to speak!'

The Conservative negotiating team, plus James O'Shaughnessy and Steve Hilton, met just before 10am at William Hague's London flat for 'a cup of tea and a chat about the day ahead', before moving to 70 Whitehall for what was billed as the first proper session of talks. Before the full negotiating meeting got under way, Cameron discussed with a key member of his team what he believed was Clegg's position. 'He clearly wants a deal,' Cameron is reported to have said, 'because he doesn't like Brown, but he can't come to an agreement without something on electoral reform. That is the sticking point.'

The Liberal Democrats' reference team met at Cowley Street, having pored over the Conservative negotiating document late into the night. The reaction to their document had been little short of astonishment. The document set out eleven policy areas with sub-headings, what the Conservative manifesto had wanted to introduce, what the Lib Dem manifesto said and where the overlaps were and where there might be compromise.

The Conservatives turned up prepared to be flexible, and there was plenty of compromise and concession in the document for the Liberal Democrats to appreciate. Indeed, one senior member of Cameron's team said: 'My view of what turned the Liberal Democrats our way were the position papers. They suddenly saw in black and white that we were serious, prepared to go issue by issue, that we really wanted to work out where we could stand together.' The Liberal Democrat strategy was simple: focus on getting the constitutional package they wanted (specifically voting reform), and don't waste political capital elsewhere that might distract matters.

As agreed the day before, the first item on the agenda was constitutional reform, but not before Sir Gus O'Donnell had once again stressed the importance of the impending pressure from the financial markets due to open the next morning and the need to come to the most stable agreement possible. The teams each had assigned to them an individual civil servant who was there to co-ordinate support in three areas on behalf of the Civil Service if a party should request it. The Conservatives had Senior Treasury official Edward Troup, while the Liberal Democrats had Caleb Deeks. The Queen's Private Secretary, Sir Christopher Geidt, was also in attendance for the talks, giving their outcome an ever greater significance.

Deeks and Troup could offer support, according to the Civil Service official papers, in three areas: advice on constitutional issues and processes; factual information about specific policy issues; and logistical support to the negotiations. Throughout Sunday though, the civil servants were largely left hovering in the waiting areas outside the main negotiating room, looking for 'signs of body language on how the session was going', as one civil servant who was closely involved said.

The two teams had agreed that the session would be about getting all the issues on the table, so that it was clear where any concessions might be and where the immovable red lines were. If the teams agreed to disagree, the issue would be moved to the two leaders to consider.

However, the Liberal Democrats wanted to begin discussions on areas of disagreement, and the Conservatives on the areas of agreement. In the event they followed the order that Letwin's paper set out. What they all agreed on throughout the day was the high quality of the biscuits as demanded by Oliver Letwin and in the main eaten by Liberal Democrat policy aide Polly Mackenzie.

If there were policy areas that needed to be clarified, both teams had key personnel on standby to assess, interpret, question and advise – Christian Moon and Chris Saunders as well as Polly Mackenzie for the Liberal Democrats, and James O'Shaughnessy and Rohan Silva for the Conservatives. The basis and order of discussion followed Letwin's paper that had been so painstakingly prepared throughout the previous day.

Having felt that constitutional reform 'might be a problem' the two teams raced through the items at a fairly brisk pace. Fixed-term parliaments, House of Lords reform, devolution and decentralisation of power, party funding, cleaning up expenses and powers of recall, and voter registration – all were large areas of policy overlap between the parties, without significant problems or concerns.

Even on the potentially difficult issue of same size constituencies, an essential part of the Conservative manifesto, the Liberal Democrats were 'perfectly amenable to that', according to William Hague. Indeed they were, as the Liberal Democrats also made the proposal that 'there should be a number of changes to the House of Commons, one of which should be a boundary change, to look at reducing the number of seats and for aligning their size.' They would support it but it would need to be part of a package of changes that would include electoral reform (with a minimum of a referendum on AV). There were some minor concerns in discussions about the timing of House of Lords reform and how quickly the Lords moved to an elected chamber, but there was no fundamental disagreement.

Electoral reform was the sticking point. Cameron's opening gambit at St Stephen's Club was an 'all-party committee of inquiry on political and electoral reform'. This was never discussed seriously at the negotiating session because it was simply a non-starter for the Liberal Democrats and would have caused an immediately negative reaction – not judged the best way to get talks off to a good start. Indeed, one of Cameron's close aides admitted: 'That was always a minimalist offer. That was an opening negotiating offer, it's fair to say.'

The Liberal Democrats had their own opening gambit on the voting system with a bid for a referendum on a fully proportional system (Single Transferable Vote or AV-plus) and the implementation of AV without a referendum. Chris Huhne argued that AV was a form of first-past-the-post, so why couldn't it simply be implemented. Instead what the Conservatives tabled, and it was the main item of discussion in the constitutional part of the negotiations, was a free vote in the House of Commons on a referendum on the Alternative Vote system.

The Conservative team held to this line because it was not believed on Sunday morning, particularly by Osborne and Hague, that the Conservative Parliamentary Party was likely to agree to go any further – although Osborne was already convinced that a coalition agreement would have to cede a referendum to the Liberal Democrats. Labour after all had already offered it as part of its manifesto commitments.

As the negotiations wore on the Conservative team did make a concession, that in the free vote David Cameron, George Osborne, William Hague and Oliver Letwin would vote positively for a referendum on AV. However, it would be a free vote so there could be no guarantee of success – in all likelihood it would have failed as a combination of Labour MPs and the majority of the Conservative backbench MPs would have sunk it.

The Liberal Democrats rejected the plan and no deal was possible on the issue of AV. They made it clear that this was a red line issue for them and 'without the ability to move forward on electoral reform we'd feel it was much more difficult to go into a coalition'. George Osborne and William Hague said that it was a similar red line issue for the Conservative Party and they could not move. William Hague suggested that the matter be 'kicked upstairs to the leaders'. Over the following negotiating sessions, several matters that were too tricky for the negotiating teams would be kicked upstairs for the leaders to try to solve. Where disagreements could not be settled, the use of the trusty old review was wheeled into action.

The leaders were quickly into action by telephone to try to sort out the problem. A call was made between Cameron at home in Notting Hill and Clegg, also at home in Putney. Cameron was expecting the Gove family as guests for Sunday lunch and Clegg had a birthday party planned for one of his children later in the afternoon. The discussion was brief and there was no firm conclusion on a way forward on voting reform – but things would gather pace through Sunday night and Monday morning.

According to both, Clegg and Cameron had felt from the very first contact very relaxed in each other's company. Clegg said: 'We are both from the same generation, we speak the same kind of language, we both have a very un-precious way of going about things; quite candid with each other about where the constraints are.' The two men would have some tough things to say to each other in the hours ahead, but it was done in a pragmatic and businesslike way, never allowing emotions to get in the way of what needed to be said or done. Both men liked to get business done at a brisk pace, deciding what the possibilities were and then exploring them.

But the issue of AV meant that the negotiations moved from being about agreeing a deal on a coalition to discussing a confidence and supply arrangement. Coalition was not ruled out, because a breakthrough might still be possible, but the focus moved to the idea of co-operating and pursuing areas of policy agreement as the basis of a programme for a minority Conservative government. David Laws said: 'It was just that, it seemed as if we had reached a position that neither party could cross and we kind of accepted that in an adult way and looked at the potential to negotiate a confidence and supply agreement.'

Work began almost immediately in the Conservative camp on drafting a supply-and-confidence agreement that it was hoped could perhaps become, over time, the basis of a more detailed and stable agreement for a full coalition. There was urgency at all times not to let the negotiations drift or run out of steam. Momentum was the key to any agreement and Cameron insisted his team keep pressing forward, demonstrating the dynamism that reaching an agreement would need. Any drift, he felt, would provide an opening to Labour. If a coalition was not possible then a confidence and supply proposal had to be on the table by the following day, and to achieve that the Liberal Democrats needed to see the document before the day was out.

Unfortunately for the Conservative negotiating position on AV, David Laws later got wind of the ring-round of Conservative MPs, that had taken place on the Sunday afternoon, asking a series of open questions including about AV. David Laws said: 'This bolstered our view that we needed to go back to the leader of the Conservative Party and make clear how important a referendum was to us.' Clegg held vital knowledge of the Conservatives' potential willingness to concede something on AV, and in important conversations later on Monday, he would play the card expertly.

After several hours of negotiation, the two teams broke for lunch, going to their separate rooms at 70 Whitehall. The morning had gone well for both sides. The spirit in which the negotiations were being conducted was excellent, there were no cross words or – voting reform apart – any seemingly impossible bridges to cross. Furthermore, the teams liked each other. The Civil Service laid on the sandwiches and the lunch break was used to catch up on conversations with party leaders, former leaders and senior policy advisers. There were also discussions to prepare for the afternoon session, which would now be looking to maximise areas of agreement for use in a confidence and supply arrangement between the parties being drafted while they spoke.

The second big item on the agenda was the economy, and first up was deficit reduction. George Osborne made this an absolutely non-negotiable core for the Conservatives because he believed that any government formed would fall apart without taking the action deemed necessary by the Bank of England. There had been a preliminary discussion about the economy in the Friday night meeting when the Liberal Democrats had been offered and had declined briefings with the Treasury and the Bank of England. Governor Mervyn King had been on standby to speak to negotiators. The Conservatives thought that they would need independent corroboration of the fact that 'we need to make public spending cuts quickly, but we didn't need to do that,' one of the Conservative team said.

The Liberal Democrats, intellectually at least, had moved on the issue of spending during the election campaign. As with most of the constitutional reform programme items, the teams moved briskly through the economic issues in Letwin's document. On the Conservative side there was an immediate willingness to concede to the Liberal Democrats their manifesto commitment on the personal tax allowance. Osborne knew it was key to the Liberal Democrats' manifesto, but that it was very expensive. However, for a deal to be done, he knew 'we would just have to find a way to afford it', thus making it a spending priority. In the event it would not be done in one big bang, but bit by bit over the period of a five-year parliament as resources would allow. This was a policy that most Conservative MPs felt should have been in the Conservative manifesto, but was considered by the party leadership to be unaffordable in the current economic circumstances. It was a concession likely to be welcomed and even popular among Conservative MPs.

The next concession, on inheritance tax, was likely to receive a more mixed reaction. It was something that was popular with William Hague personally, as well as a number on the right of the Parliamentary Party. There was some affection for an inheritance tax cut, not only because it was believed to be fair, but this had been a policy that had saved the Conservative Party from a general election early in Gordon Brown's tenure in 2007. It had turned around the opinion polls enough to stop Brown taking a gamble, a gamble that probably would have resulted in a Labour parliamentary majority, or at least in Labour returning as the largest party. Osborne believed though that he would find it difficult to get inheritance tax through the House in a minority government and that his marriage tax proposals were more important. Osborne negotiated that the Liberal Democrats would abstain on Conservative marriage tax proposals, meaning the policy was deliverable. It was quite a coup in the circumstances.

The third early concession by the Conservative team was on Capital Gains Tax, and one that would not go down well with the Parliamentary Party. Osborne had to take a calculated risk. He had reviewed Liberal Democrat tax policy and was concerned by the party's huge array of green taxes and pensions. He therefore agreed to concede a move towards the Liberal Democrat policy on capital gains tax, meaning a significant rise from its level at 18%. Even in the honeymoon period of a new coalition government, this issue was to cause rancour on the Conservative back benches, almost to the same extent as the perceived coup by the leadership of the influential 1922 Committee.

The Liberal Democrat team also agreed to stop the Labour government's proposed National Insurance rise, or 'jobs tax' as the Conservatives called it throughout the election. It was believed that this was a red line issue for George Osborne, and there was never a chance of persuading him to change his mind and drop it altogether. However, Osborne did make a small concession as he left part of the National Insurance rise in place to fund some of the money that was needed for the raising of personal allowances.

As the Conservative leader in the negotiations, William Hague was simply realistic about making concessions. His view was that with 307 MPs the Tories would not be able to get everything they wanted through the House of Commons, so giving up some policies because it was impossible to get the Liberal Democrats to agree was simply a recognition of the fact that the Conservative Party could not get the legislation through Parliament, however much it may want it. His view was that some Conservative MPs, when they talk about the concessions the party made at the time, compare what would have been implemented with a majority Conservative government. That was never the choice; the comparison had to be between the coalition and a minority Conservative administration.

The Liberal Democrats had raised Value Added Tax as an important issue during the election. However, during the negotiations on the economy and despite the speedy progress across issues, it was never raised. One negotiator told me: 'We had no discussion at all on VAT, but we did say in the agreement that the deficit reduction processes would have to take place in a way to protect those on lower incomes and key public services.'

In return for Conservative concessions the Liberal Democrat negotiators conceded that they were 'happy to start the deficit reduction process this year [2010–11] rather than next year [2011–12] and also have a more rapid pace of reduction this parliament'. This was seen as an astonishing turnaround by the Liberal Democrats, as the party had argued consistently that in-year cuts would be devastating, putting economic recovery at risk, and that any increase in the pace of deficit reductions would do the same.

However, Danny Alexander pointed out in their defence that the Liberal Democrats were clear in their manifesto that 'we wanted to eliminate the deficit as quickly as possible, consistent with what the economy would allow. We also said that we wanted spending to bear the lion's share of that. In fact we always presented ourselves as the most hawkish party in setting measures to tackle the deficit.'

However, even during the election, Clegg had been moving on the issue – but without telling the electorate. He later told the BBC that he had changed his view during the general election: 'Remember between March and the actual general election, a financial earthquake occurred on our European doorstep … we were all I think reacting to very, very fast-changing economic events.'

Apparently as the euro crisis unfolded, this affected the Liberal Democrat leader's thinking as it was 'much, much more serious than we had previously been led to believe'. But it was George Osborne who strikingly played a key role in changing Liberal Democrat hearts and minds on the issue in the negotiations. One Clegg aide said: 'The thing that changed minds was George Osborne saying that he had seen the figures and it was quite horrific in real life as opposed to spin life. He wasn't saying these things as points of dogma or to win us over; he was genuinely describing to us the state of the economy.'

Surprisingly the arguments presented by Osborne did not appear to have been rigorously or independently checked by the Liberal Democrats. None of the negotiating team had presentations from the Treasury or the Bank of England during the negotiating sessions, despite several offers from civil servants. Vince Cable did have several conversations with Treasury officials, but never saw the Governor of the Bank of England. But what limited discussions there were came after the negotiations on the economy had been completed and agreed by the two parties. Whatever information both Clegg and Cable received, it was almost irrelevant because it was subsequent to what they had already agreed.

As if to emphasise the budget deficit and economic crisis shaking Europe, Osborne was called out of the talks to take a call from the Chancellor, Alistair Darling, who was in Brussels with his European counterparts having talks about Greece and the potential financial rescue package. The Chancellor called to ensure that Osborne was in agreement with his negotiating position, which was to try to keep the UK out of the main European rescue package. Darling had not expected to be Chancellor on the Sunday and clearly did not have much confidence that he would be continuing in his role. Osborne informed him that there could be only one Chancellor at a time and that he should make his own judgements and he would either support or criticise them depending on his view.

It is perhaps worth noting at this point that what were considered the two potential areas of conflict, in constitutional reform and on the economy, had proved to be no such thing. Neither of the negotiating teams was putting up serious resistance on issues that had been the cause of enormous conflict only days earlier. The impression is that both sides were much keener on coming to an early agreement than perhaps they led their Parliamentary Parties to believe either at the time or subsequently.

Education was the next big policy negotiation to be tackled. As their parties' education spokesmen, David Laws and Michael Gove had got to know each other reasonably well. There was a high degree of mutual admiration and trust between the two men. Gove was frequently generous and complimentary about Laws in public, while Laws respected Gove's intellect and admired his genuine reforming zeal.

The gaps in policy were not large and the main area of discussion was a pupil premium, as it would be with Labour's Ed Balls. George Osborne had questions about where the money to finance it would come from, because Laws was insistent that this money must be additional to the schools budget.

After education funding there followed in fairly quick succession banking reform, the environment, nuclear power, civil liberties, and international democracy (the Human Rights Act). By 6pm enormous progress had been made, and both teams seemed heartened and satisfied by the day's work.

The final thing to do as negotiations closed for the day was to agree a line for the enormous media scrum awaiting the teams as they left the building. The Conservatives left first and Hague said: 'Well, we've had some very positive and productive discussions over many key policy areas. The issues we have covered include political reform, economic issues and reduction of the deficit, banking reform, civil liberties, environmental issues. So we've had good discussions about all those areas. We intend to meet again over the next 24 hours. We are agreed that a central point of any agreement that we make will be economic stability and the reduction of the budget deficit. But each negotiating team is now going to report back to our party leaders – so my colleagues and I are on our way to discuss where we have got to with David Cameron, and the Liberal Democrats will also be meeting Nick Clegg. So as I said, we intend to meet again over the next 24 hours and we'll keep you updated.'

It was an honest assessment of the day's negotiations. The Conservative team though had to go back to David Cameron and give a more private assessment. William Hague's humorous assessment of the day was that 'it appears we have Conservative Party policy that only Oliver Letwin knows about'. George Osborne was surprised by the negotiation and was reported to say: 'This should be the happiest day of our lives, because it's all our policy that's being agreed.'

Everyone who had set out on the process of trying to bring about a deal between the Liberal Democrats and Conservatives had begun with scepticism. Events were proving everybody wrong.

When Clegg met Brown

As the Conservative and Liberal Democrat negotiating teams resumed after lunch, another key meeting was taking place close by in the Foreign Office. The tide seemed to be going the Conservatives' way, and Gordon Brown had been yearning for the chance to get into a room one-to-one with Nick Clegg – which may appear strange in light of the Prime Minister's appalling reputation for interpersonal skills.

However, Brown knew that when he was focused and had decided on a plan of action he could rise to almost any occasion. According to Clegg's aide, the two men met for around 45 minutes, about half the time Cameron spent with Clegg, in the oak-panelled office of Sir Peter Ricketts, permanent under-secretary at the Foreign Office.

Brown was very friendly and began a charm offensive heavily laced with persuasion. 'We don't know each other well Nick, but I know we can work together effectively,' he began. 'I know there is a lot at stake for the country and in British politics and I really want you to know that I intend to press ahead with reform.' Brown was showing himself as willing, co-operative, flexible and charming.

Clegg's response was to emphasise that his party was in a process with the Conservatives and it was going reasonably well, with the odd glitch. But Clegg continually said that he couldn't see 'how the numbers could possibly stack up'. He continued: 'It is not an issue of policies, it is an issue of how it would be perceived if we prop up a defeated government; the public would not perceive it as legitimate.' Brown's response was: 'It can be, it can, I believe we can make this work for the country.'

But it would be wrong to believe that Clegg was not affected by this first meeting. Brown was at his best, as Clegg said himself, 'Brown was very persuasive, very persuasive in that first meeting in the Foreign Office.'

Brown's pitch was good as he said: 'I'll move heaven and earth to make this happen. It's a big moment in British politics, this is an important once-in-a-generation crossroads. We can either go the regressive direction with the Conservatives, which I know you don't want to do, after all the Liberal and Labour parties are cousins in the progressive cause. I know there are sceptics, but I really believe in the case for major political reform. I know we should have done more in office, but I have a plan for a jumbo referendum that will cover a number of areas that need constitutional change.' There was no mention of Brown stepping down.

The meeting had gone extremely well for Brown, and Clegg had been given food for thought. It was felt a further meeting would be worthwhile and it was quickly arranged for 9.30pm the same day, with Peter Mandelson and Danny Alexander present.

Clegg denies that personality played any part in his decision-making when choosing Cameron and the Conservatives before Labour and Brown. But when listening to Clegg talk about his relationship with both men it is striking how easy-going and congenial the relationship is with Cameron, while with Brown it 'took a lot longer because there was an awful lot of him wanting to tell me things. He would get quite fixed and I would ask him questions and he just repeated what he had said.'

Conservative disquiet

While the negotiating team continued its work, David Cameron was often left waiting around for when his services would be called in to action. He had spent part of the Sunday afternoon playing tennis with a close friend. The following day Conservative MPs were likely to start arriving in Westminster, and many had questions and concerns. There were worries about the deal, about the start of a bidding war, about consultation – and the list went on.

Knowing that the Liberal Democrats had already started a thorough consultation with their MPs, one Conservative rang a whip to ask what arrangements had been made for a meeting of the Parliamentary Party. The answer given was that the party was not due to meet until Parliament formally resumed in several weeks! This was relayed to the leader's office, which suggested that the whips would not know it, but that a consultation would begin shortly.

The Cameron team were taking a number of calls, so it was felt that the leader's time could be productively spent soothing the party's nerves. All Conservative MPs were then informed that Cameron would see anyone who would like to drop in on Sunday evening. Some were specifically invited in to speak to Cameron one-to-one. Chief Whip Patrick McLoughlin was present during every party meeting.

There was a meeting for half a dozen members of the shadow Cabinet including Dame Pauline Neville-Jones, Andrew Mitchell, Dominic Grieve, Eric Pickles and Chris Grayling. Malcolm Rifkind, former Foreign Secretary and senior member of the party, held a private meeting with Cameron. He had taken to the airwaves fairly early on in the process, not trying to sell a particular way forward but realising that it was a sensitive time for the leadership, so his intention was to simply give an analysis of what was happening.

Rifkind had always assumed a hung parliament was the likely outcome, not due to any mistake with strategy, merely the huge size of the task. 'I had assumed ... that Britain does not like coalitions and that a minority Conservative Government was the most likely option. I did not think a coalition with the Liberal Democrats could be delivered. Not on any issue of principle, but because I couldn't see how the Liberal Democrats themselves could make the necessary concessions, for example on economic policy. The idea of Cabinet posts would be very seductive to them, but I couldn't see how they could carry their party.'

Cameron made clear to Rifkind that his preferred option was a coalition, as long as it didn't involve too many concessions, but this was by no means certain. Cameron indicated that he did not want to make any concession on electoral reform, but in his judgement felt it was likely to be necessary to offer something. Given the huge importance of electoral reform to the Liberal Democrats, he told Rifkind, something on it would have to be part of the package if there was to be any prospect of Clegg being able to sell it to his own people.

Cameron also indicated that the most likely candidate already emerging on the constitutional side was some aspect of the Alternative Vote, because the Liberal Democrats knew that there was no way that the Conservatives would ever concede the Single Transferable Vote. Cameron felt there may need to be a discussion on whether it was reasonable to offer a referendum on AV.

Other MPs turned up, including Hugo Swire and Greg Barker. As friends of the leader, Swire and Barker met Cameron together to offer their support. The rest had a larger group meeting around the huge table in the Leader of the Opposition's office in Norman Shaw South. This included Bernard Jenkin, Damian Green, Alan Duncan, Lee Scott, Nick Boles, Rehman Chishti and Nadhim Zahawi.

When Cameron spoke to the larger group of mainly backbench MPs he was keen, as one MP remembered, to stress how the preferred aim was a coalition. 'Cameron used hand gestures to talk about confidence and supply down here, while a full blown coalition was up there [holding his hand high by his head]. He was clear what he wanted, but there was no mention of AV that I remember.'

There was a range of responses to Cameron, mainly positive. Lee Scott said he had consulted his association members, and councillors were very positive about what the leader had done so far; he and they would support David, he said, before urging him to 'do the deal'.

Nick Boles wanted as firm a deal as possible, the longer and deeper the agreement the better. Bernard Jenkin, sitting beside David Cameron and opposite the Chief Whip said: 'David there is absolutely no doubt you are going to be Prime Minister. All you need to do is wait.' He thought there was no chance of the Labour Party stitching up a rainbow coalition to form a majority government, and Gordon Brown was finished. He told Cameron that he would need just the minimum agreement with the Lib Dems to get into government and once in office he would have the authority of government. He could open the books, have the emergency budget within fifty days, and dare the Liberal Democrats to vote against it. His calculation was that they dare not, as they were in no position to fight a general election and would be responsible for plunging the country into an economic and political crisis. If there were an election in July, the Conservatives would win it. A more likely date for calling an election though would be October, which he believed the Conservatives would be in a good position to win outright.

Cameron's response was, 'I think some of the people around this table were hoping for a bit more incumbency than that' – a remark which had several meanings. First, George Osborne had been advising Cameron and the team around the leader that the most important thing in this negotiation was simply to get into government. Once in government, he believed, 'the rules of the game changed'. Government brought with it the levers of power and a massive shift in how the Conservative Party would be perceived.

Sir Alan Haselhurst reinforced the point when he said that a substantial period of incumbency was going to add authority to the Conservative Party in government and to the leader of the party. There were still concerns within the leadership that the Conservative brand needed further decontamination. A period of government might convince people that a Conservative Party led by Cameron had changed.

Second, in recent years the longer the incumbency of a hard-working MP, the better he or she did in elections. (It is believed that this was the reason that a number of Labour MPs survived the election when they should have lost their seats.) There developed a lively debate about whether the party would win an October election, with the Chief Whip of the view that the Conservatives would be unlikely to win. It was felt that the Unite campaign had been quite effective in London and parts of the north, even though it was based exclusively on scare stories. Cameron was of the view that it was the leaders' debate that tied Brown down and stopped him getting his cuts agenda off the ground. Everyone left feeling they had had an opportunity to fully express their view.

This is important as it has been argued that Conservative MPs were not consulted and were steamrollered into a coalition agreement. Although it is true that the party's consultation was not as frequent or as detailed as the Liberal Democrats', Cameron did take pains to engage the party on all the major decisions. It was much worse for Labour MPs as they had no formal consultation process during the entire five-day period.

Cameron meets Clegg

After Cameron finished with his MPs he met with his negotiating team for a report back on proceedings. The report was positive, and Cameron was delighted, feeling that on the current trajectory he was heading for Downing Street: 'Everything was falling into place nicely,' he said.

Cameron was to have a one-to-one meeting with Clegg at 7.45pm in Room 391 in Portcullis House, and then two phone calls at 9.15pm and 22.55pm. It was this meeting and the subsequent phone calls that covered important ground that made both leaders confident a deal was moving within their grasp.

The negotiating teams had been unable to come to an agreement on the Liberal Democrats' big issue – reform of the voting system. Chris Huhne had made a series of proposals to the Conservative team at the morning session, including legislation without a referendum; legislation but with a confirmatory referendum; even a Constitutional Convention where the result would be put to the public in a referendum. All had been turned down and kicked upstairs for the leaders to argue over.

To the great disappointment of both leaders, the stalemate had moved the negotiation from coalition to one of confidence and supply. Now the leaders tackled the key issue between the two sides head on. The bottom line was that Clegg would accept nothing less than a referendum on AV, as he argued this had been in the Labour manifesto and would certainly have been delivered by Labour in any agreement as a minimum. He also said he would need to have something to convince his party that the risk of forming a government with the Conservatives was worth taking. In their conversations, Clegg was also clear he ideally did not want a confidence and supply agreement as he believed his party would get all of the downside and none of the upside. He said: 'I just thought that's not what the country wanted, what the party wanted and not frankly what I thought David Cameron would want either.'

Cameron was sympathetic, but he was not totally sure he could deliver a referendum. Privately, Cameron knew that the huge ring-round of over three hundred of his MPs carried out by the Whips's Office earlier in the space of a few hours that afternoon had delivered quite unexpected results.

As well as asking for views, the Whips's conversations with Conservative MPs were designed stealthily to guide them, particularly new ones, in their thoughts. So the conversations began with the offer of congratulations on their election and then proceeded to outline that this was a really important time for the country. The party had fought a strong and positive election campaign, and although it had fallen short of an overall majority, it had gained more seats than at any election for the last eighty years. The most important thing was for Britain to have a strong, stable and decisive government. The Conservatives have always been a party that puts the national interest first, and the best thing for Britain now was a new government that worked together in that national interest. There was mood music about how important it was to keep people informed in the fast-moving situation, but the message for MPs to say nothing and let the negotiators get on with it was also there.

The views that came back were better than the leadership had hoped. As one aide put it: 'We had a very detailed read-out on the mood of the Parliamentary Party, including on AV. A referendum was probably doable, but anything further than that would not fly.' Cameron knew the position from his discussions with Clegg, but the data was raw and he did not want to have to row back from any agreement. George Osborne had informed him that he believed that a referendum on AV would have to be offered to ensure a coalition deal. He was absolutely clear about that.

Cameron made no promises, but agreed to consult further. At some point he knew he would have to secure agreement from his shadow Cabinet and the Parliamentary Party if he wanted to make an offer. Cameron was willing to consider the option only on the basis that this would secure the deal, subject to the negotiation's small print. Clegg was clear that there would be no coalition deal without it.

After the disappointment of the move to confidence and supply, both men found themselves getting what Clegg described as 'a second wind'. Clegg said: 'I remember over the phone saying "No, let's just go for it", and remember both of us being quite uplifted that we'd both independently come to the decision that the only logical thing to do was to try again.' A Cameron aide put it this way: 'It was a joint decision as we felt that we should not give up on the coalition plan, as a lot of us always thought it was a much better option. But none the less, we would work up the other track, which we did.'

Following the meeting and phone calls, where excellent progress had been made with tremendous goodwill between the two leaders, Cameron left for home on Sunday night 'feeling we were heading for government.' Clegg also felt a deal was almost there and told his reference group that the concession on a referendum on AV from the Conservatives was 'likely'. Although the negotiating teams would meet the following morning to discuss confidence and supply, Cameron and Clegg were still convinced a bigger prize was possible.

Late night: Brown and Clegg meet

At 9.30pm Gordon Brown and Peter Mandelson met with Nick Clegg and Danny Alexander in the Prime Minister's office, behind the Speaker's Chair in the Commons. It was a good location, well away from the prying eyes of the media. Brown and Mandelson had made sure they would not be seen leaving No. 10 by using an underground tunnel to the Ministry of Defence, where a car had been waiting.

Brown's hopes were high. The meeting earlier in the day in a one-to-one with Clegg had been friendly and had gone probably better than either man expected. But it had made Clegg think that the fact that the meeting had gone so well made the Liberal Democrat leader determined it was time to talk tough. The Liberal Democrat team had previously tip-toed around the issue of 'personnel' (that is, Gordon Brown's continued position as Prime Minister), hinting at it, saying 'We will come to that', confirming it was a 'problem', but refusing to discuss it as part of any formal or informal talks (which many would argue were the same thing). Clegg was also feeling emboldened as his talks with Cameron that same evening had gone very well.

Now Clegg had become determined: 'After the meeting with Brown in the Foreign Office, I had concluded that it was necessary to be open and blunt with him about the dynamic that I thought was inescapable – as far as any kind of co-operation with Labour, he had somehow to be taken out of the equation.' With as little as 23% of the popular vote and 57 MPs, Clegg and his team had concluded it was right for them to choose who should not be the leader of the Labour Party and who should not be Prime Minister of the UK.

This was to leave lasting anger and a bitter taste in the mouth for Labour MPs, many of whom disliked Gordon Brown and thought him a poor Prime Minister. It was for them as members of the Labour Party to say who was their leader, not Nick Clegg, or a small party. Tom Harris MP blogged about the issue, and later said: 'The idea that the leader of the Liberal Democrats can have any say whatsoever who leads the Labour Party is an utter anathema. It just crystallises the reason why I am so against electoral reform, the idea that we should give small parties a veto over who leads the main parties is shocking. In effect after years of senior Labour people asking Gordon to go, suddenly this jumped-up little scandal-waver from Sheffield jumps in and says "You've got to go", and he says "OK, I'll go!"'

Brown had once again repeated some of the things he had said to Clegg that morning: moving heaven and earth to get a deal, delivering more than the Conservatives would, that the parties had a great deal in common and so on. He consistently thumped home that the country was at a crossroads and that a deal must be done between the progressive parties. 'It would be a very big mistake indeed to allow the Conservatives to govern,' he said: 'Don't you realise, Nick, that if the Conservatives get in everything we have fought for will go backwards.' It was heartfelt and said with fire, but it was essentially tribal.

The initial conversation on electoral reform had gone well. Labour was offering a better deal than the Tories. A referendum on AV had been in the party's manifesto and would get through the Commons – Chief Whip Nick Brown believed that something that was in Labour's manifesto would be delivered by the party in the Commons. But the Prime Minister was offering more. The referendum would include a question as to whether there should be a further referendum on a proportional electoral system – the Liberal Democrat holy grail.

The conversation on the economy did not go quite as well. Brown was arguing forcefully that 'what is important is what happens in Europe and the United States, but what we must not do is take money out of the economy now. The Conservatives have got this wrong.'

Clegg, however, was not willing to be rolled over on this issue, as he had already changed his mind about deficit reduction plans. He was concerned about the firestorm engulfing Greece, and worried that it would spread across Europe, as Spain appeared vulnerable. Therefore the idea that there could be no fiscal contraction this year simply could not have been possible, Clegg thought. He felt that if an incoming

government did not do something more than the previous government, the country would find itself pushed around by the markets.

Clegg said to Brown: 'If doing some fiscal contraction this year
keeps the markets at bay, surely it's worth it.' Mandelson has since
suggested that the Labour Party had not taken the issue of the deficit
seriously enough and that in government more should have been done.
At that meeting Mandelson sat nodding as Clegg set out what nobody
had anticipated. The economy had now become a central dividing
issue between the Liberal Democrats and Labour.

Then Clegg raised the issue of personnel. Mandelson from the
first text sent to Danny Alexander knew Brown the man was an issue
for Clegg. He had been told so frequently, both during the election
campaign and since, via the industrious Liberal Democrat–Labour
back channels.

Mandelson personally was torn between loyalty to the man who
had brought him back to the mainstream of British politics, furnish-
ing him with enormous power as effectively Deputy Prime Minister,
and the knowledge that no deal was possible with Brown still as leader.
It was a challenge to square that circle, even for a man as Machiavellian
as Mandelson. It was the question that preoccupied him most during
the Friday, Saturday and Sunday: how could he come out of this difficult situation looking as if he had 'done the right thing'?

One Downing Street aide said: 'Peter always knew that Brown
would have to go. He'd lost the election and Clegg was never going
to agree to share power with him. But Peter didn't want to be seen
ratting on Brown, so he played the loyal no. 2 and tried to give Brown
a dignified exit, while maintaining his own reputation.'

Who knows what was really in Mandelson's mind? If that was
his aim, he failed. Brown was humiliated during the meeting that

followed, and Clegg had had to steel himself before putting the issue on the table: it was not an easy subject to talk about, and Brown still hoped it would not be discussed.

Brown had said earlier in the meeting that he did not wish to be a barrier to an agreement, so Clegg began, as recounted in Mandelson's memoirs: 'Please understand I have no personal animosity whatsoever, but it is not possible to secure the legitimacy of a coalition and win a referendum unless you move on in a dignified way. You have said you don't want to be a barrier. You've been an incredible catalyst in reshaping politics, but we cannot persuade the public of renewal unless you go in time.'

Brown's response was typical Brown. He did not want to go despite all that he had said about not being a barrier. As one of those present said: 'Brown did not want to hear the message.' While he took what must have been a shattering personal blow in his stride, Brown made clear that he wanted to stay on to make sure the referendum worked out. He said: 'I want to get this referendum won before I step down.' Danny Alexander's response was short but withering: 'But we can't win this referendum with you as Prime Minister.' Brown looked at Alexander, genuinely shocked by the brutality. He recovered his composure quickly and stressed that he also wanted the economic recovery in place before he went.

Brown was now effectively begging his executioner for a stay of execution, arguing for his own political survival, arguing that only he could deliver the Labour Party for a 'Yes' vote on electoral reform. Clegg tried to pin Brown down on the timing of how long that might take, and Brown eventually agreed to announce that he would step down, but that he would not go until he had dealt with 'the tasks in hand'. Clegg feared the Liberal Democrats would be legitimising a continuing Brown premiership, which would do untold damage to his party. This was not tenable.

The humiliation worsened for Brown as Mandelson intervened to 'try to steer Nick away from pushing too hard at this meeting'. But inadvertently Mandelson started to talk about Brown in the third person, as if Brown were now invisible. For example: 'He doesn't want to stand in the way of a deal.' Mandelson did however make the important point that surely Clegg would not want a Labour leadership campaign in the early stages of a new coalition government. But Clegg was clear: Brown had to go and go soon if any arrangement with Labour was to work. However Clegg's belief that this was essential so that the country's 'fundamental desire for change' was recognised rang slightly hollow. If he were truly worried about the will of the people, would he have forced another unelected Labour Prime Minister on the country?

Clegg has since said: 'I remember thinking that perhaps it was unfair that I had said all this about Brown in front of other people, because he is a proud man and I felt for him. Afterwards I apologised that I had been so blunt with him in front of other people and that I should have said it one-to-one. I didn't want him in any way humiliated. I said to him if he were to go he should go with dignity. I felt no animus towards him but he was clearly taken aback by what I'd said.'

Whatever his intention or regret, the Prime Minister had been humiliated and hurt by what had taken place. One can argue that he brought it on himself by his unwillingness to cede power, but can also understand his desire to continue in the job he loved. Sunday had moved quickly for Brown from being a high point in the morning to being a miserable low point by the end of the day.

As was now the habit, Clegg returned to Cowley Street for a late-night discussion with his reference group. There was some consternation that Gordon Brown did not appear that easy to shake off. He was not meekly sailing into the sunset, making both a deal with Labour difficult and at the same time preventing a Labour–Liberal Democrat deal seeming realistic enough for it to be used to apply pressure in negotiations with the Conservatives – what they termed 'sweating the negotiations'.

It was felt that the back channels could be used to good effect, as they already had been, and that Clegg should not be involved directly in any back-channel contacts. So David Laws, Paddy Ashdown's successor as MP for Yeovil, went round to Ashdown's flat late that night to see what pressure could be applied.

Ashdown's role, blessed directly by Clegg, was to keep alive the prospect of a Labour deal, something he genuinely wanted but something the party leadership needed for its negotiating position with the Conservatives.

While Clegg's discussions with Brown had been under way, the Conservative leader reviewed and signed off a confidence and supply draft agreement shortly after 10pm. It had been worked on quickly, and the Liberal Democrats were pressing the Conservatives to deliver it as soon as possible. There was a whole team of Liberal Democrats loitering in Nick Clegg's office waiting to see it.

Eventually word came from Cameron's team in their second-floor Norman Shaw South office that it was ready and signed off by Cameron, Osborne and Hague. The Liberal Democrats sent their talented policy adviser Polly Mackenzie across to pick it up. Speed was of the essence, and she was met on the stairwell by Steve Hilton (in his shorts) and Ed Llewellyn. Mackenzie raced back to the Cowley Street HQ so that the document could be pored over by the reference team and Clegg. Over curry, the reference team digested the document's

content, which seemed far less tasty than their previous discussions
– or the curry.

As a Clegg aide confessed: 'There was a lengthy discussion about
the document and the choice we would now have to make. It was a
question between what we wanted and what we thought we could
get from the Conservatives. We believed there was scope to get more
concessions on some of the sticking points, and leaving the question
open about the type of agreement we might reach left the Conservatives with some uncertainty that would help us to squeeze those
concessions.'

While Cameron had gone home feeling positive, the only person
sensing that the deal was in danger was George Osborne. He had been
working flat out with colleagues, and a day of negotiation had been
particularly exhausting. After Cameron's team had handed over the
draft confidence and supply proposal to Polly Mackenzie at around
10pm, he waited in Cameron's Norman Shaw South Office for the
Liberal Democrat reference meeting to give its feedback.

As they sat there eating pizza in a now empty office with no
pictures on the wall, Osborne felt depressed. The deal, he felt, was
drifting, slowly slipping away – and with it his getting the Conservatives back into power. As he left the office at 2am, Osborne's intuitive
feeling was that the Labour Party was back in play.

DAY 4

– Monday 10 May –

Clegg and Brown agreed late on Sunday to meet again the next morning to continue their discussions, but events were moving fast, and were overwhelming Brown.

His apparent desperation to hang on had caused consternation within the Liberal Democrats' top team meeting late on Sunday night into Monday morning. Laws went round to see Paddy Ashdown in the early hours to see what he could do to stop Brown clinging on to power. Ashdown agreed with Laws that he would ring Tony Blair, somebody he knew well from previous talks about bringing the Liberal Democrats into government and a realignment of the left in British politics.

Blair was in the Middle East, but returned Ashdown's call at around 2am. Ashdown said: 'If this thing is to fly at all, Brown must go, as his continuation is poisoning the prospect of a deal.' Blair said he would see what he could do and to leave it with him.

Blair was as good as his word and rang Brown hours later to say that in principle a new centre-left coalition government was a good idea, but when he had held talks with Ashdown in 1997 it was on the basis of having won the election. 'Trying to do it from a position where we have clearly lost was unlikely to work or be acceptable to the public,' he said. Blair's view was that it would be better to go into opposition and let the Conservatives form a weak minority government and the likelihood was it would quickly be overwhelmed by the size of the deficit and the challenges it faced. What Labour did now would be likely to affect the way people perceived the party in the months and years to come, so it was crucial to get it right, he reasoned.

Brown was still not ready to give up, despite everything he had been through. He turned to those he hoped would be supportive friends in his hour of need and woke Vince Cable at 6am. Cable had to pull his thoughts together quickly once he knew who was on the line. The Liberal Democrats' reference team had met after Clegg's meeting with Brown at Cowley Street late on the Sunday night and Vince Cable had been present, listening to the report of the Clegg–Brown meeting and the strong view that Brown must go as soon as possible if there was to be the slimmest hope of a deal. He was clear about the party leadership's thinking on the issue, even if he didn't like what he heard.

Cable told Brown that for any chance of a Lib–Lab deal he would have to go. Cable's style is not confrontational and he was not as direct as Clegg had been the day before, but he was still keen to see a deal between their two parties and could not see how it could be done with Brown as leader of Labour. He knew categorically that his own leader would not do a deal with Labour while Brown was still in charge.

Cable said: 'I wasn't getting at him [Brown] personally. I didn't say, "You have to go" in that kind of way. I said it would be better because it wouldn't be possible for our people to be in government when you were leading it.' It wasn't a bad-tempered conversation, but vague promises of a Brown departure at some point in the future would not be enough if the Liberal Democrats were to take Labour seriously in any talks or full negotiations that might follow. Brown's reaction to Cable's advice was one of sorrow rather than anger.

Danny Alexander was also quickly on the telephone to Mandelson to confirm what Clegg had said to Brown at their meeting late on Sunday. Clegg did not want the issue to drift and was keen to put maximum pressure on Labour to deal with it quickly, particularly as the two men had another meeting planned at 10.30am in the Prime Minister's

Commons office. Alexander wanted a date, mid-October after the party conferences at the latest, by which Brown would step down.

Not only would the result of Brown announcing his departure mean that a deal was more palatable to Clegg, it had the important side benefit (of which both Clegg and Alexander were well aware) that the Tories would be more convinced that a Lib–Lab deal was possible and undoubtedly put more pressure on Cameron to make concessions in the ongoing negotiations.

Ashdown also continued with his phone calls, to Alastair Campbell, Andrew Adonis and Peter Mandelson: all had the same message rammed home, that for there to be any hope Brown must go. Ashdown, in this back-channel role, acted more as a blunt, rather than precision, instrument. One wondered whether in his conversation he simply over-egged the feelings of others, and described what had happened in black-and-white language. So, for example, when he said that Clegg found Brown 'bullying and uncongenial', was this just emotions running high or exaggeration?

Ashdown is clear about his role: 'Everything I did was in close co-ordination with Nick and the team that were running this' – meaning what he said and did was officially co-ordinated and sanctioned from the very top. Ashdown was a mouthpiece, and his reason for wanting rid of Brown was different from Clegg's. Ashdown wanted to keep Labour onside in the race for power, and that could not happen with Brown as Prime Minister – Ashdown wanted his long-desired coming together with Labour. Clegg wanted options, so that he could squeeze the best possible deal from the Conservatives, while maintaining Labour as a safety net.

The problems kept growing for Brown as more of his Cabinet began to express their doubts about any deal with the Lib Dems.

Unofficial soundings had been taken throughout Sunday and the Cabinet was split. Nick Brown, the loyal Chief Whip, would of course carry out his leader's wishes, but disliked Liberal Democrats intensely thanks to his experience on the ground in Newcastle, where they were Labour's main challenger. In addition, of those whose opinions mattered, Andy Burnham, Alistair Darling, David Miliband and Jack Straw were opposed, as were heavy hitters on the back benches such as David Blunkett and John Reid. Even among those who approved of or supported a deal, of which there were only a handful, the feeling was that Brown would probably have to step down.

It would be wrong to suggest that support for Brown evaporated on Monday morning, because that would suggest it was in much evidence in the first place. One of the strange things when talking to members of Brown's Cabinet is that very few actually liked their leader after the experience of having worked for him. When it came to dumping him, there were very few prepared to fight with any relish to save him.

Brown meets Clegg

When Brown met Clegg at 10.30am in the Prime Minister's office at the House of Commons, he was clinging on to office only by his fingertips. With no support to rely on, this was Brown's last chance to convince Clegg that working with him was not a poisoned chalice. The meeting had 'an air of desperation about it as Brown sensed it was slipping away'. If a deal was possible, and in Brown's mind it still was, he had told aides that he would stand aside. But first he would make his final play.

Brown again repeated that he would be able to offer Clegg a better deal than the Conservatives: on constitutional reform, with a referendum on the Alternative Vote; he repeated again and again that the two parties could be the progressive force in British politics and that the Conservatives would wreak terrible damage on Britain. Clegg had heard this before, but now his ears pricked up as Brown made a number of offers that had not been mentioned in any of the contacts between the two parties. It was a last desperate but bold gamble.

Brown said: 'Nick, I know you are a passionate pro-European. I would be able to give you a completely free hand running what was going on in Europe for the government. You should be very happy with that role.' It was clearly designed to be something that would appeal to Clegg and be deliverable by Brown. He followed up on his offer of a referendum on AV with the offer of a further referendum on proportional representation that would be part of a jumbo constitutional package that would be put to the people.

Then Brown made a stunning offer that echoed what Mandelson had said at the first meeting with the Liberal Democrats on the Saturday afternoon. 'This government would have to be a completely new sort of government, not identified with the past, one that looked to the future.' But now he went further: 'It would be a balanced government with a balanced Cabinet.'

Clegg took this to mean that around 50% of the new government would have Liberal Democrat Secretaries of State around the Cabinet table. A complete 50:50 government was suddenly on offer. Clegg was momentarily stunned: it was difficult to take this in and compute what it meant. This would mean around 20% of his entire Parliamentary Party would be in the Cabinet, and most of the Parliamentary Party in government.

A major role in government, big concessions on constitutional reform, a free hand in Europe, an enormous leap in the relevance of his party, it was heady stuff designed to turn Clegg's head in Brown's direction. Brown had been thinking about the offer for several days and had decided to deploy it as his final resort or nuclear option. He knew following the overnight conversations with Blair, Cable and close colleagues that the walls were closing in rapidly. If he were to survive, it was now or never.

However, Clegg quickly realised that a desperate Prime Minister trying to cling on to power could make any offer he wished, but if he did not have the Commons numbers and the political legitimacy it was little more than hot air and empty promises. Clegg therefore rehearsed his now familiar doubts about how it would be extremely difficult to make it work, and it certainly wouldn't work if Brown were at its head. Brown then knew it was over: he would have to go.

Yet there still might be the possibility of a deal for his party. The tribal politician in him still wanted to keep the Tories out, and after his meeting he rang Menzies Campbell. Brown repeated his often used lines over the past few days, saying Clegg was 'making a terrible mistake'. But he had made the decision to go and believed this would jump start Lib–Lab negotiations. He was therefore upbeat about the prospects for a deal, although Brown did not tell Campbell the reason why he was optimistic.

The note of the meeting between Brown and Clegg was made by Mandelson: Clegg would put 'three options before his MPs. The first was a deal with the Tories. It still fell short of what they wanted on Europe, and left the Tories free to oppose voting reform at the time of the referendum, so he said he would not be recommending it.' It is worth pausing here to point out that at midday on Monday 10 May the Tories had not publicly agreed to a referendum on any form of constitutional reform.

It is extremely unlikely that Mandelson's note of the meeting was incorrect, so was Clegg over-egging what the Conservatives had offered? Did Clegg know something that much of the Conservative Parliamentary Party did not? Had Clegg already done a deal with Cameron that a referendum on AV would be offered? If a top-level deal had been done, where does this leave both parties' narrative that a turning point on offering the AV referendum was a conversation between Clegg and Cameron at 4pm on the Monday afternoon?

There had been a flurry of contact between Clegg and Cameron late into Sunday night, a one-to-one meeting at 7.45pm, a telephone call at 9.15pm and a further call at 10.55pm. The Sunday negotiations had encountered some sticking points, the main one being a referendum on electoral reform, which had moved a potential coalition deal to a confidence and supply one. One would have expected the two leaders to discuss how to break the log-jam, as they were both keen to have the more stable of the two potential deals.

The truth is that by midday on the Monday, Clegg was probably convinced that the Conservatives would offer his party a referendum on AV as part of any final coalition deal. Cameron was sympathetic to Clegg's position and was actively consulting with the Chief Whip and others as to whether it was deliverable. Cameron had made no promises, but had indicated that it was being actively considered and that he was minded to move in that direction if it meant a coalition deal.

The second option, outlined by Mandelson, was a confidence and supply arrangement with the Conservatives, under which the Conservatives would adopt a number of Liberal Democrat manifesto policies, but nothing on electoral reform. This meant that under any confidence and supply arrangement with the Conservatives there would be no referendum on AV. Clegg said he was not happy with either Conservative offer, as you would expect from someone trying to get the best deal for his own party. He wanted to give Labour hope of an opening that might lead to an agreement, particularly as his party was still not convinced by a deal with the Conservatives. The third option Mandelson outlined was of opening serious formal talks with Labour, as Brown had agreed to step down and have a new Labour leader in place by mid-October.

The Conservatives: things were going well but roadblock remains

At around 9am William Hague met with Oliver Letwin, Ed Llewellyn, George Osborne and Steve Hilton in Norman Shaw South, with Des Swayne joining the meeting slightly later (which is forgivable having, as he does every morning, run to the Serpentine, swum and run home before breakfast), to discuss the further negotiating session due to begin shortly after 10am. The main topic of conversation was could the Conservative Party be persuaded to agree to a referendum on AV. Various permutations were discussed – for example, just whipping the front bench as opposed to the whole party. As Cameron's PPS, Swayne keeps a close eye on what his parliamentary colleagues are thinking, and his view at the time was that the leadership would not get it through.

It was the only proverbial fly in the ointment, as reports at the meeting were unremittingly positive about the atmosphere of the negotiations, the lack of serious difficulties and the seriousness of both sides. Yet the issue of electoral reform had caused negotiations to move from a full coalition agreement to confidence and supply a day earlier. Although there was no dissatisfaction with the negotiations per se, there was already a feeling developing that 'it was slipping away' – not just a coalition deal but any deal at all. The meeting worried about the Liberal Democrats' natural inclination towards Labour, the close friendships of people like Paddy Ashdown, Charles Kennedy and Vince Cable: it was in their DNA. The tension was building within the Conservative camp as the deal seemed to drift.

After a full day of negotiations on the Sunday, the teams resumed again on Monday at 10.15am for a short session, its reduced length due to the Liberal Democrats holding a Parliamentary Party meeting. There had been a frantic effort by the Conservatives to have a confidence and supply draft agreement ready, which the Liberal Democrats had spent time into the early hours discussing. More talks had taken place that morning at Cowley Street at 7.30am.

Hague arrived at the meeting to reinforce a positive message: 'Well, the talks are going well as you've probably heard from our Liberal Democrat colleagues already, and we're meeting now to discuss some specific ideas and proposals, and we're optimistic about making further progress.'

The proposals and ideas were in fact the confidence and supply draft agreement. The discussion focused on the detail of how an agreement might work that allowed maximum openness and co-operation. For example, how could the Liberal Democrats have access to economic figures, to the budget; what would be their ability to input to key events and decisions?

The Liberal Democrat negotiators knew that this was not the option they wanted, as it would mean they propped up a Conservative government with all the problems that would bring them with the public and their membership, but were left on the outside of any decision-making. One member of the team said: 'We were always concerned that with a confidence and supply agreement the Tories could pull the rug on us at any time. The last thing we wanted was another general election this year.'

The meeting lasted around an hour and a half and had been positive, and the media scrum outside was again treated to a choreographed summary of the talks. Hague said: 'Well, we've made further progress in our meetings with the Liberal Democrats this morning. On our part we are now going to report back to David Cameron again and to have meetings with parliamentary colleagues. And the negotiating teams are working really well together.'

Danny Alexander said: 'We are working well together. Good further progress has been made. And I'm now going to report on that to Nick Clegg and my parliamentary colleagues.'

The orchestrated mood music of how the negotiating sessions were reported to the media suggested that a coalition, if it hadn't been officially announced, was perhaps almost under way.

*

At noon Clegg and Cameron met again in Room 391 of Portcullis House, and there was a bit of nifty footwork to be done as the room was situated unfortunately close to Menzies Campbell's office – although as Campbell's phone was hot with another call from Gordon Brown, they probably need not have worried about being seen.

Clegg used this meeting to ratchet up the pressure on Cameron and make him sense that a deal with the Conservatives was not the only option available to the Liberal Democrats. Despite Clegg's known personal dislike of Brown, which Cameron was aware of, 'he went on at length about the Brown meeting and where Brown said he could offer much more, much bigger and better,' said a senior Cameron aide. Clegg did not tell Cameron that Brown had offered AV without a referendum, but he was clear that Brown was putting on the table a bigger and better constitutional package.

While they continued to trouble-shoot problems and remain positive about prospects for a deal, this was not the meeting that Cameron had expected: seeds of doubt had been deliberately sown by Clegg. But Clegg was not in a position to say definitively what was on offer from Brown on constitutional reform because, as he admitted himself, he didn't understand the full package – so he used subtlety and inference to great effect.

Having met with Brown and Cameron in quick succession, Clegg made his way to the Grand Committee Room to address a 1.45pm meeting of his Parliamentary Party. As he walked, he asked one of his close aides for thoughts on what he should do. The response came without hesitation. He was told, 'We've got to go into coalition with the Conservatives. It would not be ethically right to prop up Labour. Indeed, it is morally incomprehensible that we could form a government with them.' This was what Clegg thought privately, but he still had doubts, and responded that he thought his party would not wear any alliance with the Conservatives.

Clegg's team had also just received a welter of reassurance from Labour, both through direct and indirect channels, particularly about what the minority parties would do in the event that the Liberal Democrats chose to go with Labour. The Welsh and Scottish Nationalists, with national elections on the horizon, were ready to take the default option and bash the Tories. 'Of course it [a rainbow coalition] would be tough, but it was doable', was how one Clegg aide put it.

Clegg and his aides entered the Grand Committee Room, from

which they would not emerge until several hours of fraught, bad-tempered debate had taken place among the party's MPs. So many members of the Parliamentary Party sought to have their say about the developments that not all were able to speak, and one MP recalls feeling 'very frustrated'. According to a senior aide, 'there was a slight element of alarm' within the leadership about the tone of the meeting.

Alexander began the meeting by reporting on the morning's negotiations with the Conservatives, and revealed to his fellow MPs that, after the rapid progress the previous day, the talks had reached an impasse due to electoral reform. There were 'barriers' to a full coalition, he said: 'We have got the pretty uninspiring option of something less and we can obviously progress that. But at the moment this looks like all that might be possible with the Conservatives.'

Paddy Ashdown had concerns of his own about a Labour deal. He said that a 'panjandrum' deal, one that involved everybody else (the so-called rainbow coalition) would never work and should not be pursued. Nonetheless, the party should continue talking to Labour because at the very least it offered the Liberal Democrats bargaining power with the Tories. Ashdown said later: 'I was not saying a minority deal with Labour wouldn't work and I did have a conversation with Chris Rennard, who said, although it would be very fragile, it was possible to do a deal with Labour which would produce a minority government, but which in effect would look like it had a majority in the House of Commons. We could do in Westminster what Alex Salmond was already doing in Scotland.'

Ashdown never believed that this would be 'a very seaworthy ship in which to sail', but it was worth trying, in so far as it gave the Liberal Democrats the opportunity to persuade the Conservatives that there was an alternative, and that was something that was both emotionally congenial and served their bargaining purposes.

Alexander's message triggered alarm among his colleagues. Throughout the weekend, a number of the party's MPs had been uncomfortable with the very idea of a coalition or close co-operation with one of the larger parties. But having been back to their constituencies where the idea appeared to be popular and looked at what a looser confidence and supply arrangement from Opposition would offer them, the Parliamentary Party did not like what it saw. At the minimum, they would have to vote through, and then account to their constituents for, a raft of unpopular spending cuts or tax rises. The Parliamentary Party's clear and unambiguous message to Clegg was, he recalled: 'Hang on a minute. The problem with confidence and supply is that you take all the responsibility and get no power. What's the point of that? It's even worse: you get all the downside and none of the upside at all.'

What happened at the parliamentary meeting was that, as Chris Huhne described it: 'The party decided it didn't wish to be half-pregnant,' meaning that now only a coalition would be satisfactory. Only one MP, Greg Mulholland, the party's health spokesman, spoke in favour of confidence and supply.

Those on the left of the party were heartened that a deal was looking difficult with the Tories because there was no movement on constitutional reform and now they did not want confidence and supply. This had two implications. First, to the great delight of many Liberal Democrat MPs, negotiations would be opened with Labour immediately. Indeed, many of the speeches from MPs demanded it. Don Foster said: 'I don't care how difficult it is, I don't care how many late night sittings there are, I don't care how many whipped votes, I don't care how ill I might be when dragged in from my sick bed to vote. Politics is not supposed to be easy, I didn't come into politics for an easy life, if it's the right thing for the party to do, don't let "It's difficult" be the reason to go with another party. I want to know if we can get a deal with Labour.'

Second, as one Liberal Democrat negotiator put it: 'Having moved from what was a rubbish position of confidence and supply to wanting a stable, high trust agreement, the next leap in thinking would become easy – "Right, if we can't do it with Labour, we will do it with the Conservatives."' Although the Conservatives were to move to a state of gloom and despair that Monday afternoon, in terms of the way the party was thinking, the bridge had been crossed by Liberal Democrat MPs.

'Morally incomprehensible' or not, the Parliamentary Party came to the overwhelming view that the negotiators should now open full coalition talks with Labour.

David Laws's statement

With the Parliamentary Party meeting finished, David Laws was despatched to announce the party's latest thinking to the media. Speaking on the steps leading down from the Grand Committee Room to Westminster Hall, Laws sent a coded message to the Conservatives. Despite 'very good progress on a number of points' having been achieved with the Conservative team in the talks to date, 'clarification of details' would be sought with regard to education funding, 'fair taxes', and, significantly, in relation to voting reform and 'progress on that issue'. Moreover, the Conservatives could no longer assume they were in pole position in the negotiations. While the Liberal Democrats wanted a coalition deal ('strong and stable government in the national interest'), and were conscious of the need to agree one quickly, Laws hinted that channels of communication with Labour were up and running: 'This discussion is dependent not only on the Liberal Democrat Party, but also on the proposals and discussions that are ongoing with the Conservative Party, and the representations that, frankly, are being made by the Labour Party.'

But Laws also had a warning for Labour ahead of the talks between the two parties later that day, declaring that the Liberal Democrat Parliamentary Party had 'also agreed that deficit reduction and a plan to bring down the deficit *as soon as possible* must be at the heart of any agreement'.

*

While much of Westminster heard the Liberal Democrats' position via the rolling news channels, Clegg called the Tory leader directly to relay his party's position. Cameron took the call in Osborne's office in Norman Shaw South, with Llewellyn sitting in, having just come from his own meeting of the shadow Cabinet. He was told by Clegg that there was good news and bad news following the Liberal Democrat Parliamentary Party meeting that had recently finished. The good news was that his party had collectively decided against any form of confidence and supply arrangement. They wanted the stability of a full coalition – something Cameron dearly wanted.

But Clegg then made explicit to Cameron what Laws had hinted at in his statement to the public at large: 'Sorry David, this isn't going to work with you guys, for a number of reasons. We need a lot more than what you're offering us on electoral reform.' At a tense meeting his Parliamentary Party had just told him it wanted to open formal discussions with Labour, or to do nothing, if the Conservatives' position on electoral reform remained unchanged. Brown, he told Cameron bluntly, was offering far in excess of what his party was on electoral and political reform.

However, having heard the Liberal Democrat leader's explanation, Cameron was adamant that he knew exactly what Clegg was referring to. His concerns had been further fuelled in conversations that day with Osborne. He had also been getting scores of phone calls, texts and messages from contacts in the media and 'lots of different sources' telling him that Labour was offering the Liberal Democrats a change to AV without a referendum.

Cameron never actually bottomed out with Clegg what he had actually been offered by Brown – if he had tried, it is unlikely Clegg's answer would have been illuminating because he contests he never fully understood it himself. It is certainly surprising that an offer of something of such core importance to the Liberal Democrats was never fully understood and substantiated. Throughout the negotiations, constitutional reform was the Liberal Democrat Holy Grail, and yet a full understanding of the offer being made by Brown was never reached.

Brown kept talking to Clegg about constitutional reform throughout their meetings and phone calls. It was Clegg's belief that Brown thought it was necessary to have what he termed a 'jumbo referendum' on a wide range of constitutional reform in the autumn, not just asking for a mandate for electoral reform on its own, but a wider need to change politics, giving a new government the backing to make significant change to the constitution – including, apparently, establishing a written constitution. Clegg said: 'It was his whole philosophy and thinking that it needed to be much bigger, and I was never quite clear in my own mind what he meant by that.'

Whether Cameron was outraged by Clegg's apparent willingness to prop up the defeated, widely loathed Prime Minister in order partially to secure his party's singular obsession, or whether he was suddenly facing up to the possibility of his long-cherished dream of becoming Prime Minister being snatched away from him, or a mixture of both, he responded angrily to Clegg: 'You can't possibly do AV without a referendum. It wasn't in your manifesto, it wasn't in Labour's, it would be indefensible.' Clegg fired back that it was perfectly legitimate to change the electoral system without a referendum – arguing, as Huhne had been arguing in negotiations, that AV was a form of 'first-past-the-post' and therefore was not a significant constitutional change. Clegg tried to convince Cameron that it was possible to do so, but he responded; 'There's no way I could do that.'

Cameron was so annoyed by the conversation that he said later, 'I was quite prepared to not form a government', as he had always been concerned about the risk that Clegg 'could go off with the other lot' and had been disappointed on several occasions during the negotiations when he found out via third parties that Clegg was meeting with Brown and Labour and had not informed him. It had the whiff of double-dealing.

Clegg did not want to burn his boats as he ideally wanted a coalition deal with the Conservatives, not Labour. According to one of his negotiating team, he floated once again the question, 'which was a last throw of the dice': would the Conservatives be prepared, if not to promise an AV referendum, to settle for a Constitutional Convention like Ontario and British Columbia, which would also look at the voting system, but with the commitment that the convention result would be put to a referendum? This would at least avoid the politically difficult job of putting simply one issue (a referendum on AV) to the Conservative Parliamentary Party.

The idea had been floated originally on the Sunday by Chris Huhne at the negotiating session. It made no progress there, but to see if there was a way around the impasse, Cameron asked Steve Hilton (supported by Osborne aide Rohan Silva) to look at it and put something together. The notion was treated with seriousness as Hilton liaised with Richard Reeves, the Liberal Democrat Head of Demos (later Nick Clegg's special adviser). Clegg and Cameron briefly discussed it during their Sunday night one-to-one session, and 'Clegg appeared enthusiastic'. However, events on Monday simply blew away any hopes of a back-channel solution.

Cameron continued to be extremely concerned, as he could see immediately how Labour could get away with AV legislation without a referendum. After all, Labour had supported AV; it had promised a referendum in its manifesto; a number of its senior MPs and ministers had spoken in support of it; and now Clegg was pushing for it. Cameron believed that 'things seemed to fit into place', as Clegg was seemingly trying to persuade him that AV legislation without a referendum was possible. Cameron concedes that his conversation with Clegg was not 'proof of what Labour was offering the Liberal Democrats, but it was another thing that made me think this is what's on offer'.

Osborne, listening to the call, also believed it. He remembered Cameron coming off the phone 'absolutely convinced' that Labour was offering Clegg AV without a referendum. He also believed that Brown had become so desperate, he would almost certainly have offered it – although with no back channels to Labour and little intelligence being gathered, it was almost impossible to do more than guess. Mixing this all in with the media speculation, it produced a heady cocktail, which is now universally described by those involved as 'the fog of war'.

Clegg himself acknowledges how unclear he was with Cameron

during the telephone call: 'The perception, which I think was accurate, was that there were discussions around [AV] and it might have been an offer that might have been made; it might have been considered.' This was an explanation vague enough to have led Cameron to believe that there had indeed been an offer by either Gordon Brown or the Labour Party. As Clegg has confirmed in the House of Commons since, there was never any formal offer of AV without a referendum either from Brown or his negotiating team.

During the heated exchange, Clegg told Cameron that his party was going to start negotiating in earnest with Labour. It was 'a bad call, an angry conversation', Cameron recalled later. Both he and his senior aides remember the call as a turning point. Suddenly, the Conservatives believed things were slipping away.

The Cameron reaction – and the shadow Cabinet is reconvened

Immediately after the angry conversation with Clegg, Cameron called his closest aides into his office for a quick conclave in which they discussed whether they could improve the party's offer or not. With the time pressure getting critical, Cameron's immediate team discussed the choices they faced. The Conservatives were now confronted, so the team thought, with the real prospect that the Liberal Democrats would go with Labour.

A Lib–Lab coalition would attempt to legislate directly to change the voting system to AV. Even if it couldn't get that through the House of Commons, it would easily get a referendum on AV (after all, the House of Commons had voted for a referendum on AV before the general election, only for the measure to be blocked by the House of Lords in the wash-up of Bills prior to the dissolution). There could be a referendum on AV whether the Conservative Party liked it or not.

Nor was there any guarantee that the Lib–Lab coalition would fall apart after a few months: it was equally possible that the two parties could manage to keep a coalition together for longer, even years, with the Conservatives helplessly locked out of power. Since Friday, Osborne had been driving the case for getting the party into government, for its own sake as well as that of the country.

Cameron quickly came to the decision that while the party could not and would not match the offer of AV without a referendum, they needed to move to a referendum on AV (while retaining their opposition to it in the referendum campaign) as a last throw of the dice. Cameron felt it was his duty to do the right thing and ultimately, his and his party's duty was to try to give the country a decent government that trumped its own self-interest in the electoral system that suited it best.

'Was the party so wedded to the electoral system that suited its interest best that it wouldn't even contemplate a referendum, one that could bring about a coalition government that would be good for the country?', he mused. On this basis, Cameron did not want to be the person held responsible for stopping progress towards a stable government. He wanted to go home that night with his head held high, confident at least that his party would end up with its reputation enhanced for making the right judgement calls on behalf of the country and the Conservative Party. He also knew that without the concession he would be less likely to hold power and become Prime Minister.

The decision made, as always in close concert with George

Osborne, Cameron called in his shadow Cabinet, rather embarrassingly, for the second time that afternoon. Earlier in the afternoon, starting at 2pm, Cameron had reported to his assembled team that discussions with the Liberal Democrats had been constructive and positive: they were continuing, but on the basis of a confidence and supply agreement rather than a full coalition.

Cameron's phone call with Clegg and information through Monday afternoon from other sources had suddenly changed the dynamics. Now at 4.45pm his aides had hurriedly had to get the shadow Cabinet back in his Norman Shaw South Office. Cameron, according to one member of the shadow Cabinet, told the meeting that Clegg had called him to say that 'the Liberal Democrats had changed their mind, they now wanted a full coalition agreement with a guarantee of AV. He [Cameron] said that they had been in discussions and Labour was offering AV without a referendum, and a referendum on whether there should be proportional representation. The call for those around the table was 'could we up our offer?'

Cameron said that although he felt he could not match Labour's offer, to keep the process going he would like to make the gesture of a referendum on AV, but that Conservatives could and should campaign against it. The view around the table was that this was very much the endgame, and that the Liberal Democrats had probably already decided that Labour had offered them so much they would do a deal with Labour.

William Hague said that the offer was the right thing to do and was supported by Theresa May. Several members of the shadow Cabinet spoke strongly against the offer, including Theresa Villiers and Chris Grayling. Tom Strathclyde was also said to be unhappy, and Philip Hammond was known to have concerns. Others who also did not like the offer kept quiet.

The referendum on AV had been from very early on something that Cameron was prepared to concede to the Liberal Democrats if he had to, as a last resort. His close ally George Osborne had advised him on a number of occasions that a coalition deal was unlikely to be possible without giving way on a referendum. The principal aim from the beginning was to get the Conservative Party into power, so in the naked struggle for power a referendum would be offered if the party would agree.

In shadow Cabinet it was agreed that a consensus had been reached on the AV referendum, and the matter would now go to the Parliamentary Party for discussion later that evening. However, any member of the shadow cabinet who wished to speak against it there would be free to do so. So close to being in government, most saw the option of open dissent as a career suicide note. Another member of the Conservative shadow Cabinet said: 'Clegg proved an adept negotiator, but if he did say that Labour had offered a move straight to legislation, it was a downright lie.' There is no evidence that Clegg did say this or that Labour ever made the offer either formally or informally. Even when Brown was offering Clegg more or less whatever he wanted, he never appeared to make this specific offer on AV legislation without a referendum.

As the shadow Cabinet meeting came to a close, with its decision about offering a referendum made, news came that Brown was about to set out a resignation timetable in a final bid to see off the Conservative challenge for power. The shadow Cabinet turned on the TV and settled down to watch history unfold.

It has been often repeated that the Cameron changed his view on the referendum due to Brown's resignation mid-shadow Cabinet meeting, and that the Prime Minister somehow trumped the Tories with the timing of his resignation. However, as the shadow Cabinet watched Brown's statement, the decision on offering a referendum on AV had been made and therefore Brown's act of resignation played no part in Cameron's or the shadow Cabinet's thinking.

The Brown statement

The agreement with Clegg in the morning, that formal talks between their parties would now begin, needed Brown's timetable for stepping down to be announced first. At 5pm, with Mandelson, Campbell, Sue Nye and other friends inside watching, Brown delivered his resignation speech in front of No. 10. Its aim was to remove any remaining roadblock to a coalition deal with the Liberal Democrats.

Brown, a tribal politician to the bones and advised what to say by Alastair Campbell and Peter Mandelson, was still intent on stopping the Tories crossing the threshold of No. 10. Nick Clegg had just informed him, Brown told the nation, that the Liberal Democrats now wished to take forward formal discussions with the Labour Party.

With breathtaking audacity bordering on arrogance, Brown asserted that the general election results indicated not a defeat for Labour but the existence of a 'progressive majority in Britain', and declared his belief that 'it could be in the interests of the whole country to form a progressive coalition government'. In addition to dealing with Britain's economic priorities, Brown went on, 'only such a progressive government could meet the demand for political and electoral change which the British people made last Thursday.'

Declaring his willingness to form and lead a coalition government between Labour and the Liberal Democrats (albeit on an interim basis), Brown reached what would be the most painful part of the statement for him, but also that which most rang true: 'The reason that we have a hung parliament is that no single party and no single leader was able to win the full support of the country. As leader of my party, I must accept that that is a judgement on me. I therefore intend to ask the Labour Party to set in train the processes needed for its own leadership election. I would hope that it would be completed in time for the new leader to be in post by the time of the Labour Party conference. I will play no part in that contest. I will back no individual candidate.'

Brown concluded his statement by announcing that he now intended to 'facilitate the discussions that the Liberal Democratic party has asked for'. The blunt truth was that only once he had made clear his plans to step down would the Liberal Democrats consider it possible to agree to meet with Labour to negotiate in earnest over a coalition deal.

The response from Nick Clegg made Labour think that once again it had a chance. On the phone to Brown (a phone call listened to by Ed Balls among many others at No. 10), Clegg is reported by Balls to have said: 'Of course, we should proceed on this basis. Of course, Labour and the Liberal Democrats should seek to reach agreement. We are after all the two progressive parties in British politics. And I'm clear that if my party sees me reaching an agreement with the Conservatives, I'm going to have my members leaving in droves, that is why we must make this work.'

The Conservatives had expected Brown's resignation, so it did not take them by surprise when it finally happened. Rumours had been circulating since just after midday, and there was a feeling that this was Brown playing his last card, although it was a significant one. If Labour could replace Brown in reasonably short order with somebody more congenial from the Liberal Democrat point of view, it could have proved problematic.

Mandelson believed that 'even in his going, Gordon was setting the political weather. His statement dramatically changed the context of Nick's negotiations with both of the major parties. For the first time it seemed possible – though still not likely – to me that a coalition between Labour and the Liberal Democrats might actually work.'

Brown's key lieutenants, in the bid to keep the Labour Party in power and the Tory Party out, now hit the airwaves to put the case for a 'progressive' Lib–Lab coalition. Describing a potential Lib–Lab coalition as a 'partnership of principle', Adonis told BBC Radio 4's *Six O'Clock News* that a deal under which Labour remained in power could have even greater legitimacy than a Conservative minority government: 'Ideologically and in policy terms we are very close together, Labour and the Liberal Democrats … No one party can command a majority in the House of Commons. Fifteen million people voted for Labour and the Liberal Democrats combined last Thursday. Only 10 million people voted for the Conservative Party last Thursday. There would be absolute democratic legitimacy behind an arrangement between Labour and the Liberal Democrats.'

Behind the scenes, Brown and Clegg had several further phone calls. Clegg told Brown what he had told Cameron: that his Parliamentary Party had rejected the idea of anything short of full coalition. With the Conservative talks now on hold indefinitely, it was up to the negotiating teams from the two 'progressive' parties to make a coalition happen.

The Cabinet meeting

Following his speech outside No. 10 setting out his decision to step down and after a number of phone calls, Gordon Brown met his

Cabinet at around 6pm for the first time since the election. With the walls closing in around him, and little personal support, he had thought better of bringing the Cabinet together to discuss as a group the way forward. Now all potential threat to his tenure was removed with his resignation, and a binding collective decision on the way forward was necessary.

Unlike 1990 when Mrs Thatcher stepped down, there were no Cabinet tears or grand eulogies. According to one present, 'There were no huge fiery speeches.' But there was some praise for the leadership he had shown in difficult circumstances during the campaign and the decisions he had taken in government. Otherwise, 'it was actually a very businesslike meeting.' There was little sadness in Brown's going: while some in the Cabinet certainly respected him, few actually liked him.

The main business of the meeting was Brown trying to get Cabinet agreement to talks with the Liberal Democrats (which were now an option thanks to his resignation and would begin immediately after the meeting finished in Portcullis House) and to try to form a government. Nobody tried to veto continuing talks, and Peter Hain spoke up very strongly in favour. (Although he was no fan of PR, he felt AV was a better system.)

While there was no objection to exploratory talks, some members of the Cabinet were hesitant, and raised concerns about a deal with the Liberal Democrats. Andy Burnham's view was that Labour had lost the election and it would be better if the result was accepted, rather than to put together a 'coalition of losers'. Jim Murphy, Alistair Darling, and Jack Straw felt the same. Alan Johnson was reported to be 'unhappy' with developments. However, John Denham and Ben Bradshaw were supportive, while others such as David Miliband – probably thinking ahead to the Labour leadership campaign – gave nuanced answers. Members of the negotiating team knew that Brown was due to announce they were going to begin their work.

Brown announced rather than asked for Cabinet's agreement that the negotiating team would consist of Mandelson, Adonis, Balls, Ed Miliband and Harriet Harman. It was essentially the same team as met with the Liberal Democrats on Saturday afternoon (when Harman had not been able to attend), but this was now the official line-up. Essentially the team was made up of Brown's closest and most trusted allies in Cabinet, rather than the best negotiating team, and Liberal Democrat MPs and negotiators still wonder aloud today whether the outcome would have been different if Alistair Darling and Peter Hain had been on the team in place of Ed Balls and Ed Miliband.

Still, Cabinet agreed the team was 'well balanced', with Andrew Adonis known to have a good understanding of the Liberal Democrats. Mandelson was the government's no. 2 and Harman was Labour's second-in-command, and Balls and Miliband were two of Brown's closest aides in government. There was at least some logic.

The long Cabinet meeting meandered to a close at around 8pm, when the freshly appointed Labour negotiating team strolled off to Room 391 in Portcullis House. Unfortunately they were to arrive late, and therefore got the meeting off to the worst possible of starts.

The Conservative Parliamentary Party meets

Having had only a few minutes to prepare, Cameron went over to address his Parliamentary Party, who were packed into Committee Room 14 in the House of Commons. On the way Ed Llewellyn called Paddy Ashdown and told him what Cameron was about to do. Although Clegg and Cameron had discussed this eventuality, there was never any guarantee that Cameron would deliver a referendum on AV, not least because he had no idea how the shadow Cabinet and Parliamentary Party would react, but here he was about to go before his party.

This was a momentous moment for Cameron and the Conservative Party. As one senior aide put it: 'It was a very bold thing that David was going to do, to put it mildly' – and bold in terms of the history of the Conservative Party, as (according to Conservative historian Lord Norton) it jeopardised in terms of the constitution 'things that Conservatives would be a bit wary of jeopardising'. Changes proposed to the voting system and second chamber were, in historic terms, 'profoundly un-Conservative stances'. In light of this, Llewellyn was taken aback by Ashdown's response: he neither seemed to recognise the dramatic import of what was about to occur, nor would it be 'anywhere near enough to clinch the deal'.

There was no time to tell Cameron what Ashdown had said, which left Cameron staking huge political capital with his party on a referendum that might make no difference to the progress of negotiations. One aide present said: 'That was quite a low moment personally, in the sense that we were asking this huge thing of the party, convinced it was the right thing to do, but actually thinking it wasn't going to work.'

Oliver Letwin was also gloomy, as he was now filled with doubts that his cherished project was unravelling. But that did not stop him telling an aide that if AV referendum was granted 'there would be an opportunity to change the face of British politics for generations'. One Conservative backbencher said: 'Letwin essentially wanted a realignment of British politics alongside the Liberals.'

Ashdown was only one contact, one viewpoint, and Clegg, despite the mood music of the earlier call to Brown, believed throughout the process that a deal with the Conservatives was the preferable outcome for his party.

Cameron announced to his 300-plus MPs (not everyone was there and there was still one result to come) that the negotiations with the Liberal Democrats had reached an impasse, and that he was seeking their authority to make an offer to the Liberal Democrats of a referendum on changing the voting system for Westminster elections to the Alternative Vote system as part of a coalition deal between the parties. He told MPs that there would not be a commitment to support it, and that they would be free to campaign against it if they wished. He went on to say that the party had a choice: either put up with a referendum as the price of power, or face the dead certainty from opposition of AV being imposed without a referendum by a Labour–Liberal Democrat coalition government.

One backbencher said: 'It was quite clear that the whole rationale for the meeting was to seek our agreement to offer a referendum on AV, and that Labour had offered legislation on AV without a referendum. There weren't really any questions about anything other than AV and the referendum.'

After Cameron had finished speaking, a number of the senior Conservative MPs including Stephen Dorrell, Sir Malcolm Rifkind, Peter Luff and Sir Alan Haselhurst – who had all been teed up by the party whips and Cameron's team to give supportive and helpful comments – were called on to speak first.

Having been a senior minister, Rifkind had very rarely spoken at 1922 Committee meetings, but he felt this was of sufficient importance to intervene. He said the party was being asked to make an incredibly painful decision. A party historically opposed to electoral reform, being told that the only way it could form a coalition that was in the wider public interest because of the economy, must make a huge concession in this area. 'What makes it difficult,' he continued 'is that we are being asked to make it literally within seconds [here he clicked his fingers] of hearing it for the first time, whereas the Liberal Democrats have been discussing it for years. But you require a decision now, that's the political reality. The Conservative Party's judgement has always been that in any crucial decision we have to address the public interest, not the party interest. And the public interest is economic stability, the prospect of a government that can govern at any particular moment, and if your judgement, David, is that this is the concession we must make, then, with considerable concern, you have my support.'

As the hour-long meeting played out, the leadership felt it had won the overwhelming endorsement of the Parliamentary Party to make the AV offer to the Liberal Democrats. The matter was never put to a ballot, and it was never suggested to Chief Whip Patrick McLoughlin by any member of the Parliamentary Party that it should be. Most of those who privately held dissenting opinions chose not to air them, or some – Peter Bone, for example – felt that they were not called to speak. One shadow Cabinet member opposed to the offer of a referendum on AV opted to stay silent rather than risk causing stories of a split. Members of the right-wing Cornerstone and No Turning Back groups had met prior to the meeting to discuss whether to speak against the proposed offer, but in the event, Cornerstone member John Hayes was called to speak early as a spokesman for the right of the Parliamentary Party and supported the leadership's position.

Other potential opponents feared blotting their copybook with the future Prime Minister, with only a handful raising their doubts. Bravely, in the opinion of one senior backbencher on the right of the party, only one newly elected MP rose to question the proposed offer on AV, followed by the veteran MP Sir Peter Tapsell, who warned that the offer was a huge gamble and that AV, if the referendum were lost, risked the party never being able to govern on its own again. It might even mean the end of the Conservative Party as we know it, he was reported to say.

Backbencher Christopher Chope, got up to oppose the whole idea of a coalition with the Liberal Democrats, saying that nobody was interested in AV so he hoped there would be a threshold requirement for it to pass, because it would be wrong to change the voting system on a small turnout in a referendum. For good measure he added that he did not trust the Liberal Democrats, and had just spent part of the general election campaign in a seat where the local Lib Dems had used every homophobic trick in the book to undermine the Conservative candidate. Cameron's response was clear. If we are to have a coalition it had to be based on trust and honesty; we could not go behind their back and impose a threshold requirement.

There was an undercurrent in the meeting that a minority Conservative government would be a preferable outcome to a coalition with the Liberal Democrats, so that the concession was unnecessary. Few were prepared to rock the boat, but many there thought it. Those close to Cameron argue, with some justice, that you could not choose a Conservative minority government because, in the circumstances, Labour could have cobbled together a workable alternative government, particularly with Brown resigning. Who is to know how long a rainbow coalition or a Labour minority government might have lasted? They further question what sort of government would this or a Conservative minority have provided the country with under the circumstances of an economic crisis and a huge budget deficit? Neither government would have had the strength to deal with the huge challenges the country faced, as they wondered which parliamentary votes it could get through. 'It would have been a nightmare, and I believe the Conservative Party would have been torn apart,' said one member of the now coalition Cabinet.

The offer made by Hague

Having secured the consent of the shadow Cabinet and the acquiescence of the Parliamentary Party to cross the 'red line' on electoral reform, the Conservative leadership proceeded to make its historic 'AV offer' to the Liberal Democrats. Conscious of the need to appeal to the public at large as well as the Liberal Democrats, the leadership communicated its message by means of a public statement. At 7.14pm, outside the St Stephen's Entrance to the House of Commons, William Hague told the television cameras and reporters that although the Conservatives believed from their negotiations with the Liberal Democrats that a workable agreement between the two parties was within reach on most issues: 'Clearly the situation has now changed somewhat, in that they have also opened negotiations with the Labour Party and Gordon Brown has said that he is prepared to resign. They've also said to us – the Liberal Democrats have said to the Conservative Party – that they are only prepared to enter into a coalition agreement with a party that will change our electoral system to the Alternative Vote method of voting. Now, David Cameron and the shadow Cabinet and the Conservative MPs have decided that although our concentration in all of these negotiations has been on the financial situation, on reducing the deficit, on the improvement of education, on other great issues facing our country, in the interests of trying to secure a stable, secure government we will go the extra mile and we will offer to the Liberal Democrats in a coalition government the holding of a referendum on the Alternative Vote system, so that the people of this country can decide what the best electoral system is for the future.'

However, for the moment at least, the Conservatives would go no further. Leaving the ball in the Liberal Democrats' court, Hague warned them that the 'great majority of people' would find a Lib–Lab coalition government, dependent on the support of minority parties and headed by the second unelected Prime Minister in succession, to be 'unacceptable'. Reiterating Cameron's private argument to Clegg, Hague declared that to impose electoral reform without a referendum would be 'profoundly undemocratic'.

This was the offer that would either get the Liberal Democrats over what Cameron described as 'the hump in the road', or (as it felt on Monday evening) leave them in the arms of the Labour Party.

Gloom in the Conservative camp

'Fuck it, we're going home,' a senior Conservative recalls a number of the party's MPs saying to each other at the end of the Parliamentary Party meeting. Through the 'fog of war' that surrounded the negotiations across the whole five days, the Conservatives had gained the impression that serious negotiations between Labour and the Liberal Democrats had been taking place throughout the afternoon, and that a deal may already have been on the table.

While the Conservatives were meeting to discuss the AV offer, Clegg had appeared on Sky News welcoming Brown's announcement and hinting that it could 'be an important element in the smooth transition towards a stable government that people deserve' by finally paving the way for formal talks between his party and Labour. Some

Conservatives were convinced by his absence that Vince Cable was central, busy facilitating a deal with Labour. After the 4pm phone call with Cameron, the Liberal Democrats 'had stopped taking our calls', one Conservative aide said. 'We were sitting around waiting for a call back on our track of the negotiations and nothing happened.'

Back in Cameron's office, there was a mood of resignation and plenty of gallows humour, which was not helped by Paddy Ashdown appearing on television suggesting the party's potential deal with Labour might still be on (which was not true). As his long-cherished ambition to be Prime Minister appeared to be slipping away, Cameron's calm and good humour throughout the day had impressed his close aides. Cameron's view was: 'It's not going to happen … On Sunday I was thinking I probably will be Prime Minister on Monday. I was thinking by the end of Monday, I definitely won't be Prime Minister.' Sitting with those aides in the Leader of the Opposition's office, he joked about putting the pictures back up on the walls before leaving the Westminster maelstrom for his North Kensington home.

At home, Cameron remembers talking to his wife: 'Sam and I were having supper in the kitchen, and I remember saying to her, "You know, it's not going to happen, I'm going to be Leader of the Opposition," and I remember saying to her, "I want to go on being Leader of the Opposition. I think we can defeat this new government. I'm depressed that it hasn't worked out as we wanted but we behaved in the right way. We made them a big, generous offer, to have a coalition government, they're going with the other lot, we're going to fight them all the way." And I thought, "That's it, I'm going to be in opposition for a couple more years."'

George Osborne once again took a counter-intuitive view, despite the fact that the television news that evening was unremittingly negative for the Conservatives. The narrative had become that negotiations with the Conservatives were suspended and that those with Labour would begin that evening. It looked like Brown's resignation had resuscitated Labour's chances.

Party chairman Eric Pickles went back to his flat that night convinced that the Liberal Democrats were going to do a deal with Labour. As Osborne arrived home at around 9pm, his wife Frances asked him why he was home early. She had been watching the news and thought it looked disastrous for the Conservatives. As Osborne tucked into his TV dinner of pasta, he told her: 'I think we're in. I know it looks terrible but we've made an offer on AV. We got it through the shadow Cabinet and the Parliamentary Party and it's a good offer. We are the only people who can offer a stable coalition.' Unlike his boss, Osborne was extremely optimistic in the midst of despair.

Llewellyn and other Cameron aides stayed late into the evening in Cameron's office in Norman Shaw South, mulling over the situation, eating yet more pizza and slurping Diet Coke as they waited for news. The mood of resignation became mixed with a sense of defiance. Feeling they had acted properly in their dealings with the Liberal Democrats, both morally and politically, they were convinced that their actions since polling day would reflect well on the party in the eyes of the public. One aide said: 'There appeared to be a great yearning in the country for parties to come together. I know it sounds pompous, but we wanted people to know and also to think: "Those Tories, that's impressive the way they've behaved, they've behaved properly."'

They bounced pugnacious statements off one another about how they would attack a possible Lib–Lab government during yet another period of opposition. 'The view was we were probably heading for opposition, but we were well placed to harry the government night after night in tight votes if we did!', was the determined conclusion, before they went home to rest.

Labour–Liberal Democrat negotiations

Labour and the Liberal Democrats arranged for their teams to negotiate in earnest for the first time at 8pm in Portcullis House, the modern annexe to the Houses of Parliament. On Sunday, an opening bid had been made to the Liberal Democrats by Labour in the form of a paper sent across by e-mail from Downing Street by Jeremy Heywood, permanent secretary at No. 10, to Polly Mackenzie.

Written in bold capital letters, it was obvious that the document's author was Gordon Brown. 'It was basically the Labour manifesto,' said an aide who saw the document: 'They said we'll carry on everything that we're doing and we'll have a few reviews.'

Donald Dewar had tried something similar during the negotiations that followed the Scottish Parliament elections in 1999, drafting on his own typewriter 'a one-page policy summary that was basically a blank cheque to Labour', according to Mark Oaten's book *Coalition*. If the Liberal Democrat team at that time (in which Jim Wallace and David Laws were the major players) had found Dewar's attempt to be 'laughable', the 2010 team were scathing about Brown's document. 'It was shit,' recalled a policy aide.

The Liberal Democrats decided that they needed their own negotiating document, and after the Parliamentary Party meeting concluded they rapidly went to work on it, using the Conservative document as a template to set out what they wanted and where they were prepared to make concessions. It was the Liberal Democrats' thinking that they should set the agenda for the Monday night meeting with Labour, although Labour had done further work on its response to the draft Liberal Democrat document and tabled it at the meeting.

The Liberal Democrat negotiators, who had been keen to avoid going in and out of the Cabinet Office for their meetings with Labour, noticed that the talks lacked the same formality as the talks with the Conservatives that had taken place at 70 Whitehall. Civil servants were less in evidence in Portcullis House, and the Queen's Private Secretary, Sir Christopher Geidt, was completely absent. One negotiator felt that the Monday night session, the second meeting (but first formal negotiating session) between the Labour and Liberal Democrat negotiators, and with time running out for a deal to be struck, still felt more like exploratory talks than the real thing.

Labour also noticed the different status of the talks. The Saturday talks had not been public, like Friday's talks with the Conservatives. The Labour negotiating sessions were felt to be generally quite short and therefore deliberately limited as to how far they could go towards reaching an agreement.

Liberal Democrat negotiators were left hanging around waiting as the Labour negotiators arrived around thirty minutes late, having come straight from the Cabinet meeting that followed Gordon Brown's statement announcing the opening of talks and his plans to stand down as Labour leader. The apologies were neither fulsome nor heartfelt, according to one Liberal Democrat; indeed, from the start the atmosphere was: 'Oh God, do we have to be here?'

Alastair Campbell reports that within half an hour of the meeting getting under way he was getting text messages from Paddy Ashdown and Charles Kennedy saying, 'It's not going well.' He believes that both men could only have been getting text messages from within the negotiations, which does not suggest that all Liberal Democrat negotiators had their attention on the job in hand. Campbell thought it was all 'a bit odd'.

Some Westminster wags recount an unlikely text message exchange during the same meeting, but worth repeating for its humour. The story goes during the negotiations in Portcullis House with Labour, Alexander's father sent his son a supportive text saying: 'Just remember, you are the only one in the room who knows how to get a lobster out of a rock hole.' Alexander apparently replied that he was 'in the hole with the lobster and he's called Peter Mandelson', not the first time in his career that Mandelson had been confused for a crustacean.

After this inauspicious beginning, matters soon got worse. Some of the Labour negotiators were clearly taken aback by the Liberal Democrats' bullish approach to the negotiations. Ed Balls accused the Liberal Democrat team of 'arrogantly' assuming they were in a position to make demands and of being 'dismissive' of Labour's suggestions. Balls said: 'I think by the time we had got to the meeting, we thought that there had been quite a step forward. We thought it was really difficult, but we had advanced and we went in cautiously optimistic. Compared to the Saturday atmosphere it was much more negative. It was much more difficult from their side, much more aggressive, sort of take-it-or-leave-it kind of thing and very difficult around the referendum on AV and the economy. When the reports came out later in the evening I was quite taken back – all these complaints about body language at the meeting. The conclusion that we all reached at that point was that the people who wanted a Labour–Liberal deal, who were not in the negotiating room, they had to be persuaded that it was not doable but most importantly they had to be persuaded that it was us that didn't want a deal, rather than the Liberals.'

The Liberal Democrats in turn were disappointed to find Labour divided and unprepared. Without any member of the Labour team seeming to be in charge, the two peers, Mandelson and Adonis, appeared to be 'positive' throughout and committed to making a success of the negotiations, with Adonis in particular seeking out common ground. However, the attitude and negative body language of the MPs – Harman, Balls and Ed Miliband – was much more problematic. The Liberal Democrats found their proposals met with the 'turning up of noses' and 'sneers' from the 'two Eds' who repeatedly told them that their proposals were unachievable or unaffordable. Nor did the Liberal Democrats welcome Harman's suggestion that each Labour Cabinet minister should simply thrash things out with his Liberal Democrat shadow, thereby rendering the negotiating process which they had prepared for and in which they were engaged somewhat redundant. When she suggested that Alan Johnson should talk directly with his Home Office shadow, it became clear that, rather embarrassingly, she had no idea what Chris Huhne's position was within the third party hierarchy.

If it was understandable that agreement would not be reached in all areas during the first proper negotiation between the two sides, the Liberal Democrat negotiators were none the less frustrated about how little progress was made in key areas of policy compared with what they had already agreed with the Conservatives. In their view, the Labour team were unprepared to offer additional money on the Liberal Democrats' much cherished policy for a 'pupil premium'. A proposal was made on the idea of a £10,000 income tax allowance, which the Liberal Democrats quickly concluded was both a sham and an insult to their intelligence.

Discussions on environmental policy fared little better, with even Labour sources admitting that the discussion of renewable energy sources was a particularly difficult conversation. After Chris Huhne proposed that the two parties agree on an increase in the national target for the proportion of energy to be produced from renewable sources by the year 2020, Ed Miliband snapped back, ridiculing the Liberal Democrats' policies on the issue and subjecting Huhne to a lecture on how even the current renewables target for 2020 would be impossible to achieve.

Two clear areas of disagreement were Liberal Democrat proposals for an emergency budget and for electoral reform. The Labour negotiators refused to accept Liberal Democrat proposals for an emergency budget and immediate spending cuts, and were surprised by the Liberal Democrats' apparent conversion to the Conservatives' plans for immediate and aggressive action to reduce the budget deficit. There was a long argument over whether a Labour–Liberal Democrat arrangement with no working majority in the House of Commons would have credibility in the eyes of the financial markets when it came to taking action on the deficit. Although Labour had been reluctant to make economic commitments without first consulting Alistair Darling, Balls asserted that there was 'no way' that Labour could go back on its promise not to cut spending in the current financial year.

With an offer from the Conservatives of a referendum on AV in their back pocket, and encouraged by Brown's vague assurances to Clegg of his plans for a multi-referendum on wide-ranging constitutional reform, the Liberal Democrats had hoped that Labour would go further than the Tories on the ultimate prize of electoral reform. Alexander pushed for agreement on a referendum containing multiple options for a new voting system, including proportional representation. Despite finding Mandelson 'very keen to be emollient' and to leave the matter open, resistance again came from Balls and

Miliband, who argued that the Parliamentary Labour Party would never agree to such a proposal on proportional representation.

Earlier in the day Brown had 'offered' Clegg a referendum on PR during their talks. But there appeared, as Clegg suspected there would be, a gap between what Brown said in his meeting and what Labour's negotiators were prepared to agree. Lord Adonis remembers Alexander and Huhne making proposals for a referendum on a fully proportional system: whether it would be in the form of Alternative Vote Plus or Single Transferable Vote was left open. 'We said we were prepared to go back and consider it,' said Adonis, 'and I think we would have been prepared to agree, to agree an additional question on a fully proportional system. But even if we did there would of course have been no Labour commitment to support it.'

Chris Huhne had floated the idea to Labour of legislation on AV before a confirmatory referendum at the Saturday meeting. Now he went much further, adding spice to the rumours that had been flying around Westminster that day, and which so horrified the Conservatives. He proposed an immediate change of the electoral system to AV, to take effect prior to a subsequent referendum, even if a general election preceded that referendum. The Labour negotiators were shocked. Adonis described the proposal as 'extraordinary – a complete non-starter; there was not a scintilla of possibility that such a proposal would get through Cabinet, even if we wanted to.' Adonis believes that to force through legislation before a referendum had agreed it would have been dishonourable. Balls kept saying to the Liberal Democrat team: 'That makes the referendum completely redundant. If it's law, what is the referendum for?' The proposal was left hanging in the air.

Despite the intelligence that Cameron's aides were receiving from a host of journalistic and political sources, Labour negotiators remain adamant that they never agreed to any direct move to legislation on AV, let alone offered it in the negotiating meetings. Far from securing legislation or an agreement to force through a change in the voting system, the biggest concession Labour had made on electoral reform was a commitment that the party would campaign for a 'Yes' vote in a referendum on AV.

Yet Adonis was constantly faced with journalists asking him on Monday evening if it was true – as they had been informed by the Liberal Democrats – that Labour had offered AV legislation without a referendum. He does not know for sure who briefed the press that Labour had made this offer, but he believes it was the Liberal Democrats in an attempt to bid up the Conservatives, as with the clock running down on negotiations they were anxious to get some sort of offer on AV. Adonis also believes that it suited the Conservatives to believe it, as it was a first-order concession required to deliver the coalition and it gave the message that Labour was prepared to offer anything, however unreasonable, to clinch the deal.

According to the Labour negotiators, in addition to the concession on campaigning for a Yes vote in an AV referendum, there were a number of other potential concessions during the Monday talks that Labour was prepared to consider. They told the Liberal Democrats that as they were only then having the first proper negotiating session between the two parties, they would need to consult on a number of the issues; it was only right that they would have to discuss financial issues with the Chancellor, for example. Peter Mandelson's impression of the meeting was that 'There were differences of detail, but nothing big, certainly nothing irresolvable' between the two parties' negotiating teams.

Mandelson's optimism was not shared by the Liberal Democrat negotiators. After the meeting had broken up, the Liberal Democrat team shrugged their shoulders in exasperation, barely needing to confirm to each how badly the session had gone. Jim Wallace, waiting for the group in Cable's office with a handful of colleagues, had never seen a group of people trudge through a door before looking so dejected. 'Before they even told us what had happened I could have told you,' he recalls. So bad were the talks that the negotiating group saw little point in further discussion unless there was movement from Labour. The party would look 'utterly ridiculous', thought David Laws, if it made a deal with Labour on the terms offered and then details of what had been agreed with the Conservatives, which already went 'way further' in terms of meeting the Liberal Democrats' policy demands, were subsequently published.

Liberal Democrats go back to Clegg

The meeting with Labour broke up after 9pm, and prior to reporting back to an expectant Parliamentary Party at 10.30pm, the Liberal Democrat negotiators headed straight to their leader's office in the Commons to debrief Clegg and the 'reference group', which included Cable, Burstow and party president Ros Scott.

Clegg was shocked at his negotiators' report of the talks with Labour. 'Are you really sure that the talks were as negative as you've described?' he asked the negotiators. Clegg, who by now felt acutely that time was running out to strike any deal, reminded his negotiators that a coalition would be a huge step for the party and that their parliamentary colleagues would find a coalition with the Conservatives particularly uncomfortable. He decided to seek the views of each of those present about what should happen now. The view around the table was both clear and decisive: the Liberal Democrats should join a full coalition with the Conservatives. Ros Scott, the party president, tried to take a balanced approach, but the only member expressing lingering doubts was Vince Cable. Now even he knew for certain where the negotiations would end up.

The Liberal Democrat leader told his negotiators that however badly the talks with Labour had gone, they would almost certainly need to try again the next day, even if just for the sake of the Parliamentary Party. Perhaps, he suggested, things would improve once Labour had got over the shock of Brown's resignation as party leader. Clegg was also acutely aware that it was too early to allow the negotiation to become a one-horse race.

Liberal Democrats: the Parliamentary Party

At 10.30pm, the Liberal Democrats' MPs and peers trooped into the Grand Committee Room in the corner of Westminster Hall. Nick Clegg opened proceedings with a gloomy assessment of the meeting with Labour. He spoke of the meeting as having being 'terrible', and that there had been poor body language. Labour's attitude was sneering, and they did not appear to be serious about the negotiations.

Danny Alexander reported back in detail on the Labour discussions on behalf of his fellow negotiators. Alexander put his best spin on how the talks had gone with Labour, but had little solid progress to report. Sceptics requested that Laws, Huhne and Stunell each give their own individual account of the talks to confirm the accuracy of Alexander's report. Each man in turn confirmed that little progress had been made in their respective policy areas, with more than one expressing his astonishment at how badly the talks had gone.

One member of the House of Lords present at the meeting said that the message from the negotiators was 'very important – they said, "Our information to you as the negotiating team is that we did not think Labour was serious about this." They also gave the flavour of the meeting and put into words the body language, and that had quite an influence on the Parliamentary Party.'

Shocked, dismayed and deeply disappointed by what they had heard, many of the MPs present demanded information on the sticking points, while others, including Menzies Campbell, Ed Davey, the party's foreign affairs spokesman, and Michael Moore, the party's international development spokesman, simply wanted the negotiators to try again with Labour. Among the peers, Paddy Ashdown continued to voice his opposition to a deal with the Conservatives. Some Liberal Democrat left-wingers said that this was the way that Labour negotiated, that not too much should be read into one session.

But according to those present, the Parliamentary Party as a whole began to swing behind the notion of a deal with the Conservatives. It started with two prominent MPs, Norman Baker and Don Foster, who spoke out saying that the party had little choice in these circumstances but to try to reach an agreement with the Tories. Crucially Cable, who had bided his time, now threw his weight behind a coalition with the Conservatives. He spoke for as little as three or four minutes, but with emotion. They had all agreed to the negotiating strategy, he reminded them. They could go back to Labour, but a Conservative deal is what they would end up with.

No admirer of the Tories himself ('I hate the Tories, I spent my whole life fighting them'), Cable told his colleagues that although there were things about the people in the Conservative Party that they did not like, a coalition was probably the best thing they could do for both the party and the country in the situation the Liberal Democrats found themselves in. 'I think we could be quite influential with the Tories,' he said, but according to colleagues he appeared devastated.

He, perhaps more than anyone, had been working behind the scenes to keep a Lib–Lab deal alive, and even now he still believed it should be pursued. He later told BBC Political Editor Nick Robinson: 'It was emotionally a very turbulent time for me. As somebody who had spent all my political life fighting Conservatives, it was quite difficult to face the fact that we might be working with them in a coalition arrangement.'

As the meeting stretched into the early hours of Tuesday morning, the Liberal Democrat Parliamentary Party demanded that the leadership exhaust all other possibilities before settling on a deal with the Conservatives. They insisted that there would have to be at least one last go at negotiating with Labour to demonstrate to the party at large that a Lib–Lab agreement could not be achieved, but also with the hope of pushing for further concessions on electoral reform. One MP characterised the mood: 'I think there was an expectation to have one more go, but there was an expectation that nothing would come of it.'

With the prospects of a deal with Labour heavily damaged but still just about alive, the pro-Labour Liberal Democrats such as Ashdown and Campbell, tried to salvage the situation. Numerous private calls were made to contacts in the Labour Party, with several MPs reporting back to Labour the brutal verdict on the talks that their negotiators had just delivered to the Parliamentary Party. Adonis and Mandelson were urged to try to sort out as far as possible any personal and policy issues that stood in the way of a deal prior to the parties' teams next meeting later in the day.

But all the back-channel contacts in the world could not reverse matters now. Essentially it was hopeless for Labour. One senior Liberal Democrat painted the picture as Tuesday morning dawned: 'As long as the Labour Party was in the game it kept the pressure up on the Conservatives. I'm not saying a formal decision had been made [about the Conservatives], but there was the sense that there was no doubt about that.'

*

Labour reaction

Adonis was called by Paddy Ashdown late on Monday night (going into Tuesday morning), upset and annoyed at what he had heard at the Liberal Democrat parliamentary meeting. He complained of the 'terrible body language' and that the 'negotiating session had gone badly'. Adonis replied: 'Your people must have been at a different meeting.' He was astonished.

Hearing of the version of events that their Liberal Democrat counterparts had described to their parliamentary colleagues (and to journalists), both Adonis and Balls claim then to have come to the conclusion that the talks were a charade. The Liberal Democrats they felt to be most in favour of a deal with Labour were not in the negotiating room.

The Liberal Democrat negotiators were briefing colleagues that the session had gone badly at a personal level. For three negotiators, there were false accusations of a negative attitude, particularly Balls and Miliband. There were some frank views exchanged, but there was nothing unreasonable, they thought. There was also the accusation at the Liberal Democrat meeting that Labour was saying 'No' to a whole range of reasonable Liberal Democrat requests. Not true, says Labour, they merely needed time to consult, as it was our first proper session.

It was concluded that this was nothing other than the Liberal Democrat leadership trying to pin the blame on Labour as an 'alibi' for their decision to proceed with an agreement with the Conservatives. Earlier Labour had believed that there was a serious game on, and what it had to do was some serious work overnight to respond to Liberal Democrat concerns raised at the evening meeting. The Liberal Democrats were deliberately creating a narrative of unsuccessful negotiations. It was now clear to Labour there was no deal to be done.

The Conservatives react

It was not until after 1.30am on the Tuesday morning that Llewellyn took a surprise call from Danny Alexander. It was clear to Llewellyn from Alexander's conversation that the Liberal Democrats' talks with Labour had gone extremely badly. Alexander expressed the Liberal Democrats' desire to 'get going again' with the Conservatives, with a further meeting of the negotiating teams the next day. The two counterparts agreed to speak again in the morning. Alexander was also clear that negotiations over the detail of the final coalition agreement should recommence and be concluded and announced the following evening. The Liberal Democrats had essentially made their choice.

Llewellyn sent Cameron, Hague and Osborne a lengthy message with the news to 'call me in the morning', as the rollercoaster ride was continuing and the deal was not only back on but that the final decision by the Liberal Democrats had been taken. The text included the information conveyed by Alexander that negotiations were to be completed and announced on Tuesday. A coalition deal would now be done.

DAY 5

– Tuesday 11 May –

On Tuesday, the country woke up to its fifth morning since polling day without knowing who would form its government, or what form that government would take. BBC Radio 4's *Today* programme told listeners that the Liberal Democrats were expected to make a decision that day on whether they could work with the Conservatives or Labour to form the next government.

A decision from the party leadership was expected that night, BBC Political Editor Nick Robinson told the programme, although it might yet be the following day. But, Robinson told the nation's listeners, the terms of the contest had changed, perhaps decisively: 'The contest frankly is nothing to do with negotiations, it's no longer about detailed policy – this is a contest between head and heart. The Liberal Democrats' head tells them very clearly that there is only one stable governing arrangement because of the numbers; that is Liberal Democrats and Tories together. Their heart says, and their gut frankly, we can't stomach going in with the Conservatives, we've always longed to have this so-called "progressive alliance". Today they've got to make their minds up.'

Robinson was being told by 'some senior Liberal Democrats' that morning that they had doubts about the seriousness of the new generation of Labour politicians in making a Lib–Lab deal work. 'They believe that Gordon Brown is very serious indeed, and admire him for the decision he took yesterday,' Robinson reported, but 'some of them are worried that the next generation of Labour politicians have their mind on a leadership contest, not on making a coalition government work or indeed on the necessary measures for the deficit.'

The Liberal Democrats were briefing to the media, but only part of the story. The late-night telephone conversation between Danny Alexander and Ed Llewellyn meant that both the Conservatives and Liberal Democrats knew that the choice had been made, the decision reached, subject to the final policy detail. A flurry of phone calls around dawn confirmed matters. But to satisfy Liberal Democrat MPs, in case anything went wrong with the Conservative negotiations, and to continue to squeeze further concessions, the Liberal Democrats would continue with its morning negotiations with Labour. It was highly unlikely it would amount to anything. Ed Balls characterised his party's three meetings with the Lib Dems as: 'Saturday, warming up positive; Monday, cooling down negative; Tuesday, going through the motions – we didn't believe they were serious at all. Our assumption was that the deal was just about done, the die had been cast. We don't think they were serious at all on the Tuesday.'

Even before the 10am negotiating session began, the cracks in the so-called 'progressive majority' that had emerged the previous day became increasingly evident for all to see. Another Labour heavyweight, this time former Home Secretary David Blunkett, told the *Today* programme of his opposition to his party's involvement in negotiations. They should accept defeat, he argued, before launching a vitriolic attack on the Liberal Democrats: 'We see now what it would be like with fully fledged PR don't we, we see what we would have to put up with.' He charged: 'Can we trust these people? Can you trust the Liberal Democrats? I mean, they're behaving like every harlot in history.' A Liberal Democrat aide at the heart of the negotiations remembers 'half a dozen Labour backbenchers' on College Green telling the media: 'Over my dead body will we do a deal with the Lib Dems.' With a need for the Labour party to be strongly and uniformly behind a coalition deal for it to have any chance at all of being able to govern, it was becoming more and more obvious that the arithmetic just wasn't going to work. A Clegg aide, somewhat disingenuously, rang Downing Street to ask 'what the hell was going on, why were there all these negative voices attacking a deal?'

Peter Mandelson, aware of John Reid and David Blunkett's public opposition to a deal with the Liberal Democrats on top of the 'private reservations' that existed within the Cabinet, felt a change of mood that morning. As he recalled in *The Third Man*, he had been surprised to read reports in the day's newspapers that the Liberal Democrats had found his negotiating team 'negative and even disengaged' – although it should be said that a re-reading of the newspapers on that Tuesday morning suggests that there was little in the way of negative reports of the negotiations.

Ed Balls, interviewed on the morning outside his home, made an altogether more revealing remark about the Labour team's mindset ahead of the last-minute negotiations. While he and his colleagues would 'see if' they could achieve a deal with the Liberal Democrats to provide a stable government, Balls told television reporters: 'I'm very clear my job is to be there with the whole negotiating team to make sure that we protect our manifesto.' This was a reference to the Liberal Democrats' change of emphasis on deficit reduction, and as both Andrew Adonis and Ed Balls have since made clear, they were not prepared to row back from their view that cutting too soon and too fast would endanger the economy.

Most remarkably, the leading contender to replace Brown as Labour leader (and therefore the likely replacement Prime Minister under a Lib–Lab deal once Brown had stood down), was an almost entirely absent figure over the five-day saga, having not been chosen to be part of the team that would take part in the talks that would determine that party's immediate future. Speaking to the media that Tuesday morning, David Miliband, an as yet unannounced candidate for a leadership contest that as yet had not commenced, all but let slip that his attention was now on the forthcoming contest: 'I'm certainly not going to be saying any more; none of the candidates are going to be saying anything more.' The Liberal Democrat negotiators' suspicion on the Monday night had been that Brown's resignation had turned Ed Balls and Ed Miliband's focus onto the leadership race – a suspicion apparently with some justice.

By contrast, having been frozen out by the Liberal Democrats the previous day, the Conservative camp was justifiably optimistic from the very first. Cameron phoned his chief of staff in the early hours to learn more of the latest twist in the saga. In public at least, Cameron would continue to play with a straight bat, while taking the opportunity to ratchet up the pressure on the Liberal Democrats. Interviewed later as he left his home, Cameron told reporters: 'It's now, I believe, decision time – decision time for the Liberal Democrats – and I hope they make the right decision to give this country the strong, stable government that it badly needs and it badly needs quickly.'

If Alexander and the Liberal Democrats held to their word there would indeed soon be a decision. Having talked things through with his leader, Ed Llewellyn contacted the Liberal Democrats to arrange for the Conservative–Liberal Democrat negotiations to be reactivated. A third and final session was arranged for early that afternoon, again at the Cabinet Office buildings on Whitehall.

Clegg too gave his view of the state of play early on the Tuesday morning. He also affirmed what was the general sense: that the time for talking and debating was drawing to a close. The message that neither the public nor the City would tolerate a longer period of uncertainty had hit home. There was to be no Continental gestation period for the birth of a new government. The discussions between the political parties had, he told the listening media, reached 'a critical and final phase … The discussions between the political parties has [sic] now reached a critical and final phase. I'm as impatient as anybody else to get on with this, to resolve matters one way or another. My Parliamentary Party was up into the small hours yet again discussing things. We will act, as ever, responsibly. We will act to try to do our bit to create a stable, good government that the British people deserve. And I really hope that we will be able to make an announcement so we clear up everything and explain to people exactly what our thinking is as quickly as we possibly can.'

Publicly at least, using its back-channel spokesman Paddy Ashdown, the Liberal Democrats were maintaining the stance that a grand 'progressive alliance' was possible and legitimate. Ashdown had told the *Today* programme that in the event of a coalition made up of Labour and the Liberal Democrats, although there would be a technical majority which could vote down such a government, in reality that majority would never be assembled. In particular, Ashdown argued, the SNP would never vote with the Tory Party, having suffered bitterly from doing that in 1979. In terms of legitimacy, Ashdown continued, 'we [sic] would be representing a progressive coalition that had 51% of the people of Britain behind it. For the very first time, you would have a government that had the majority of support in Britain. I call that legitimacy.' This is the line he had peddled since discussions with Lord Rennard, through meetings at his house and now in the media. He hoped for it and wished it to be true, but the reality of Tuesday morning was that it had drawn its final breath the previous night.

As agreed with their parliamentary colleagues late on Monday night, the Liberal Democrat negotiators would have one more attempt to negotiate a deal with Labour that morning. Having entered the 'final' phase, it was now up to Labour to come up with a 'game-changing' offer. Could there realistically have been a game-changer at this late stage for Labour? The only thing that would have made a difference was a tangible commitment to go significantly further on electoral reform. Clegg said that Brown was very insistent that he could go much further than the Conservatives, but crucially he didn't go further than AV, 'because of course if he'd gone further, then I don't know.'

However, behind the scenes, even before the four Liberal Democrat MPs met with their five Labour counterparts, key policy aide Polly Mackenzie was tasked to work alongside Jim Wallace in drafting a document identifying, from the negotiators' notes, what the party had and had not agreed so far with the Conservatives, a document the party leadership hoped would have the potential to evolve into a final coalition agreement some time later that day. Mackenzie had sent across a draft of the document to Oliver Letwin's e-mail earlier in the morning. Letwin then met Jim Wallace (while the negotiations with Labour continued) at around 11.30am in Norman Shaw South, only to find that the document had not arrived with the Dorset MP and was 'missing'. There was some alarm that nobody knew where it had ended up, but for the purpose of the meeting with Letwin copies were made and circulated. The two men went through it methodically for over an hour, leaving only a few loose ends to tie up. There was, for example, a figure of 75% of MPs in agreement for the vote for dissolution of parliament to be passed, which Letwin felt needed further consideration. Substantially, this was to be the document that formed the content of the coalition deal later in the day.

On the Tuesday morning, even while continuing negotiations with Labour, the Liberal Democrats had met and largely agreed with Oliver Letwin what they hoped would be a document that finalised their arrangement with the Conservatives. There was still to be one more negotiating session, but the document produced by Letwin and Wallace was described by one senior aide to be 'over 90% unchanged'.

Clegg left his home for a further session of face-to-face talks at midday with David Cameron. As he was being driven into the House of Commons through the Old Palace Yard entrance in Parliament Square, he was photographed through the window of his car holding what looked like a handwritten list of outstanding negotiating points to be dealt with by him and David Cameron. The first point on his list was 'Red Lines', followed by what appeared to be 'Europe', 'Immig[ration]' and 'Trident'.

The red lines Clegg's note referred to were Conservative red lines: David Cameron had made it clear from the outset during his Friday afternoon speech at the St Stephen's Club that these issues were ones on which he was not prepared to compromise. These issues, arguably the ones on which the two parties were (and remain) the furthest apart, had been parked in the talks between the Conservative and Liberal Democrat negotiating teams up to that point. Clegg, for whom Europe is a particularly important issue, sought to find any possible areas of movement or common ground that could have made the terms of a final deal more palatable in these areas. In light of what the leaders reported back, the two parties' negotiating teams would pick up these difficult issues that afternoon as they scrambled to finalise a deal.

The next item on Clegg's list read 'AV', and what appeared to be 'wider constitutional convention'. The idea of an independent constitutional convention was to be proposed again at the afternoon negotiations by Chris Huhne. Any proposals agreed, the Liberal Democrats hoped, would be put to the people in the form of a referendum. As the Conservative leadership recognised, an offer of electoral reform involving a referendum on AV, as big a step as it was for the Conservative Party, was the very least that the Liberal Democrats would find acceptable as the price of a coalition. The Liberal Democrats had not sought electoral reform in isolation, but as part of a wider package of political reform, including the introduction of fixed-term parliaments to prevent a Conservative Prime Minister dissolving parliament at a time that suited the Conservatives at the Liberal Democrats' expense. (This was a common fear among Liberal Democrat MPs over the five days.)

The list also made reference to the inter-party talks on party funding, chaired by the former civil servant Sir Hayden Phillips. The Liberal Democrats had long sought to reduce the gap between themselves and the Conservative and Labour parties on party finance, and had proposed to the party funding review a £10,000 cap on all donations to political parties. The eventual coalition agreement would contain a commitment to 'pursue a detailed agreement' on limiting donations and reforming party funding 'to remove the big money from politics' – though not a commitment to adopt or take forward the draft agreement Sir Hayden had put to the three main parties in August 2007.

However, what was most revealing about Clegg's note was an entry letting slip just how advanced the talks with the Conservatives were. In a strong indication that a deal was nearing completion between the two party leaderships, he now proposed to discuss with Cameron the actual make-up and working arrangements of a coalition arrangement, not merely whether such an arrangement was possible. Under the heading 'Posts', Clegg had written 'ratios' and, intriguingly, 'me' – a reference to his own precise role as the party leader of the junior party in a coalition government. Clegg had asked Jim Wallace to put together a paper for him to use as a basis for discussions late on the Monday night.

Meeting with Labour at 10am, once more in room 391 of Portcullis House, the Liberal Democrat team immediately felt that the atmosphere had improved since the previous day. Adonis was once again enthusiastic. Ed Miliband, perhaps having reflected on his trenchant performance the previous evening, bought a round of coffee and pastries for both teams and appeared to the Liberal Democrats be 'trying to be much more positive'.

But for a party with a historic decision to make, the time for pleasantries had passed. There was no longer time for misunderstandings. Andrew Stunell was asked by his colleagues to open the meeting with the group's collective assessment of the previous day's negotiations and where things stood. He did not hold back, making it perfectly clear that from the point of view of the Liberal Democrat team the previous session had not gone well: he and his colleagues had been surprised and disappointed by the attitude of their Labour counterparts. The Liberal Democrats were not in these negotiations to sell themselves short; the party would not now pitch its tent beside Labour's mansion in exchange for a handful of 'policy reviews'. Casting minds back, Stunell reminded the five Labour ministers that the Cook–Maclennan process prior to 1997 had eventually brought about major advances on the constitutional reform agenda, of which the devolution project in the UK – with a parliament for Scotland and an independent assembly for Wales – was the most striking example. The Liberal Democrats, Stunell emphasised, were looking for something on a similar scale, and now was the time for Labour to make its bid.

Stunell was probably chosen to deliver the message because it would be least expected to come from him, as he was likely to have been considered the most polite and understated of the Liberal Democrat team. It appeared to Labour that the Liberal Democrats were immediately setting out to be difficult. In truth they probably were, as the meeting was really a case of going through the motions. Andrew Adonis believes that the Liberal Democrats needed this meeting to go badly to continue its narrative that a deal could not be done with Labour. If not entirely true of their earlier meetings, it was almost certainly true of this one. These suspicions would hardly have been allayed by a leak, barely an hour into the second session, from a source 'inside Lab–Lib talks' to Channel 4 News that Ed Balls was once again 'sneering' at the Liberal Democrats.

Shocked by Stunell's chutzpah, Labour replied that they were less than pleased to find that such views had already been leaked to the press the previous evening. (If, as Oliver Letwin remarks, the lack of calculated leaks to the press had aided the building of confidence between the Conservative and Liberal Democrat teams, the opposite was true in the case of the Labour and Liberal Democrat negotiations – though those responsible for the leaks might argue that they were a response to what was already an unhelpful atmosphere, rather than the root cause.) Mandelson made clear his displeasure at what he perceived as a 'new attitude of prickliness, even truculence' from the Liberal Democrats, and sent a text message across the room to Danny Alexander, telling him that Stunell was being overly obstreperous, and 'if this continues we'll get nowhere'.

But overall, Mandelson's colleagues agreed that the second meeting between the Labour and Liberal Democrats was somewhat less difficult than the first, if only because they had little if any expectation of success.

As we have seen, probably even at this late stage in the negotiating process the one area where a game-changing offer could be made was electoral reform. Chris Huhne pressed again for the Liberal Democrats, arguing that there should be legislation on AV with a confirmatory referendum, but on the face of the Bill making clear that if a general election intervened it would take place under the new electoral system. It was a difficult discussion because Balls in particular did not understand the point of a referendum if the changes were already made and then potentially used at a general election. The Liberal Democrats also requested a referendum on a fully proportional voting system, which Labour might have accepted as the price for a deal.

Adonis is still insistent today that the Liberal Democrats got a much worse constitutional deal from the Conservatives. He argues that while the Labour Party would have campaigned for the AV referendum the Conservatives will campaign against, and that the Liberal Democrats would probably have got the additional referendum on full PR and Labour would not have wanted fewer MPs. The redrawing of boundaries, he believes, will wipe out the party in Parliament: 'The deal they got from the Conservatives was a whole category worse than they would have got from us.'

Adonis soldiered on, trying to present a package of concessions that would placate the Liberal Democrats. Having been able to go away and consider and consult on the Liberal Democrats' demands overnight, he and his colleagues felt in a better position to give more a conclusive and positive response. Labour agreed to drop plans for a third runway at Heathrow Airport. They would agree to the Liberal Democrat position on identity cards for UK nationals, although they would not move on the issue of the cards to foreign nationals. The party was prepared in principle to move to the Scottish system for the DNA database.

Adonis recalled that Labour were prepared 'in principle' to discuss the Liberal Democrats' proposals for a pupil premium and higher income tax thresholds on the Tuesday morning. But a vague willingness to discuss was not going to change the path of the negotiation at this late stage. The Liberal Democrats were unimpressed that Labour had again come up with so little by the way of concrete, 'bankable' offers on these two core manifesto policies. Nor were they persuaded by a vague suggestion that a Lib–Lab coalition would discuss further the issue of replacing the Trident nuclear weapons system, which the Liberal Democrats had committed themselves against. The suggestion was that it could be part of the Defence Review. Their environmental proposals, including a proposal to support a unilateral increase in the EU emission reduction target to 30% by 2020 as well as for higher targets for renewable energy, again drew resistance from Ed Miliband.

Generally there continued to be unresolvable problems on economic policy. The Liberal Democrats had been convinced by Conservative arguments on cutting the deficit. David Laws and Chris Huhne wanted further and faster deficit reduction, which had by Tuesday morning evolved into the elimination of the structural deficit. The talks were suspended before it was clear, according to Labour, whether this was a red line or a negotiating position. However, both in-year cuts and the elimination of the structural debt in one parliament were non-negotiable to Balls and the Labour team. Labour simply would not agree to the new Liberal Democrat position.

Balls also challenged the Liberal Democrats on the details of the pupil premium policy, asking them whether or not the money to be spent on poor pupils was to be additional to the rising profile of overall education spending over the next three years that Labour had set out in the pre-Budget report, which he believed the Conservatives had refused to match. He recalled that the Liberal Democrat team confirmed to him that the additional money they proposed for the pupil premium would come on top of a rising schools' budget.

But curiously for someone who had so actively sought Alistair Darling's job for himself the previous year, Balls was still insistent on referring almost any matter involving finance to the Chancellor (a tactic employed likewise by his colleagues). The fact that the Labour team were still saying on Tuesday, 'Oh, that would be a matter for Alistair,' is remembered now by the other side as a source of significant annoyance and mistrust. It baffled and frustrated the Liberal Democrat team, who had assumed – not unreasonably – that any questions of finance relating to the Liberal Democrat demands (the pupil premium, issues of tax relief and so on) would have been referred to Darling overnight on Monday, after the teams' first meeting.

It was also indicative of a fundamental difference in the two sides' attitudes to the negotiating process, which at least partially explains their failure to strike a deal. As far as the Liberal Democrats were concerned, the point of a negotiating team was that it would be competent to make decisions on behalf of the party, and empowered to do so (with the sole exception of certain key issues which inevitably would need to be referred up for decision by the respective party leaders). If Darling's say-so was required, he should have been on the team. And besides, the composition of the Labour team led some of the Liberal Democrats at least to assume that this was simply a fudging tactic. As one of them now remarks: 'I remember saying at one stage, "We have probably got the economist in this room who knows more about these issues than anyone else in the country, who has been in the Treasury for years – why can't he speak for the government as a member of the negotiating team?" And Mandelson said, "Who are you talking about?" and I said, "Well, obviously Ed Balls!"'

'Are you the negotiating team or aren't you the negotiating team?', thought another Liberal Democrat negotiator to himself of his Labour counterparts.

This was another instance of the fundamental psychological gulf between a party which had become used to seeing itself as the serving government and a party which had been in opposition. The Labour negotiating team, hastily assembled after polling day from individuals who had been busy serving as government ministers, had not had time to develop any group approach or philosophy distinct from their individual identities as ministers who still saw themselves as part of the Cabinet of a serving government. One Liberal Democrat further speculated that after thirteen years in government, Labour ministers were not used to operating without civil servants at their side.

Looking at the concessions that the Labour team offered on the Tuesday morning, it struck one member of the Liberal Democrat team once again that there was a fundamental division within Labour ranks – and within the Labour negotiating team itself – in terms of a willingness to make the negotiations work. The concessions Labour offered, it was noticed, were all made in the areas that Andrew Adonis and Peter Mandelson could control. However, in terms of those Liberal Democrat demands which would impact upon Labour's broader social and economic policy strategy – where Darling's and perhaps Brown's approval would be required – there was no sign of a willingness to be flexible.

And as it happened we now know – what the Liberal Democrat team then did not know – that the Chancellor was in fact otherwise engaged. With the official negotiating channel proving unexpectedly difficult, Brown would simply try to open up a separate one. In public Brown had stated his willingness to let the Conservatives and Liberal Democrats talk; in private he was desperate from the start to open all lines of communication, direct or otherwise, to the Liberal Democrat leadership. And since the official negotiating channel – the talks between the Liberal Democrat and Labour teams – was proving unexpectedly difficult and the atmosphere unconstructive, he was quick to look for other channels which might advance his cause. Once again the Prime Minister called his old confidant Vince Cable, who at least until the party leaders' TV election debates had been considered the Liberal Democrats' real heavyweight, eclipsing Clegg both in terms of authority and star quality, and who could be expected to exert considerable influence in the party if he could only be convinced about the merits of a Lib–Lab deal.

Brown rang Cable several times, initially to say, 'For God's sake don't commit yourself to working with the Tories – you must think about the future, try harder, talk to our team, you're not doing enough to secure a deal.' He then urged Cable to meet with Darling to discuss the economic situation and explore possible common ground. Surely Cable did not want to renege on the Liberal Democrats' election promises on deficit reduction? Cable agreed, managing to slip into the Treasury unnoticed, so he thought, while the party's official negotiators were holed up in Portcullis House.

The first the Liberal Democrat negotiating team knew about this was when they received a call from Cable to say that a car was outside waiting to take him to the Treasury. To the consternation of the Labour team, Danny Alexander had already announced to the negotiating meeting that Cable would not be allowed to hold separate talks with Darling. When Alexander heard of Cable's proposed meeting he was 'apoplectic', according to one colleague, and was determined that there could be no parallel negotiation. Labour's bid to set one up served only to reaffirm the mistrust which had been developing between the leadership of the Liberal Democrats and the Labour Party.

As far as Cable himself was concerned, the Liberal Democrat leadership's message had been unequivocal. Clegg sent the order, via Alison Suttie, that Cable was 'not to get in the car' that Darling had sent from the Treasury. Cable apparently ignored the order, and after arriving at the Treasury met with Darling for around fifteen minutes. What was discussed? Not a lot, apparently. Cable has since asserted that it was 'all a bit pointless' and 'we were just sharing views on the world in an amicable way'. It was obvious to him that the meeting with Darling would not lead to anything. Any negotiations that Brown may have anticipated failed to materialise with Darling, and neither man apparently tried to persuade the other of anything.

Cable's disobedience was curious, at the very least. Was it because he felt awkward spurning the invitation, or because he did sincerely believe that it might yet advance the cause of the deal he personally favoured, that Cable ignored his party leader and accepted Darling's invitation? Cable had made an influential, perhaps decisive intervention at the meeting of the Liberal Democrat Parliamentary Party on the Monday night, telling his colleagues he realised that a deal with Labour was 'not a goer', but nonetheless believed that the party should 'genuinely keep trying [with Labour, to] see what came of it' on the Tuesday. 'I was all for that,' he later recalled. He would later have 'very mixed feelings' before agreeing to join the coalition Cabinet.

Darling, whatever the role Brown had envisaged him playing (he had in all likelihood refused to join Labour's negotiating team), gave the strong impression to several of the leading players in the saga that in his opinion, Labour had lost the election and had to go. The Chancellor had intimated to his Conservative shadow George Osborne over the course of the weekend that he had not thought he would still be in office on the Sunday and he didn't expect to be there on Monday or Tuesday. Osborne's impression was that Darling found his party's attempts to put a deal together with the Liberal Democrats something of an embarrassment. This episode confirmed that Brown was fighting an increasingly lonely battle in his bid to thwart the Tories.

As the second proper meeting of the Labour and Liberal Democrat negotiating teams broke up, the two sides tentatively agreed to meet again, but in truth both knew that time had run out. Mandelson recalled that 'the tide, on all sides, was running away from us.' Adonis felt the process was a charade. Balls was clear that the Liberal Democrats were now playing with Labour in order to drive a harder bargain from the Tories. He returned to Downing Street confident in his view 'that Brown and the party should now get out'.

Cable was hauled in for a hastily arranged one-to-one meeting with Nick Clegg just after 12.30pm, when it was likely that he had the error of his ways that morning explained to him. Then the Liberal Democrat reference group met in Clegg's Westminster office at 12.45pm, but when Wallace turned up he found nobody around so he nipped off to get a sandwich. Suddenly an avalanche of texts and calls came through: 'Get to the leader's office at once.' There followed a quick update to receive feedback from the morning meeting with Labour and the meeting between Wallace and Letwin.

Brown, despite being on the verge of calling it quits, had earlier tried to rescue the situation and spoke to Clegg by phone, attempting to reassure him that Labour could still deliver a deal, and that voices such as Blunkett and Reid were a side issue. Clegg, knowing that a broad agreement was in place with the Conservatives and that his negotiators were finalising matters, wanted time to secure a few final concessions. He desperately needed Brown to be kept in-play a bit longer before he would ready himself to sign off the final deal with the Conservatives – it was still a huge and momentous decision. Needing to keep the game alive for the political pressure it applied to the Conservatives (much as Balls surmised), he agreed to meet Brown again.

After a debrief with his negotiating team following their morning session with Labour, Clegg paid a visit at 1.15pm to the Prime Minister's office in the House of Commons. He found Brown in a lather, repeatedly demanding: 'Why aren't your people cooperating? Why aren't your people cooperating?' Clegg replied: 'Your team wasn't prepared to do business.'

Understanding that his negotiators had gone into the meeting that morning armed with concessions, Brown was baffled and frustrated that the Liberal Democrats had not reciprocated. Unable to comprehend, as ever, how any leader of a progressive party could contemplate getting into bed with the dinosaurs of the Conservative Party – how what seemed mere matters of process could be allowed to stand in the way of defeating the Conservatives – the Prime Minister proposed that he and the Liberal leader sort the matter out man to man, there and then. 'You know, we can sort this out now' he told Clegg. 'Let's just sit down now. You and I can write out the policies.'

Rather than tear up his party's entire negotiating strategy at the eleventh hour, Clegg batted Brown away. His concern was not about policies, he told him: 'I'm sure we could come up with a policy agreement, but it's the legitimacy of it…'

Though he remained Prime Minister five days after his party had suffered a historic battering at the polls, Brown's power was now almost gone. The tone of the meeting oscillated violently as the PM veered between moments of bluff acceptance of his fate (superficially at least). 'I could give this up any minute now. I can walk away from it,' he told his younger counterpart, before showing flashes of impassioned perseverance: 'We could do it, we could sort it out. This is a big mistake you're making.'

Brown was now on the edge emotionally as it looked as if a deal had slipped through his grasp and after the battering he had received over the past five days.

Thanks to the discussion between Alexander and Llewellyn during the night, the Conservative leadership, indeed confident, had been optimistic from the outset on Tuesday morning. By lunchtime, they were all but certain. Desmond Swayne, Cameron's PPS, recalled: 'Once it gelled, from the very first there was optimism on Tuesday and by the end of the morning it was a done deal, and it was just a question of tying it down.' However, some of Swayne's party colleagues were less enthusiastic. Over lunchtime, the Thatcherite group 'Conservative Way Forward' issued a statement calling for David Cameron to become Prime Minister at the head of a Conservative minority government. 'We do not believe a formal coalition with the Lib Dems is an appropriate way forward that would produce the necessary stability our country needs,' the statement ran.

A quarter of an hour after Clegg had sat down with the desperate Prime Minister, his negotiators reopened talks with the Conservative team to try to thrash out the final details of a joint coalition agreement. The Conservatives' confidence was apparent. On entering the Cabinet Office, William Hague told reporters: 'We believe very strongly that there should be a government with a strong and secure majority in the House of Commons and of course with an elected Prime Minister, and we remain very, very firmly of that view. We set out proposals to achieve that yesterday and we have come here to hear the Liberal Democrat response.'

Bizarrely, given the later dramatic and emotional events for which the day would be remembered, the Conservative and Liberal Democrat teams recall the mood as subdued and businesslike: they simply 'trundled along' as before for the first few hours as the teams attempted to finalise the language in the document and flesh it out where there were gaps. Numerous advisers, led on the Conservative side by James O'Shaughnessy, were brought in to work on individual sections. The section dealing with Europe was lengthened and extended. Lines were sought on issues not yet covered, such as the benefits system (an issue barely mentioned in the Liberal Democrat manifesto).

There were minor differences on how to empower schools. The Conservatives wanted to give schools the option effectively to opt out of local authority oversight, making schools that meet the criteria 'independent'. The Liberal Democrats wanted to give freedoms to all schools rather than a selected group who opted to go down a particular route. Laws also wanted to retain somebody between the market and central government to have some strategic oversight of schools, to make sure performance was good. It was felt that Ofsted, with its light-touch model of inspection and irregular inspection of schools that reach a high standard, was not effective.

Laws felt that there ought to be a more restricted and defined local authority role which was to do with holding schools to account, and he also wanted an educational standards authority to ensure local authorities were doing their job. This difference meant that there ensued a philosophical discussion between Laws and Letwin about the extent to which the market could sort these things out and still have some sort of local oversight. As one Lib Dem aide put it: 'They could both bore for England on this subject and unfortunately they both did.'

As the final act played itself out behind closed doors, the media was hungry for public developments, having had remarkably little to report to a public, which (according to the media at least) was similarly expectant. Suffering from the unfamiliar lack of leaked material, journalists were only too happy to seize on the colourful commentary provided by party figures on all sides (who in truth were often as disconnected from the core process as those outside). Clegg was also beginning to feel the pressure. He felt the media was clamouring for a decision and taking the line that 'the country's going to hell in a handcart'.

One colourful episode had occurred earlier in the morning, when Conservative grandee Sir Malcolm Rifkind, betraying the nerves and frustration felt by many of his colleagues, angrily denounced Labour and the Liberal Democrats' attempts to put together a 'coalition of the defeated'. Rifkind had been getting numerous calls from the media about how the negotiations were developing and did he want to comment? Watching how things had developed he thought: 'Bugger it, yes I do. These guys are two-timing.' He compared Brown's attitude to the election result to that of Zimbabwean dictator Robert Mugabe: 'The idea that the two parties that suffered most in this election, that were rejected by the electorate, should put together an illegitimate government – this is Robert Mugabe-style politics. That's exactly what Mugabe did. He lost the election and scrabbled to hang on to power in the most illegitimate way.'

Gordon Brown called Paddy Ashdown once more in the early afternoon. Brown wanted to discuss the necessity of his having to leave as Prime Minister. Ashdown told him it was a must, but furthermore, if he wanted the Labour–Liberal Democrat process to survive, the potential leaders of the Labour Party must come out and support it. 'Failure to do so,' he said, 'would kill that prospect completely.' But the next generation of potential Labour leaders now had little or no interest in a coalition. It was over.

From a Labour point of view, the sporadic denunciations by a few high-profile figures began suddenly to turn into a steady stream – making a nonsense of any claim that the party could be kept on a tight and disciplined leash in any rainbow coalition. As the day progressed, more and more Labour MPs came out of the woodwork to join the public opposition to a Lib–Lab deal, opposition that had been initiated (separately) by John Reid and David Blunkett. A *Guardian* journalist reported that there was now 'a large group in the Parliamentary Labour Party' that did not want to do a deal with the Liberal Democrats at any price. One 'senior Labour MP' told the *Guardian* that he was 'not in favour of Lib–Labbery, full stop. I think they are our political enemy. There is a massive problem with their attitude to the trade unions.'

Later in the afternoon, Health Secretary (and future leadership candidate) Andy Burnham became the most high-ranking Labour MP to indicate his opposition to a deal with the Liberal Democrats. He backed his senior colleague David Blunkett – 'David has spoken with real authority on this matter' – and called on his party to accept the verdict of the polls: 'I think we have got to respect the results of the general election and we can't get away from the fact that Labour didn't win.'

Clegg's rejection of Brown's emotional appeal at their lunchtime meeting had not put an end to the contacts between the two men. Brown returned to Downing Street, from where he would hold on to power for the rest of the afternoon. While his other senior aides were sceptical, Adonis still fought with Brown throughout the afternoon to rescue the prospect of a deal with the Liberal Democrats. From his office, Brown held a series of phone calls with Clegg over the afternoon and into the early evening, in a final push to talk round the Liberal Democrat leader, who continued to resist Brown's overtures.

Clegg knew things were coming to a head that day but still wanted more time to complete the coalition settlement. He felt it would be wrong for the Prime Minister to simply chuck in the towel before another government was formed. After all, these were the rules that all parties had accepted from the Civil Service and had guided the behaviour of all involved in the negotiations.

The Labour negotiating team had reported back to Brown after the morning negotiations (with Balls and Mandelson particularly vocal) that it was extremely unlikely that a deal would be done with the Liberal Democrats. Clegg knew from early in the afternoon that Brown felt that he was no longer interested in a deal. Clegg kept to a mantra, that his team was still in negotiations with the Conservatives, that he did not know how it would turn out yet and 'it wasn't agreed until it was agreed'.

As the afternoon wore on and with the extent of Labour opposition to a deal with the Liberal Democrats now clear, Clegg told Brown he had 'reluctantly' concluded that Labour could not deliver on a coalition agreement. 'The reality', Clegg said, echoing what one of the candidates in Labour's subsequent leadership election had told former Liberal Party leader David Steel, 'is that your party is knackered after thirteen years in power.'

Clegg now felt that Brown had finally recognised his decision to reject a deal with Labour, and openly told the Labour leader that Lib Dem negotiators remained locked in ongoing talks with the Conservatives. However, Clegg was still aware of the mammoth task he faced in selling a coalition deal with the party's historic enemies to his MPs and activists. Aware that the work to finalise a deal with the Tories would need to be accelerated – not least because of Brown's earlier threat to head to the Palace at any moment – Clegg still sought as much time as he could get to ensure the final agreement was in the best possible shape before being put to the party and the public. Sensing Brown's desperation for even the smallest glimmer of hope, Clegg held out the possibility that the advanced talks with the Tories could yet come to nothing, telling Brown he would only know whether a deal was possible when it was actually agreed.

Over the course of the day, and particularly after Labour's negotiators reported back that the Liberal Democrats had seemed less interested and somewhat disengaged in the morning's session of talks, Brown's Downing Street aides had begun to assume that the Conservatives and Liberal Democrats would complete a deal. By mid-afternoon, with the writing on the wall, Brown rang Clegg to say: 'I want to resign, I want to go. I need your answer now, Nick, I need your answer now.' Clegg, who was in his Commons office, said that he would give him his answer in one hour. Clegg rang him back several times to try to buy more time, but Brown was becoming increasingly emotional: 'Nick you're a good man, but I need an answer. I can't keep hanging on. I don't want to be humiliated.' Clegg was clear to Brown that he should not step aside until it was clear who would govern.

The mood inside Brown's 'bunker' that afternoon was surprisingly relaxed: Brown's political fate and Labour's chances of remaining in government were now largely out of their hands. By the early evening Brown was surrounded by nearly all of the staff from his years in Downing Street, with groups of aides sat around the Prime Minister's office, chatting away, cracking jokes and retelling anecdotes. One of

Brown's more endearing habits in the eyes of his colleagues and aides is a tendency to tell the same jokes over and over again. Aides primed Brown to tell them particular favourites – including a gag about Ronald Reagan and former Swedish Prime Minister Olof Palme – both for their own amusement and to stop this proud man from withdrawing into himself to reflect on his impending ejection from the office he had so long craved.

Five hours after Brown's face-to-face rejection by Clegg, while the still Prime Minister continued to flip between hope and despair, Brown's closest lieutenants, Adonis aside, sought to persuade him to make his exit. They had become frustrated at being reduced to waiting for news of a deal between the Liberal Democrats and the Conservatives. Brown, in their eyes, was being 'used' by Clegg. Mandelson told the Queen's Private Secretary Sir Christopher Geidt that the situation was 'really getting quite difficult for the Prime Minister'. Geidt reminded Mandelson of the Prime Minister's constitutional obligation to remain in his post until the Queen was able to ask somebody to form an administration. Following his return from that afternoon's meeting of the Privy Council, Mandelson recalled urging Brown to call time on the process. Summoning his spin doctor's instincts, Mandelson had turned his mind to the image Brown's departure would create. Brown, whatever the experiences of his aides, colleagues and rivals over the years, has always sought to carve out a public image of himself as a great man, proud and dignified. If the Prime Minister delayed his announcement much longer, Mandelson reckoned, he would end up leaving Downing Street in the dark, like a burglar leaving the scene of a crime.

Media reports had reached the Conservative–Lib Dem negotiation room of rumours that Brown was set to announce his immediate resignation as Prime Minister at around 4.30pm. The reports were soon confirmed to the room by 'official contacts'. Civil servants, including the Cabinet secretary started to pop into the room, telling the negotiators they had 'a very upset Prime Minister' on their hands, whom they were trying to hold on to but who could be off to Buckingham Palace any moment. Within the hour, helicopters were hovering over the Cabinet Office, conjuring visions in the mind of one negotiator of the dramatic evacuation of the US Embassy in Saigon in 1975.

Agreeing a deal was now a matter of urgency. For all Brown's protestations of his determination to ensure a stable government, he was preparing to resign, and force the Queen to appoint a new Prime Minister without any agreement in place between the parties to sustain a new government. With at least one side feeling that a coalition document was 'nearly there', the negotiating teams continued to try to finalise an agreement amid the mounting drama, although Ed Llewellyn, Cameron's chief of staff, was summoned away from the talks to help his boss prepare to assume the premiership.

At 5.30pm Clegg once again called Downing Street, repeating his request for more time, with his negotiators still seeking to push the Tories for a softer line on Europe (something that in the event Clegg would have to resolve himself with William Hague). But the desire for a dignified exit that Brown's aides had urged on him now trumped considerations of constitutional propriety and Brown's public commitment to make sure that the country ended up with a strong and stable government. With no final deal to support a government even agreed, let alone ratified by any of the parties, Brown decided to pull the plug and caught everybody on the hop in the process.

In the BBC documentary *Five Days That Changed Britain*, Alastair

Campbell recalled Brown's last phone call to Clegg, when the Prime Minister demanded: 'Time for what? Unless you can tell me you've broken off with the Tories in favour of discussion with us, I'll assume you're going with the Tories.' According to Clegg, he said to Brown: 'Why are you doing this, because the automatic upshot is that David Cameron will be Prime Minister and you said you didn't want that.'

Brown continued, according to Campbell: 'I'm now in an impossible position. I have to go to the Palace … Nick, Nick, Nick, I have to do this now, I can't stay on. It's a choice now one way or the other. You've made the choice, I'm not going to hold on.' Campbell recalled: 'His final words were: "OK, thanks Nick, goodbye." And he turned to us and said, "OK, let's do it."'

Clegg was invited to Cameron's office (taking Wallace along with him), where he remembers that everyone was wildly excited and that he was met with an enormous roar as he entered. Cameron had himself been at Conservative HQ throughout the afternoon and had been called by Gus O'Donnell to say Brown was about to resign, although he was trying to put him off, but he should be ready. Ed Llewellyn got a text from Christopher Geidt asking Cameron to 'call the Palace'. He therefore headed to his office in Norman Shaw South and then called Clegg to join him.

As he rushed to perform his constitutional duties and finish negotiations with Clegg, Cameron had to squeeze in a call to his wife, who would be accompanying him to Buckingham Palace, and found Samantha at home helping their daughter Nancy with her homework. 'Well,' he suggested to her, 'you'd better get your frock on as we could be going to the Palace!'

It was only now that Clegg started the negotiation about what he would do, and Brown had left him in a fairly weak position: there were no more aces up Clegg's sleeve. Indeed, as Clegg, Wallace, Cameron and Llewellyn continued their talks, Brown was on the television in the background making his final speech from Downing Street. Nobody paid the slightest attention. Power had now shifted, and what was happening in Downing Street was largely immaterial. The British constitution is merciless to the outgoing Prime Minister.

Clegg told Cameron that he did not want to run a department, and that as a leader of one of the two parties in a coalition government he felt that he should be Deputy Prime Minister. There was little discussion: Cameron did not negotiate, he simply agreed. While putting on his tie before going to his audience with Her Majesty, Cameron discussed with Clegg how many Cabinet ministers would be Liberal Democrats. There was more debate about this, with Cameron trying to keep broadly to the mathematics in proportion to seats won. However, once again Cameron's view was that he would be reasonably accommodating because 'we wanted to start with good grace'. But Brown's sudden collapse meant that decision-making became suddenly concertinaed.

Brown called his Downing Street staff together to announce his farewell, making a speech remembered with fondness by his aides. As he posed for final photos with his wife and sons, many were in tears. The mood was lightened by Brown's son Fraser calling out, 'Come on Daddy, we're going!' – perhaps a sign that his son was eager for more time with a father without the weight of prime ministerial responsibility.

For some of those inside No. 10, Brown's resignation marked not just the culmination of a long campaign and an exhausting few days, but the end of thirteen years in power and the end of an era in the lives of those who worked for him.

One senior Cabinet member under Brown summarised his tenure

in this way: 'At the end people felt benign towards the guy. Things had not worked out as expected with the Brown premiership but the circumstances had been more difficult than anticipated. He handled the financial side well, but his failure to call an election in 2007 and MPs expenses were bloody awful. But he had the additional challenge that he just wasn't clubbable.'

At 7.19pm, Brown, accompanied by his wife Sarah, walked out of the door of No. 10 to announce his resignation. 'I have informed the Queen's Private Secretary that it's my intention to tender my resignation to the Queen,' he declared. Unable to bring himself to mention his successor by name, he said that: 'In the event that the Queen accepts, I shall advise her to invite the Leader of the Opposition to form a government. I wish the next Prime Minister well as he makes the important choices for the future.'

In perhaps the most tellingly honest part of his statement, Brown said that 'Only those who have held the office of Prime Minister can understand the full weight of its responsibilities and its great capacity for good. I have been privileged to learn much about the very best in human nature, and a fair amount too about its frailties, including my own.' Brown's voice cracked as he talked about his family. The raw emotion of the past days was revealing itself.

William Hague is critical of the manner of Brown's going. He said: 'I think he should have stayed a few hours longer and gone in an orderly fashion. Rushing out was just face-saving. He could have gone the next morning, and that would have been orderly instead of having to start forming a Cabinet at 1 o'clock in the morning – which is what we ended up doing.'

The Conservative and Liberal Democrat negotiating teams, who had for five days been central in the scramble for power, stood together now as spectators, watching the transfer of power on a television, just like anyone else. Alexander and Liberal Democrat policy aide Polly Mackenzie took photographs to capture the moment. For minutes afterwards, Hague, Alexander and Letwin stood looking out of the window reflecting on what they had just witnessed. In the BBC Television documentary *Five Days that Changed Britain*, David Laws recalled being gripped by a sense of excitement as he looked round the room pondering the situation: 'My God, what has happened here?', he asked himself. 'We've ended up in a situation where we could well have a Lib Dem–Tory government which I never expected was likely to happen. We've changed the government. The future of British politics is going to be very, very different. Are we doing the right thing or the wrong thing?'

As Peter Mandelson left 10 Downing Street to clear his things from the Cabinet Office, Nick Clegg was heading over to Cameron's office in Norman Shaw South to finalise the coalition arrangements. While they waited for their negotiating teams to return, the two leaders turned their attention to how many and which ministerial jobs each party would get. A quarter of an hour after Clegg had walked into the Leader of the Opposition's suite of offices to an enormous roar from Cameron's excited staff, the scene became almost surreal when Osborne, Hague and Alexander walked into Cameron's office at 7.45pm, just as he was trying to finish his conversation with Clegg while simultaneously readying himself, including putting on his tie, for his visit to the Palace.

The negotiators had wrapped up their discussions after watching Brown's departure. Despite the distraction of knowing throughout the last hour of their talks that Brown's resignation was imminent, the teams strove to tie down the remaining loose ends while they were still in the room together. They turned again to the issues of the future of Trident and nuclear power, which had been parked earlier in the process, and decided ultimately to 'agree to disagree' on both. Hague told reporters on his way back out of 70 Whitehall that his team now had 'some recommendations' to take back to David Cameron and to their parliamentary colleagues.

When Hague arrived, Cameron and Clegg had also been trying to resolve some of the outstanding issues. During discussions, Cameron was called away to speak to Buckingham Palace, and returned coolly to tell colleagues: 'We can keep going for another ten minutes, as I don't have to be there until ten past eight!'

But when Cameron did head off to the Palace to receive the Queen's invitation to form a new government and 'kiss hands' on his appointment as Prime Minister, there were still a few issues to be ironed out between the party leaders. In Cameron's place, Hague was left to finalise the few outstanding details of the coalition with Nick Clegg, Jim Wallace, Oliver Letwin and a small group of others, with the two men marking up changes to the near-final version of the document in their own handwriting. The major issue remaining was Europe with Conservative demands for a United Kingdom Sovereignty Bill to make it clear that ultimate authority remains with Parliament, rather than the institutions of the European Union. Clegg didn't understand what the case for a Sovereignty Bill was, so the parties eventually agreed to 'examine the case' for such a Bill.

Cameron was insistent that there would still be a referendum lock: it was an absolute red line for him. His government would not pass power from Westminster to Brussels and if it tried there would have to be a referendum so that the people would ultimately decide. Clegg was worried that the Conservatives were viscerally more hostile to Europe and sought reassurance that the party would be reasonable and engage with the European Council meetings in a positive way. Cameron agreed, but was delighted that his bottom line, no transfer of powers to Brussels within this parliament, had been negotiated into the deal.

In the short time before going to the Palace, with most of his aides flat out negotiating or making arrangements on their phones, Cameron had time to prepare his first words as Prime Minister that he would later deliver on the steps of 10 Downing Street, and he worked with Steve Hilton to prepare something appropriate. A quarter of an hour after Brown's twenty-minute audience with the Queen, Cameron set off for Buckingham Palace. Having been invited by the sovereign to form a government, Cameron accepted but added he couldn't be totally sure about what sort of government he was going to form. He later recalled the scene in the documentary *Five Days that Changed Britain*: 'I said I *hoped* to form a coalition government but I might have to come back in the morning and tell [the Queen] it was something rather different.'

Cameron entered the gates of Downing Street with his wife Samantha at 8.44pm. In his first public words as Prime Minister, he confirmed that he aimed to form 'a proper and full coalition between the Conservatives and the Liberal Democrats'. He explained: 'I believe that is the right way to provide this country with the strong, the stable, the good and decent government that I think we need so badly. Nick Clegg and I are both political leaders who want to put aside party differences and work hard for the common good and for the national interest. I believe that is the best way to get the strong government that we need, the decisive government that we need today.'

Cameron's top aides had already migrated from Norman Shaw

South to Downing Street in anticipation of his arrival back from the Palace, and clapped him in. On his arrival into No. 10, Cameron, still pinching himself, sat down for talks with Jeremy Heywood and Sir Gus O'Donnell. Within twenty minutes he accepted his first congratulatory call from a foreign leader: US President Barack Obama. The new Prime Minister would have little time to get used to his new surroundings: soon after receiving Obama's congratulations, he had to gather his thoughts before heading back to the Commons to present the coalition agreement to his Parliamentary Party.

Cameron meets the Conservative Parliamentary Party

The triumphant Prime Ministerial entourage made its way through the Members' cloakroom area and up the stairs at the back of the Members' Lobby area, where a group of Conservative MPs including Bernard Jenkin congratulated the Prime Minister. Jenkin then walked with Oliver Letwin up the stairs from the Tea Room. As they climbed, Letwin said: 'Politics in this country is going to be unrecognisable after this parliament,' with Jenkin believing this to mean the change wrought by constitutional changes such as a new electoral system, elected House of Lords a written constitution and perhaps a permanent 'Lib–Con' alliance. Jenkin protested: 'But Oliver I'm a Conservative!' which caused both men to laugh.

'Colleagues, the Prime Minister,' announced the Conservative Chief Whip as Cameron entered the Committee Room accompanied (in an unusual departure from custom at such moments) by his wife Samantha. The Tory MPs greeted their new Prime Minister with rapturous and euphoric cheering and the banging of desks. Cameron made a typically impressive speech, but in contrast to the Liberal

Democrats there was no detailed discussion, let alone a vote on, the coalition agreement or any of its individual provisions. Cameron was none the less treated to another standing ovation as he left the room, stopping to give Desmond Swayne, his PPS, a bear hug along the way.

As the realisation of what was happening hit the two 'centre-left' parties, bitter recriminations broke out between the party leaderships, in a war of words and two different narratives that has continued ever since. Mandelson took to the airwaves to accuse the Liberal Democrats of favouring a deal with the Tories. He told the BBC: 'In the final analysis, I'm wondering though whether that's what they actually intended. When I think about it, I think they were creating so many different barriers and obstacles that perhaps their instincts and perhaps they thought their interests lay on the Tory side, on the Conservative side, rather than on the progressive side.' Labour figures briefed the press accusing the Liberal Democrats of proposing spending pledges worth £20 billion during the negotiations without any explanation of where the money would come from. Some attacked Nick Clegg personally, describing him as a 'Tory in all but name'.

The Liberal Democrats hit back later that night, accusing the Labour Party of never having taken seriously the prospects of forming 'a progressive, reforming government' with the Liberal Democrats. The statement accused 'key members of Labour's negotiating team' of giving every impression of wanting the process to fail and the Labour team of making 'no attempt at all to agree a common approach with the Liberal Democrats' on issues such as fairer schools funding for the most deprived pupils and taking those on low incomes out of tax. In line with the leaks and reports that had emerged from the negotiations earlier that day, the party pointed accusations at Ed Balls (and to a lesser extent Ed Miliband), accusing 'certain key Labour

Cabinet ministers' of being determined to undermine any agreement by holding out on policy issues, suggesting that Labour would not deliver on proportional representation and might not marshal the votes to secure even the most modest form of electoral reform. 'It is clear', the statement concluded, 'that some people in the Labour Party see opposition as a more attractive alternative to the challenges of creating a progressive, reforming government, not least in the context of a Labour leadership election campaign.'

The Liberal Democrat Parliamentary Party meeting

When it became clear that Gordon Brown was minded to go to the Palace, the Liberal Democrats called a meeting of their Parliamentary Party (both MPs and peers) and Federal Executive that evening at Local Government House. Under the rules of their by now infamous 'triple lock' arrangements, any coalition agreement would require the approval by three-quarters of each of the Parliamentary Party and the Federal Executive in order to come into effect. After being put back several times, the session finally got under way at 10pm.

The meeting was to prove a long one for a party that had met the previous day until the early hours of the morning. Party managers took the view that faced with such a momentous decision, it was better to let anyone speak who wanted to, rather than shut conversation down.

Indeed, the Liberal Democrats' careful approach to internal communications was a strength throughout the five days. Liberal Democrat parliamentarians were not only briefed on developments but had the opportunity to question proposals; the whole Parliamentary Party took part in the major decisions. Some Conservative MPs recalled feeling envious of the opportunity their Liberal Democrat counterparts had to scrutinise the individual provisions of the agreement and vote on the document. And at the other extreme, the Parliamentary Labour Party met only after the results of the five days of negotiation were known at 2.30pm on Wednesday 12 May. Gordon Brown's Cabinet met only once during the period, on the Monday evening, after Brown had announced his resignation and immediately prior to the opening of formal negotiations with the Liberal Democrats.

At the Liberal Democrat Parliamentary Party meeting, Clegg announced that an agreement had been reached with the Conservatives to go into government on a coalition basis. Not everyone was happy. A fed-up Adrian Sanders waltzed out and went home, and several others made their displeasure known. Paddy Ashdown said he didn't like it, that he had spent his life fighting the Tories and Mrs Thatcher and didn't believe they had changed. He felt it was an abandonment of the strategy of realignment of the left and made the Liberal Democrats akin to the SDP – a makeweight to power. He thought Cameron was using his party to change the Conservative Party, believing himself to cut a Disraeli figure, but Ashdown believed he would ultimately be a Gladstone. Finally, Ashdown said, he had spent the last thirty years driving Labour out of the south west, and this agreement would allow them back in.

Copies of the four-page coalition agreement were handed out to the Liberal Democrat parliamentarians, who were given about fifteen minutes to read it through before copies were collected back in to avoid leaks to the media. Many quickly found themselves pleasantly surprised by the contents. Some let out gasps of amazement on finding that large parts of the party's manifesto had made it into a programme for government.

Previously sceptical MPs (some remarkably left wing) felt they could justify and defend the deal if it was fully implemented. A significant number came to the conclusion that the party would be crazy to turn their backs on what was on offer. Others were content and somewhat relieved that an end to the tortuous process was now in sight.

Even Paddy Ashdown, who had consistently argued against a deal with the Conservatives in the meetings over the five days, reckoned, having read the agreement, that '80%' of the contents were Liberal Democrat policies. A 'masterpiece' he declared. 'Fuck it,' he told his colleagues. 'I am prepared to fight with you even if it is inside the Tory Party. I can never resist a fight, and if this is what you are fighting for you'd better count me in.'

The MPs were first to vote. Fifty voted for the agreement with none voting against, although former party leader Charles Kennedy was one of a handful who abstained. The peers were next, giving a near-unanimous support to the deal. Finally, it was the turn of the Federal Executive, a 35-member elected committee responsible for the running of the UK-wide party. Only one member, former MP David Rendel, voted against the deal.

12.38am – the Clegg press conference

The Liberal Democrats emerged from their Parliamentary Party meeting in the early hours of the morning for the second day running. Nick Clegg gave a press conference half an hour later, saying that the Liberal Democrat Parliamentary Party and the federal executive of Liberal Democrats had 'overwhelmingly accepted' his recommendation to enter into a coalition government with the Conservative party. Addressing the 'nearly seven million people' who had voted for the Liberal Democrats in the general election the previous week, Clegg acknowledged that there would be many questions and 'many, many doubts' about the new government. He would not, he said, have entered into the agreement with the Conservatives if he had not been genuinely convinced that it offered a 'unique opportunity' to deliver the party's goals of 'fairer taxes'; 'a fair start in life for every child in this country'; 'a new start for the country's discredited banking system'; 'the prospect of new, sustainable growth in the economy'; and 'a new hopeful politics' that people could trust once again.

But it was the Conservatives who were back in No. 10, getting to grips with the business of government for the first time in thirteen years. Cameron, Llewellyn, Hague and Osborne returned to Downing Street after the meeting of the Parliamentary Party, where until the early hours of the morning they set about the work of forming a Cabinet. They were later joined by Clegg and Alexander.

David Cameron felt that it was absolutely vital to form the Cabinet quickly and to get the right people into the right positions – 'round pegs in round holes,' as he put it. He appointed the entire Cabinet late into the night, and through the Wednesday he saw or spoke to all his appointees. The way the appointments worked is that Cameron agreed with Clegg which jobs Cable, Laws, Huhne and Alexander would have. They then moved on to their departments and sorted out the ministers of state, parliamentary under-secretaries and whips. The number of positions the Liberal Democrats got was done on a pro rata basis in relation to seats won, although they came back to ask for more – for example, more whips.

POSTSCRIPT

The immediate aftermath of the five-day scramble for power would be remembered principally for the remarkable joint press conference in the Downing Street rose garden a day later, on Wednesday 12 May. The positive chemistry and personal ease between David Cameron and Nick Clegg would colour many people's perception of the new coalition government, rather than the fraught negotiations that had gone before.

In fact, the negotiations themselves were not yet quite over. In the week after the struggle for power had finally been concluded, Conservative and Liberal Democrat staffers continued to work to turn the coalition agreement into a full department-by-department list of commitments. Supervised by Alexander and Wallace on the Liberal Democrat side, and Letwin for the Conservatives, Polly Mackenzie and James O'Shaughnessy, together with numerous other officials, hammered out a document that would be called the coalition's 'Programme for Government'.

Unveiled at a press conference on 20 May, this was, according to Nick Clegg, a 'unique document'. Compromises had been made on both sides, he declared, but those compromises had 'strengthened, not weakened' the final result. Clegg said the two parties would be defined by three words: 'Freedom, fairness and responsibility'. The Deputy Prime Minister looked forward to 'five years of radical, reforming government, a stronger society, a sound economy, an accountable state, and power and responsibility in the hands of every citizen'.

The new Prime Minister observed that the events of the last two weeks had been 'extraordinary'. The United Kingdom had seen the first hung parliament in over three decades, Conservatives in government for the first time in thirteen years, the first coalition government in over 65 years, and the first Deputy Prime Minister from another party since the Second World War.

Having seen it in action, albeit for just under two weeks, Cameron expressed his belief that the Conservative–Liberal Democrat coalition government had the potential to be a 'great reforming government'. Reflecting on the hung parliament negotiations, Cameron said that 'the more we talked, the more we listened, the more we realised that our visions for this country and the values that inspired them are strengthened and enhanced by the act of the two parties coming together.'

Only time will tell if the coalition government lasts the five-year course or lives up to the expectations that its leaders have set out for it. As one of the key players in the new government said to me, reflecting on the events of the five days, 'Nothing unfolds as you expect.'

The lessons of history

The coalition of 2010 is different from what had gone before in two main ways.

First, this one is purely the product of parliamentary arithmetic, unlike those of the twentieth century where one party could have governed alone with an absolute majority. Second, this coalition is far more codified and structured, as what has been agreed and how the structure of that agreement works in government is extremely detailed. These factors make the coalition of 2010 highly unusual in historical terms.

We also had, for the first time, a Civil Service active not just in policy terms (for example, drafting Queen's Speeches from party manifestos) but in providing the structured framework for the actual coalition discussions.

There is one other – and quite disconcerting – aspect of this particular coalition in British history. When looking at previous British coalitions, the personalities and the personal chemistry of the two leaders of the parties has been extremely important.

One could point to Andrew Bonar Law and Lloyd George, Baldwin and MacDonald, or Churchill and Attlee. In historical terms, it is striking that in the case of 2010 the two party leaders are very similar, while previously they were often opposites, or at least complemented each other through their differences. This time around, Cameron and Clegg appear to work well together because of their similarity, which is historically significant in that it has not happened before.

It may be that the similarity of their background bonds them and will keep them close together in their purpose. But there is also a potential danger: the closeness to one another in government is greater than their closeness to their parties. Both would be wise to pay great attention to the management of their MPs as well as to the wider management of their party.

Clegg and Cameron will also have different but ongoing challenges. Clegg will have the constant danger that as a smaller and junior party in the coalition it will be swept up by the Conservative Party and will be largely forgotten by the electorate. There is always the danger that by serving within the coalition the Liberal Democrats will lose their own identity. Even in the Lib–Lab pact in the mid-1970s, Liberals felt that their identity was being subsumed by association with Labour, causing a rift within the party.

Certainly one of the themes from previous Liberal–Conservative coalitions is how a section of the party has been absorbed by the Conservatives. However, Clegg can take comfort from two quantitative differences this time around. First, there is no split in the Liberal

Democrat ranks as there was with the Lloyd George Liberals or the National Liberals. Although the Liberal Democrat Parliamentary Party is a coalition of views (as are most political parties), it is a unified party within the government coalition.

The other difference is that it could be argued that although the Liberal Democrats lost seats, the party is on an upward trajectory relative to the previous periods. When the party split on previous occasions it was in decline, overshadowed by the other main parties. In 1922, for example, Labour had overtaken the Liberals as the second largest party. There is also a potential opportunity for the Liberal Democrats: if the referendum on AV is won, the electoral system will start to favour the election of the party's MPs and more coalition governments would probably follow. The current first-past-the-post system has favoured an outcome of single-party government.

David Cameron's challenge is to maintain the support of his party, while amending the country's constitution and leading a coalition government. A number of Conservatives regard both the election of a second chamber and the reform of the voting system as fraught with danger – both for the Conservative Party and the country. One constitutional historian has described the Conservatives' proposed reforms as 'profoundly unconservative'. If we are to learn anything from our history, these issues will cause considerable tension within the Conservative Parliamentary Party in the coming months and years. Fortunately for Cameron (unlike, for example, Tony Blair), he is rooted in the history and traditions of his party and is likely to understand the significance of these changes.

*

As I said in the Preface to this book, I would like readers to draw their own conclusions from these historic events. But I will venture to share some forward-looking thoughts – which can, at this stage of history, only be preliminary.

What can we safely conclude about each of the parties and the Civil Service?

Labour

I think it is probably safe to conclude that Labour was psychologically not prepared to do what was required to secure a coalition with the Liberal Democrats from the position it found itself in. From the Cabinet down, while a few zealously chased the dream of a Lib–Lab alliance, more people probably felt better to conclude they had lost. Some were opposed to giving away too much on electoral reform; some were viscerally opposed to the Liberal Democrats and to Clegg in particular. After thirteen years in power, the party was arguably 'knackered'.

The negotiations also highlighted both the strengths and weakness of Gordon Brown's leadership. On the one hand, he deserves to be judged harshly. Deluded enough to think he could hang on as a sort of 'Father of the Nation' figure, he was too slow to go; yet he had dismally failed to prepare Labour for the negotiations. His conduct was at times chaotic and desperate – making wild offers while failing even to convene a meeting of the Parliamentary Labour Party. On the other hand, perhaps only someone of Brown's determination, focus and conviction could have persuaded the political class that a Lib–Lab deal was a possibility. By keeping Labour in the game, Brown ironically pushed the Liberal Democrats and the Conservatives closer together. On his political deathbed, Brown can perhaps be seen as the accidental godfather of Britain's new politics.

With Brown gone, Labour may well be in a stronger position at the next election, at least in terms of momentum and seats. But as Mandelson has remarked, coalition may be the only way, or at least the next way, that Labour gets back into power. Labour needs to sort out its identity and its attitude to the Liberal Democrats: does it represent tribal working-class politics or is it a progressive party in the same space as the third party? For Labour to go into future hung parliament negotiations divided and disorganised would put at risk its ability to negotiate itself back into power. A period in opposition though, should help focus the mind.

Liberal Democrats

The relationships between Clegg and Cameron and indeed between the negotiating teams were crucial to achieving early momentum behind a deal with the Conservatives, and to getting the deal done. It will also be crucial to sustaining a deal in the more difficult times ahead. The negotiations changed the long held perceptions of each other for the better.

This may well also be reflective of longer-term changes in the Liberal Democrats as the party has moved from its left-wing core of MPs. Its experiences of the realities of local government and the rise of the new and ambitious generation, suggests that its approach is likely to be practical rather than ideological over whom it partners in future.

The front-facing relationships with the Conservatives were all positive, but the Liberal Democrats also had a plethora of back channels outside the main negotiation. Paddy Ashdown in particular was used by the leadership to undermine Brown, but their noise added to the ability of the Liberal Democrats to negotiate a slightly better deal with the Conservatives.

Clegg's ability to deliver is indicative of a changed dynamic in the Liberal Democrats. They are not traditionally a 'hierarchical party', and most MPs do not feel they owe their election to the party leader. The leadership has been often defeated at the hands of the membership at conferences. But after the 2010 campaign, Clegg's standing in the party was sky high. He was able to get his chosen negotiators approved, and his strategy to talk to the party with the most seats/ votes was backed without question.

He was then able, at the crucial Monday meeting, to guide his Parliamentary Party towards a coalition deal with the Conservatives and secure remarkable consensus within his triple lock of a Parliamentary Party meeting, Federal Executive and special conference. His stature with the other parties and the media was massively enhanced, strengthening his hand. Arguably, Clegg's ability to lead his party into coalition was a direct result of the TV leaders' debates. The relationship between the party leadership and the rest of the Liberal Democrat Party will be key to the future of this coalition and to future coalitions. More than one MP has already complained about feeling bounced into things by Nick Clegg.

Conservatives

For David Cameron and his close circle, the challenge of the hung parliament negotiations was the same as it had always been since the start of his leadership bid. Get the party back into power. Show people the Conservatives could govern and be decent.

The negotiations showed off the strengths of David Cameron, as does the story of his leadership to date. From a position of huge difficulty he was bold and executed his plan with brilliance, capturing the public imagination. His masterstroke was his superb speech on the Friday afternoon, as by taking Liberal Democrats seriously and giving them an opening, he made them feel comfortable and brought them into substantial negotiations.

In the months since he first took office, Cameron adjusted to the position of Prime Minister as if to the manor born. His Liberal Democrat Cabinet colleagues are effusive in their comments about working with him, and it does not appear manufactured admiration.

Cameron's position in some way was similar to that of Disraeli at the time of his 'leap in the dark'. Disraeli had run the numbers and eventually saw his gamble pay off, but it took time, and there was a price to pay. As events unfold there is a question whether Conservative MPs, activists and supporters will give Cameron the same time and room for manoeuvre in dealing with restive Liberal Democrats.

The Conservatives and Liberal Democrats may be locked in a temporary embrace, but they are also engaged in a battle for the same voters. Clegg has renounced running to the left of Labour in an audacious bid to park his party on the centre ground of British politics. He will therefore need a new set of voters, or be forced to join with a party that also represents them. The Conservative Party is still trying to detoxify its brand and appeal to the middle classes who could deliver them the parliamentary majority. The likelihood is that both cannot win unless the Liberal Democrats split, as they have done in the past.

*

Civil Service

Probably the influence of the Civil Service, including the Cabinet Secretary, in pushing the Liberal Democrats and Conservatives together to avoid a financial crisis has been overplayed. After all, the parties rejected civil servants being involved in the negotiations. However, its influence before the election outcome proved to be profound, in setting and controlling the rules of engagement.

None the less, the economy was clearly a factor in the outcome. As an issue it came between Labour and Liberal Democrats and did not put up the expected boundary between Liberal Democrats and Conservatives. Nick Clegg has been pressed by the media and in Parliament about his and the party's conversion with regard to cuts. It is likely that the consideration of a coalition played at least some part in this decision, that the markets would demand more evidence of determination to act from a coalition as opposed to from a majority government. There was a need to act tough early on to offer reassurance.

The experience of these five days may help establish new precedents going forward: whether the incumbent government should have the first stab at staying on; whether a Prime Minister should remain in office until resignation; how long negotiations should take; and should people have more time to overcome post-election tiredness?

Finally …

Fundamentally neither Cameron nor Clegg fancied any of the alternatives to a coalition between the two parties. Perhaps if the other options had not been so unattractive they might not have been ready to take what seemed the bold path.

Clearly for Clegg and the Liberal Democrats the prospect of another election in a few months was appalling: they could not afford it, and they expected the result to be far worse than May 2010. Another election would have been proof that coalitions are not something for Britain.

Mathematics, or electoral arithmetic, was the key ingredient that made Nick Clegg decide from very early on that a coalition deal with Labour was not possible. His party needed a strong and structured deal, as opposed to a looser fragile one. In principle, he was always trying to secure a deal with the Conservative Party.

To a point therefore, Andrew Adonis was right in his analysis of events that the Liberal Democrats had decided in principle to go with the Conservatives if they could, but needed two conditions: a good enough deal to sell to their party, and a narrative about Labour to convince their MPs. This is why Liberal Democrats never briefed on policy after meetings with Labour as such a course could not sustain the argument that (a) the offer was worse than the Conservative offer, and (b) they could not get an agreement.

Interestingly, the Conservative leadership (like the Liberal Democrats) seems to have reacted against another quick election, though there were those in their Parliamentary Party who thought this would work to their advantage. They had waited for and expected power for too long to risk ending up with tenure of only a few months: hence the willingness to do a deal.

The Liberal Democrats would not have done a coalition deal (as opposed to confidence and supply) without a referendum on the Alternative Vote electoral system. Both David Cameron and George Osborne knew this and also knew it would be a challenge (given the history of the Conservative Party) to persuade MPs. They were therefore only ever going to concede it when they absolutely had to, and the belief that a deal could be done with Labour forced it into the open.

There is absolutely no evidence that Gordon Brown or his negotiators ever offered Nick Clegg legislation on the Alternative Vote electoral system without a referendum. In fact the evidence is clear they did not. However, back-channel briefings (more accurately chatter) and a conversation with Nick Clegg were significant. In their conversation Clegg deliberately left the question open, leaving Cameron to assume the worst. It would be true to say, as things stand today, that Cameron was in his own mind 'absolutely certain' that Labour had made an offer, but was wrong.

So perhaps, taking history into account, it was rather a one-off set of circumstances that all happened to push in the direction of a full coalition – a set of circumstances which, for all the thinking and planning that had gone on, few had predicted.

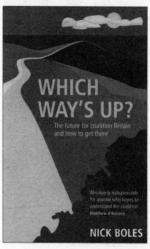

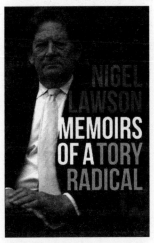